ThemeStorming

ThemeStorming

How to Build a
Theme-Based Curriculum
the Easy Way

By Joni Becker, Karen Reid,
Pat Steinhaus, and Peggy Wieck

Illustrated by Rebecca Schoenfliess

gryphon house
Beltsville, Maryland

Published by Gryphon House, Inc.
10726 Tucker Street, Beltsville MD 20705

Cover Design: Graves, Fowler & Associates
Text Illustrations: Rebecca Schoenfliess

Library of Congress Cataloging-in-Publication Data

ThemeStorming : how to build a theme-based curriculum the easy way /
    by Joni Becker . . . [et al.] ; illustrated by Rebecca Schoenfliess.
        p.   cm.
    Includes bibliographical references and index.
    ISBN 0-87659-170-5   : $24.95
    1.   Early childhood education—Curricula.   2.   Creative activities
and seat work.   I. Becker, Joni, 1953-
    LB1139.4.T45   1994
    372.5—dc20
                                                    94-21490
                                                    CIP

Table of Contents

Introduction

The Themestorming Process 15

Chapter 1—
Sticky

Theme Objectives 18
Learning Centers 18
  Dramatic Play 18
  Manipulatives................ 18
  Writing 18
  Library 19
  Science 19
  Blocks 19
  Art 19
Snacks 20
Discovery Activities
  2+ Gel-O 21
  2+ Sticky Socks 21
  2+ Sticky Hunt............. 22
  3+ Goop I and II 22
  3+ Opposites Attract 23
  3+ Good Clean Fun 23
  3+ Sticky Icky 24
  3+ Nature's Nasties 24
  3+ Poor Old Peg........... 25
  3+ Sticky Fingers 25
  3+ Tacky Dough 26
  4+ Stick to Your Plan 27
  4+ Birds of a Feather 27
  4+ Static in Your Attic 28
Art Activities
  2+ Ooey Gooey............. 28
  2+ Sticky Side Up 29
  2+ Rainbow Glue 30
  3+ Tape Tangle............ 30
  3+ Eat It Up............... 31
  3+ Almost Good Enough to Eat 31
  3+ Goofy Glue............. 31
  3+ Lick 'Em and Stick 'Em 32
  3+ Sticky Surprise 32
  4+ Catch a Ray 33
  4+ Stickers by Me 33
  4+ Magnetic Mounts......... 34
  4+ Toothpick Stick 34
Music and Movement Activities
  3+ Bee Dance 35
  3+ Jump the River 35
  4+ Friendly Attraction........ 35
  4+ Human Web 36
  4+ Three-Leggedness 36
  4+ Human Sandwich 37
  4+ Weave-a-Web........... 37
Math Activities
  3+ Calendar 37
  3+ Bandaid Match 39
  3+ Bees Are Buzzing 39
  4+ Guessing Box 40
  4+ Count and Clink 41
  4+ Sticky Feet 41
  4+ Sticky Guesses 42
  4+ Sticky Tally 42
Language Activities
  3+ Sticky Stuff 43
  3+ It Hurts................. 43
  4+ Catch a _____. 44
Transition Activities
  3+ Sit on It 44
  3+ Blow It Up 44
Songs and Chants
Theme Extensions and Variations
Bibliography
Recordings

Chapter 2—
Crash, Bang, Boom

Theme Objectives 50
Learning Centers. 50

Table of Contents

Dramatic Play 50
Library 50
Writing 50
Science 50
Blocks 51
Snacks 51
Discovery Activities 52
3+ Fruit Smoothie 52
3+ Fizzy Juice 52
3+ PVC Pipe Phone 53
3+ Tornado Tube 53
3+ Shake an Egg 54
4+ Windy Ping Pong 54
4+ Guess Who? 55
4+ Guess What? 55
4+ Blow Your Top! 56
4+ Whistling Steam 56
4+ Ocean Waves 57
Art Activities 57
3+ Place 'n Trace 57
3+ Have You Lost Your
Marbles? 58
3+ Mix It Up 59
3+ Crumpled Paper Painting . . 59
3+ Swat Team 60
3+ At the Races 60
4+ Puff 'n Paint 61
Music and Movement Activities . . 61
3+ Sit on It 61
3+ Pop Goes the Weasel 61
3+ Song Can 62
3+ Name That Tune 62
4+ Homemade Band 63
4+ Tinkle Tunes 64
4+ Tell-a-Phone 64
4+ Balloon Race 65
4+ Stormy Weather 65
4+ Leader of the Band 66
Math Activities 66
3+ Our Favorite Songs 66

3+ Calendar 67
4+ Guessing Box 68
4+ Corny Counting 69
4+ Weather or Not 69
4+ Pop Up 70
4+ Noisy Graph 70
Language Activities 71
3+ Fire Drill 71
3+ Wild Rumpus 72
3+ Shout It Out 72
4+ My Noisy Family 73
4+ Angry Pictures 73
4+ Shout or Whisper 74
4+ Muddy Pig, Muddy Pig, What
Do You Hear? 74
4+ Parading Around 75
Transition Activities 75
3+ Read My Lips 75
3+ Cattle Call 76
4+ Acting Up 76
Songs and Chants 76
Theme Extensions and Variations . . 77
Bibliography 77
Poems 78
Recordings 79

Chapter 3—
Giant Teeny Tiny

Theme Objectives 82
Learning Centers 82
Dramatic Play 82
Manipulatives 82
Library 82
Blocks 83
Writing 83
Science 83
Art 83
Snacks 84
Discovery Activities 85

Table of Contents

3+ Giant Sandwich 85
3+ Cookie Contrasts 85
3+ Mouse Hunt 86
3+ Wrap It Up 86
3+ Stuff It 87
3+ Hauling Big and Small 87
3+ Big-Little Surprise! 88
3+ Teeny Tiny Town 88
3+ Flower Power 89
4+ Super Food Bar 90
4+ Blow-Up 90
4+ Cooperation 91
4+ Let's Pretend 92
4+ One Drop at a Time 92
4+ Oh Say, Can You See? 93
Art Activities 93
3+ Giant Collage 93
3+ The Enormous Turnip 94
3+ Chalk Maze 95
3+ The Giant Paper Sandwich . 95
3+ Finger Prints 96
3+ Larger Than Life 96
3+ Giant Canvas 97
4+ It's Small 97
4+ Teeny Picture Page 98
4+ Giant Paper Dolls 98
4+ Little People 99
4+ Stuffed Animals 99
4+ Giant Crayons 100
4+ Petite Puppets 100
4+ Colorful Confetti 101
Music and Movement Activities . 101
3+ Giant Squats 101
3+ Moving From Here to There 102
4+ Full-Bodied Sandwich 102
4+ Step Aerobics—Dinosaur Style 102
4+ Limbo 103
Math Activities 103
3+ Calendar 103

4+ Guessing Box 105
4+ Giant Bean Count 106
4+ Bean Mix-Up 106
4+ Can You Believe Your Eyes? 107
4+ Order This! 107
4+ One Giant Step 108
Language Activities 109
3+ The Big Stuff 109
4+ Germ Warfare 109
4+ Other Words for Tiny 110
4+ Giants, Giants and More Giants 110
4+ Think Big, Think Small 111
4+ Inching Along 112
4+ Sketch Pad 112
Songs and Chants 113
Theme Extensions and Variations . 114
Bibliography 114
Poems 115
Recordings 115

Chapter 4— Muddy Puddles, Soap & Bubbles

Theme Objectives 118
Learning Centers 118
Dramatic Play 118
Science 118
Art 119
Writing 119
Library 119
Manipulatives 119
Blocks 120
Snacks 120
Discovery Activities 120
3+ Bury It! 120
3+ Water on the Glass 121
3+ Water Under the Glass 121

Table of Contents

3+ Muddy Footprints 122
3+ Rub-a-Dub Classroom 123
3+ Car Wash 123
3+ Blowing Bubbles 124
3+ Bubbling Raisins 124
3+ Effervescent Eggs 125
3+ Splish, Splash 125
3+ A Can of Worms 126
3+ This Is the Way We Wash 126
3+ More to Wash 127
4+ Muddy Brew II 127
4+ Washing Water 128
4+ Plant Pudding 128
4+ Sandy Cups 129
4+ Soapy Mud 130
4+ Dirt, Dirt and More Dirt 130
4+ Cake, Slime or Pie, Please 131
4+ Robin Red-Breast's Nest . . 131
4+ Bubble Mountains 132
4+ Veggie Scrub 133
5+ Bubble Gum Chew 133
Art Activities 134
3+ Rain Painting 134
3+ Muddy Tire Tracks 134
3+ Squish Painting 135
3+ Muddy Playdough 135
3+ Slippery Soap Paint 136
3+ Catch the Bubbles 137
3+ Pack a Bubble 137
4+ Clean Collage 138
4+ Magic Drawings 138
5+ Michelangelo 138
5+ Catch That Muddy Track . . 139
5+ Dig That Soap 140
Math Activities 140
3+ Bath/Shower Line-Up 140
3+ Calendar 141
4+ Guessing Box 142
4+ Catch That Drop! 143
4+ Rain or Shine 143

4+ Bubble Gum Tally 144
4+ Soap Sort 144
5+ Evaporation Investigation . . 145
5+ Where Did It Go? 145
Language Activities 146
4+ It's Raining Pizza 146
4+ Stormy Weather 147
4+ Sail Away 147
4+ Pick a Seed 148
Transition Ideas 148
Theme Extensions and Variations . 149
Bibliography 150
Poems 151
Recordings 151

Chapter 5—
Meanies, Monsters
and Make-Believe

Theme Objectives 154
Learning Centers 154
Dramatic Play 154
Blocks 154
Manipulatives 155
Library 155
Science 155
Art 155
Writing 156
Snacks 156
Discovery Activities 156
3+ Jack's Beans 156
3+ Monster Toast 157
3+ Princess Pea Soup 157
3+ Dragon Eggs 158
3+ Hungry Thing Foodles 158
3+ Me and My Shadow 159
3+ Growing a Beanstalk 159
3+ Magic Crayon Mixture 160
3+ Watch It Grow! 161
3+ Monster Crayon Mess 161

Table of Contents

3+   Slime!. 162
3+   Slime Two!. 162
3+   Making Meanie Bathwater. 163
4+   Cooperative Castle Building 164
4+   Dragon Burgers 164
5+   Monster Tracking Tool 165
Art Activities. 165
3+   Princess' Nightmare Collage 165
3+   Touch of Gold 166
3+   Nasty Faces. 167
4+   Castle Caricature. 167
4+   The Dragon's Lair 167
4+   Monster Mache 168
4+   It's a Dragon 169
4+   Dragon Wigglers 170
4+   Getting a Head. 170
4+   Green Sculpture. 171
4+   Beastly Bubble Bath 171
4+   King (or Queen) for a Day . 172
4+   Coat of Arms 172
Music and Movement Activities . 173
3+   Magic Carpet Ride. 173
3+   Hocus Pocus 173
3+   Wild Rumpus 174
Math Activities 174
3+   Calendar 174
3+   How High Will They Go? . . 175
4+   Guessing Box 176
4+   Bean Sort. 177
4+   Who's the Best Guesser? . 177
Language Activities. 178
4+   What's a Monster Look
Like? 178
4+   Penned-Up Monster. 178
4+   Mean, Nasty, Downright
Disgusting Germs 179
4+   The Fifth Dragon Story . . . 179
4+   If I Were a King/Queen . . . 180
4+   Once Upon a Time. 180
4+   A Dragon's Fare. 181

4+   How to Catch a Dragon. . . . 181
4+   Make-Believe 182
4+   It Didn't Frighten Us! 183
Transition Ideas. 183
Songs and Chants. 184
Theme Extensions and Variations. 185
Bibliography 185
Poems 186
Recordings 186

Chapter 6—
Surprises and Celebrations

Theme Objectives 188
Learning Centers. 188
Dramatic Play 188
Manipulatives 188
Writing. 188
Art. 188
Library. 189
Snacks 189
Discovery Activities 190
3+   Surprise Pudding 190
3+   Racing Colors 190
3+   Filter Fantasy 191
4+   Marshmallow Surprise 191
4+   Surprise Muffins 192
4+   How Many Are 100? 193
Special Days Activities 193
4+   Weird Week 193
4+   Hat Day. 194
4+   Pajama Day 194
4+   Picnic Day. 195
4+   100th Day 195
4+   Unbirthday Day 196
4+   Tea Party Day 197
4+   Wedding Week 197
Art Activities 198
2+   Surprise Pictures. 198
3+   Lace Rubbing 198

Table of Contents

3+ Flower Power 199
3+ Where Did the Color Go? . 199
3+ Gift Wrap Collage 200
3+ Tilt-a-Swirl 200
3+ Salty Surprise 201
3+ Party on a Plate 201
4+ Decorate the Cake 202
4+ Secret Surprise Messages 203
4+ Surprise! One, Two
Drawings 203
Math Activities 204
3+ Calendar 204
3+ How Old Are You? 205
3+ Match the Gifts 205
3+ Match the Bows 206
4+ Guessing Box 206
Language Activities 207
3+ Wacky! Wacky! Wacky! . . . 207
3+ Let's Celebrate 208
4+ Eating Big 208
4+ Make a Wish 209
Songs and Chants 209
Theme Extensions and Variations 209
Bibliography 210
Poems 210
Recordings 211

Chapter 7—All Tied Up

Theme Objectives 214
Learning Centers 214
Dramatic Play 214
Manipulatives 214
Library 214
Blocks 215
Art 215
Writing 215
Science 216
Snacks 216
Discovery Activities 216

3+ Tie It, Twist It 216
3+ Take It Apart 217
3+ Race to the Top 217
3+ Don't Forget the _____ 218
3+ Cut It Out 218
3+ Hang It Up 218
3+ Grand Opening 219
4+ Weave a Nest 219
4+ Line Them Up 220
4+ Over and Under and
Under and Over 220
4+ Darn It 220
4+ Unstring It 221
4+ Measuring Up 221
4+ String Kabobs 222
5+ Floaters 222
Art Activities 223
3+ Tangled 223
3+ Hanging by a Thread 223
3+ Beautiful Bows 224
3+ Crazy String 224
3+ Sticky String 225
3+ String of Pearls 225
3+ What's the Catch? 226
3+ Spin Me a Home 226
4+ Flying High 226
4+ A Tisket, a Tasket 227
4+ Rippling Ribbons 227
4+ Merrily We Roll Along 228
4+ Gee! Oh! Board 228
4+ Disappearing Ball 229
4+ Tie a Creature 229
4+ Sew It Up 230
4+ Tie Dye! 230
Music and Movement Activities . . 231
2+ Tightrope Tricks 231
2+ Stringing Along 231
2+ You've Got the Beat 232
3+ Jump the River 232
3+ Getting in Touch 233

Table of Contents

3+ Stompers 233
4+ Roll It Out. 234
4+ All Tied Up 234
5+ Three-Legged Walk 234
Math Activities 235
3+ Calendar 235
3+ Suits Me. 236
4+ Make a Guess 236
4+ Square One 236
4+ Presents. 237
4+ Guess My Rule 238
4+ Finish the Bows 238
4+ Guessing Box 239
Language Activities. 240
3+ Catch of the Day 240
4+ Sneakers 240
Transition Activities. 241
2+ Keeping Us in Stitches. . . . 241
2+ Crank It Up. 241
3+ Muscle-Up 241
Songs and Chants 242
Theme Extensions and Variations 242
Bibliography. 242
Poems 243
Recordings 243

Chapter 8—
Through the Looking Glass

Theme Objectives 246
Learning Centers 246
Dramatic Play 246
Blocks 246
Manipulatives. 246
Writing 247
Science 247
Art 247
Environment 247
Snacks 248
Discovery Activities. 248

3+ Peanut Butter Squeeze. . . . 248
3+ Through the Looking Glass. 248
3+ Shake-Ups 249
3+ Glass to Glass. 249
3+ Color Race 250
3+ Here's Looking at You. . . . 250
3+ Solar Power 251
3+ Watch It Sprout 251
3+ Bean Sprout Salad 252
3+ Guess Who? 252
3+ Hatch a Rubber Egg 253
3+ Mirror on the Wall 253
3+ State of Attraction 254
3+ Sound of Music 254
4+ Picture It!. 255
4+ Drink Up! 255
4+ Tops and Bottoms. 256
4+ Glass Magic 257
4+ Mirror Skating 257
4+ A Cold Look 258
4+ Fun House Mirrors 258
4+ Greens Under Glass 259
4+ Zip It Up. 259
4+ Who Nose? 260
Art Activities 261
2+ See-Through Painting 261
3+ Window Painting 261
3+ Catch the Sun #1 262
3+ Catch the Sun #2 262
3+ Shady Deal 263
3+ Reprints. 263
3+ Stained Glass Windows . . . 264
3+ Rose-Colored Glasses 264
4+ Frame It. 265
4+ I See Stars 265
4+ Kaleidoscope 266
4+ Seascape in a Jar 266
4+ See-Through Sea Creatures 267
4+ Blizzards 267
4+ Mirror Images 268

Table of Contents

4+	Foiled Again	268
4+	Jack Frost	269
Music and Movement Activities		269
2+	Copycat	269
2+	Mirror Maniacs	269
3+	Dot to Dot	270
Math Activities		270
3+	Calendar	270
3+	Cover-Ups	271
4+	In and Out the Windows	272
4+	Guessing Box	272
4+	Thoughtful Reflections	273
4+	Guess What I See?	274
4+	Clearly a Guess	274
Language Activities		275
2+	I Spy	275
3+	Window Watching	275
4+	All About Mirrors	276
4+	A Hole in One	276
4+	Magnificent Magnifier	277
4+	Night Critters	277
Transition Activities		278
3+	Looking at Plans	278
3+	Magic Window	278
3+	Looking Around	279
Songs and Chants		279
Theme Extensions and Variations		279
Bibliography		279
Poems		280
Recordings		281

Chapter 9—Picture This!

Theme Objectives		284
Learning Centers		284
Dramatic Play		284
Manipulatives		284
Library		284
Blocks		284
Science		284
Writing		284
Art		285
Snacks		285
Discovery Activities		285
3+	Masterpiece Sandwiches	285
3+	Making a Rainbow	286
4+	Blended Paper	286
Art Activities		287
3+	Puff Paint	287
3+	Scribble Pictures	288
3+	Whip It Up	288
3+	Clay Play	289
3+	Watercolor Impressions	290
3+	Shiny Art	290
3+	Bumpy Pictures	291
3+	Upside Down Drawings	292
3+	Brushless Painting	292
3+	Action Painting	293
3+	Geometric Pictures	293
3+	Don't Lose Your Marbles	294
4+	Get to the Point	295
4+	Recycled Sculptures	295
4+	All Wired Up	296
4+	Fold 'n Cut	296
4+	Freeform Cutting	297
4+	Finish the Masterpiece	297
4+	Copy Cat Drawings	298
4+	Soft Sculpting Clay	298
4+	Mache Masterpieces	299
4+	True Blue Drawings	299
Math Activities		300
3+	Calendar	300
4+	Guessing Box	301
4+	Tally ho!	302
Language Activities		302
3+	Simple Simon	302
3+	A Fistful of Markers	303
3+	Purple Painting	303
4+	Wall to Wall	304
4+	What Does an Artist Do?	305

Table of Contents

4+ Things Are Looking Up . . . 305
4+ Mixed-Up Paint 306
4+ Signs, Signs, Everywhere
Signs 306
4+ Brett's Borders 307
Transition Activities 307
4+ Mime It 307
Theme Extensions and Variations 308
Bibliography 308
Poems 309
Teacher Resources 309
Books 309
Catalogs 310

Chapter 10—Mini-Units

3's Weeks

Theme Objectives 312
Learning Centers 312
Dramatic Play 312
Blocks 312
Art 313
Manipulatives 313
Writing 313
Discovery 313
Library 313
Snacks 314
Discovery Activities 314
3+ Just Like the Pigs 314
3+ Soup—Goat Style 315
3+ Just Visiting 316
3+ Three Bears Porridge 316
4+ Which Is Stronger? 317
4+ The Grass Is Greener 317
4+ Bubbling Berries 318
Art Activities 319
3+ Yarn Mosaic 319
4+ Make a Wish 319
4+ Picture Me Ugly! 320

4+ Corn Mosaic 320
4+ Mitten Lace 321
5+ Let's Make Plans 321
Music and Movement Activities . . 322
3+ Pigs in Hiding 322
3+ Mouse, Mouse, Cat! 322
3+ Hide the Mitten 322
3+ Bear Hunt 323
Math Activities 323
3+ Mitten Safari 323
3+ Calendar 324
3+ Mitten Match 325
3+ Tally the Goats and Cows . . 325
4+ Size Sort 326
4+ Small, Medium, Large,
Mmmm! 326
4+ Guessing Box 327
Language Activities 328
4+ Act It Out 328
4+ Troll-n-Tell 329
4+ Corny Recipes 329
4+ Bear Drama 330
4+ An Then What Happened? . 330
4+ Goat Stew Recipes 331
4+ Let's Compare! 331
Transition Ideas 332
Theme Extensions and Variations . 332
Bibliography 333
Recordings 333

Pockets

Theme Objectives 336
Learning Centers 336
Dramatic Play 336
Blocks 336
Discovery 337
Work Bench 337
Library 338
Writing 338

Table of Contents

Art 338
Snacks 339
Discovery Activities. 339
   3+   Liquid Gold. 339
   3+   Guess Who I Am (#1) 340
   3+   Guess Who I Am (#2) 340
   3+   Guess Who I Am (#3) 341
   3+   Something in My Pocket . . 341
   3+   Be Our Guest. 342
   4+   Shave It Off 342
   4+   Me, a Builder!. 343
   4+   It Says Me 343
   4+   Flip It 343
Art Activities. 344
   3+   Print It 344
   3+   Painted Dust 345
   4+   Stamps Galore. 345
Math Activities 346
   3+   Calendar 346
   3+   Count Your Pockets. 347
   4+   Guessing Box 347
Language Activities. 348
   4+   Exactly Right 348
   4+   What's a Wocket? 349
Transition Ideas 349
Theme Extensions and Variations 349
Bibliography. 350
Recordings. 350

Wheels

Theme Objectives 352
Learning Centers 352
   Dramatic Play 352
   Writing 352
   Blocks 352
   Manipulatives 352
   Library 353
   Discovery. 353
Snacks 353

Discovery Activities 353
   4+   Find the Wheel 353
   4+   An Edible Wheel 354
   4+   Tire Rubbings 354
Art Activities 355
   3+   Wheels on a String 355
   3+   Rounds of Paint 355
   4+   Making Circles 356
Math Activities. 356
   3+   Calendar 356
   4+   Guessing Box 357
   5+   Wheel Tally 358
Language Activities 359
   4+   Truckload 359
Transition Ideas. 359
Theme Extensions and Variations. 359
Bibliography 360
Recordings 360

The Themestorming Process

Why should I "themestorm?"

Even the best teachers get bored with the same lesson plans year after year. If the teacher has lost his or her "spark," it will show in the children's lack of enthusiasm. Just examining ideas in a different perspective can awaken both the teacher's and children's interest.

How is "themestorming" different from traditional themes?

"Themestorming" looks at curriculum in a different way. Because it is open-ended, "themestorming" accommodates children's interests at different levels. It also encourages the use of new materials as well as utilizing traditional materials. Language and literacy are vital ingredients to the concept of "themestorming." It is not intended to be a formula but a springboard for creative thinking. "Themestorming" is not meant to be a daily or even weekly plan, but one of longevity, flexibility and adaptability.

What do you need to "themestorm?"

There are three criteria for successful "themestorming." One important factor is selecting a theme that can be experienced in many curriculum areas, especially literature. Plenty of good books and poems are essential to the overall theme. A second ingredient is time. Time is vital so the theme may be explored, processed and expanded, according to the needs and interests of the children. While four weeks is usually sufficient time for three, four and five year olds to experience a theme to its fullest potential, older students can easily explore a theme for six or eight weeks or even a semester! The last consideration is to "themestorm" with at least one other person. The more ideas and viewpoints, the better!

When implementing the "themestorming" technique, a teacher must immerse the classroom in visible and tangible materials which relate to the theme. Young children integrate what they see and hear tactually. Providing materials which the children can use and explore and with which they can interact and experiment is the teacher's way of providing guided discovery opportunities for children.

I don't know if I have enough ideas or materials for a certain theme for a month. Can it be shortened?

Certainly! One or two week units are just as much fun and beneficial as the longer themes. See the chapter on mini-themes.

How do I "themestorm?"

A good way is to create a "web" or a "network," which is simply a brainstorming process. Jot down any idea, book, materials, experiment, etc. that comes to mind. Later you can "weed out" the useless ideas. Next, start categorizing by curriculum areas, such as language, art, music, etc. Now you are ready to begin your daily lesson plans. It is helpful to make out a weekly or monthly calendar to post in the classroom and to send home to parents. (See the calendars for each theme.)

Where can I find new "themestorming" ideas?

We get several of our ideas from books children love, topics we would like to explore as well as other teachers. Always be on the lookout!

Where do I find materials to support my theme?

All around you! Be sure to consider:

- pictures from magazines
- writing to "Library Promotions Director" of a publishing company and requesting posters and bookmarks, etc.
- activities and ideas from your carefully collected teacher files
- public and school libraries
- local colleges and universities
- local museums
- high school science departments
- local stores and businesses (they often are willing to donate items)

Mondays	Make homemade peanut butter Read *Peanut Butter and Jelly*	Make a Tape Tangle Play Jump the River	Do Stickers by Me	Do Human Web Read *The Very Busy Spider*
Tuesdays	Read *Bartholomew and the Oobleck* Do Sticky Socks	Make your own jam Read *The Giant Jam Sandwich*	Do Lick 'em & Stick 'em	Do "Eensy Weensy Spider" Do Catch a _____
Wednesdays	Honey & biscuits for snack Do Bees Are Buzzing	Do Good Clean Fun ~ Play Threeleggedness	Read *Pancakes for Breakfast* Make pancakes for snack	Go for a nature walk, collect pine cones Tally items we collect
Thursdays	Go on a Sticky Hunt	Do Ooey Gooey Read *Oh, Were They Ever Happy!*	Read *Bread and Jam for Frances* Play Poor Old Peg	Guessing Box Do Birds of a Feather
Fridays	Do Bandaid Match Read *The Prince Has a Boo Boo*	Do Rainbow Glue Read *Mouse Paint*	Do Almost Good Enough to Eat Finger Jello for snack	Read *Strega Nona*

Theme Objectives

- To discover "sticky" things in the environment
- To experience the different possible meanings of the word "sticky"
- To explore the physical properties connected with the word "sticky"

Learning Centers

Dramatic Play

- empty plastic syrup, honey, chocolate syrup containers
- sticky notes
- magnets and magnetic chalk board
- velcro fastened dress-up and doll clothing
- tape dispenser and tape
- disposable doll diapers
- roll of plastic food wrap
- hand cream (supervise closely)
- hair gel (supervise closely)

Manipulatives

- magnetic pattern blocks
- interlocking plastic miniblocks
- interlocking plastic blocks
- waffle blocks

Writing

- labels
- envelopes
- stamps
- stickers
- glue and tape
- magnetic board and alphabet
- name labels
- address labels
- sticky notes

Library

- puppets with velcro attachments
- flannel board
- puppet mitts with velcro attachments
- velcro loop board and attachments

Science

- Goop I and II (see activities in Discovery section)
- magnets
- hair gel (supervise closely)
- seeds
- milkweed pods
- sweet gum pods
- pine cones and branch
- mud

Blocks

- tape to post signs
- velcro target game
- traffic signs with velcro attached
- hat/helmets with velcro-attaching signs

Art

- colored glue (glue with food coloring added)
- transparent tape
- two-sided tape
- toothpicks and styrofoam packing pieces
- labels (for making stickers)
- contact paper
- clear art glue
- glue sticks
- clay
- playdough
- bread dough for sculpting

- papier-mache materials

Snacks

- honey and bread
- caramel apples
- roasted marshmallows
- finger gelatin (recipe on box)
- homemade jelly or jam (recipe on pectin box)
- giant jam sandwich
- fresh-squeezed fruit juice
- popcorn with syrup poured over it
- rice cereal treats
- caramel popcorn
- oatmeal
- raisins
- homemade peanut butter
- pancakes and syrup
- fruit salad
- cotton candy
- sweetened cereal

Discovery Activities

Gel-O

Materials

- hair gel
- recloseable plastic bags, one per child

What to do

1. Have each child feel the texture of the hair gel.
2. Have each child spoon some hair gel into a recloseable plastic bag.
3. Close the bag and let the child use his fingers to draw on the bag for some clean artwork.

More to do

- Add a tablespoon of powdered tempera paint to the gel in the bag, close, and let the child manipulate the bag to mix the paint.

Sticky Socks

Materials

- pair of old socks, one per child

What to do

1. Put a pair of socks over each child's shoes.
2. Go outside on a "sockwalk" and see what "sticks" to the socks.

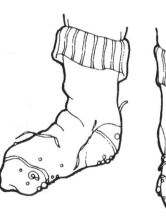

Sticky Hunt

2+

Materials

- one roll of wide masking tape

What to do

1. Give each child a piece of masking tape about six inches long.
2. Let each child go on a "Sticky Hunt" on the rug to see what sticks to her tape.

More to do

- Make a list on a chart of things that stuck to the tape. Go on a "Sticky Hunt" somewhere else, in the classroom or outside.

Goop I and II

3+

Materials

- white school glue
- liquid starch
- cornstarch
- water

What to do

1. To make Goop I, mix equal parts of school glue and liquid starch. Let the mixture sit overnight. By morning, it will stretch very thin and then return to its original shape.
2. To make Goop II, add water to cornstarch until it is the consistency of mashed potatoes. Try to pick it up—it slips through your fingers!
3. Use Goop I and II separately to explore their different properties: how does each mixture look in its bowl? How do they feel? How do they change consistency as they are handled?
4. Compare Goop I and II: Which one is stickier? Which stretches more? Which is harder to hold?

Opposites Attract

Materials

- purchased bingo wands
- magnetic bingo disks
- magnets of assorted sizes and shapes

What to do

1. Place the magnet, disks and wands on a table or tray.
2. Ask the children, "What can stick to a magnet?"
3. Let them experiment with items from different areas to see if things "stick."

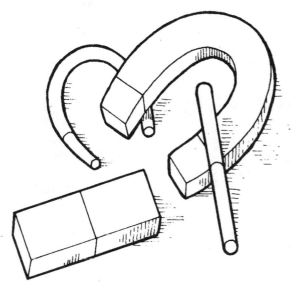

More to do

- Have the children order the magnets from smallest to largest. Create a structure with magnets. Compare the magnets' strengths—which is strongest? Which is weakest?

Good Clean Fun

3+

Materials

- bubble solution
- bubble wands
- straws
- pipe cleaners
- paper cups
- shallow pie pans

What to do

1. Pour the bubble solution into two or three pie pans.
2. Bend the pipe cleaners into various shapes to form loops.

3. Remove the bottoms of the paper cups.

4. Use pipe cleaner shapes, straws, bubble wands and paper cups to dip into bubble solution and blow bubbles.

More to do

- Try to blow bubbles with your fingers formed into a circular shape. Open and close your hand to feel the stickiness of the soap.

Sticky Icky

Materials

- six small bowls
- syrup
- honey
- gelatin
- marshmallow creme
- pasta

What to do

1. Cook the pasta, drain it, but do not rinse it.
2. Prepare gelatin according to package directions.
3. Put each one of these items into a separate bowl. Let the children feel each of these sticky items for sensory exploration.

Nature's Nasties

Materials

- cock-a-burs
- thorns
- mud

What to do

1. Let the children explore and touch these natural materials.
2. Vote on which one is the stickiest!

Poor Old Peg

Materials

- one brave volunteer
- one roll of masking tape

What to do

1. Tell the story of "Poor Old Peg" while taping the body parts named in the story "back on" the volunteer.

   "Peg woke up this morning and got out of bed, but when she tried to put her slipper on, her foot fell off. Poor old Peg!" (Put some tape around the volunteer's foot.) "She went in the bathroom to brush her hair and her arm fell off. Poor old Peg!" (Put tape around his arm.) "Peg went to the kitchen to eat breakfast, but when she lifted her spoon, her fingers fell off. Poor old Peg!" (Put tape around his fingers.) Her day continues as long as the teacher wants to make it. After each part of her body falls off just say, "Poor old Peg!" and tape it back on.

More to do

- Substitute any child's name for Peg. Let the children suggest parts of the body that need to be tape back on. Let the children make up the story.

Sticky Fingers

Materials

- 4 cups flour
- 4 cups water
- 1/2 cup salt
- 4 tablespoons oil
- 4 tablespoons cream of tartar
- 15 drops of food coloring
- electric skillet
- chart paper
- markers

What to do

1. Have the recipe written out in pictures on a large chart for students to read.
2. Let the children measure and mix ingredients in the electric skillet.
3. Turn the skillet on low and let the children stir the playdough mixture until it begins to form and stick together.
4. Put a small amount of flour on the table in front of each child. Put a small amount of the warm playdough on the flour. Let cool.
5. When cool, let the children knead the playdough. It will be "sticky" at first, and more flour may have to be added as the dough is kneaded.
6. Let the children make sculptures with the resulting playdough.

Tacky Dough

3+

Materials

- 1 cup peanut butter
- 1 cup honey
- 2 cups powdered milk
- posterboard
- markers

What to do

1. Using pictures, draw the recipe on the posterboard for the children to follow.
2. Mix all the ingredients together in a bowl.
3. Add more powdered milk if necessary to make a workable dough.

4. Let the children form the dough into any shape they wish.
5. The children can eat the dough after they are finished playing with it. (Remember: children should wash their hands before beginning any recipe!)

More to do

- You may substitute one cup of corn syrup and one cup of powdered sugar for the honey if you wish.

Stick to Your Plan

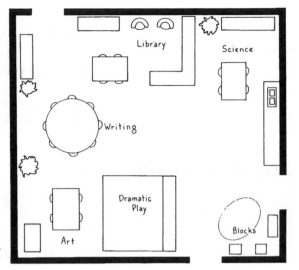

Materials

- large plan sheet showing the various centers in your room
- assorted stickers

What to do

1. When the children come into the classroom, have each child put a different sticker in the center that she would like to start playing in during choice time.

More to do

- Laminate or cover with contact paper a small picture of each child. Put a piece of tape on the back of each picture. The child can use her picture to indicate which center she will begin to work.

Birds of a Feather

4+

Materials

- assorted pine cones, one per child
- peanut butter
- wooden popsicle sticks
- birdseed
- string
- pan
- recloseable plastic bags

What to do

1. Tie a string around each pine cone for hanging.
2. Let each child spread peanut butter on her pine cone using a wooden stick.
3. Roll the pine cone in a pan of birdseed.

4. Place the child's birdfeeder in a recloseable plastic bag with her name on it to take home and hang in a tree.

More to do

- Spread a slice of bread with peanut butter and sprinkle with bird seed. Poke a hole in the bread and hang it on a tree with yarn.

Static in Your Attic

Materials

- balloons, one per child

What to do

1. Blow up a balloon for each child.
2. Have each child rub their balloon on his hair.
3. See their hair "stick" up!
4. Try to get the balloon to "stick" on the wall.

Art Activities

Ooey Gooey

Materials

- light corn syrup
- food coloring
- paper
- four paint cups
- paintbrushes

What to do

1. Pour a small amount of syrup in each paint cup.
2. Color the syrup by adding four or five drops of food coloring to each cup.
3. Let the children paint with the syrup on paper. The paintings will be beautiful, shiny, and sticky!

4. Let the artwork dry overnight. The paintings will become sticky again if the weather is humid!

More to do

- Cut paper into different shapes depending on the season of the year, such as: leaves or pumpkins for fall, Christmas trees or bells for winter or flowers or Easter eggs for spring.

Sticky Side Up

Materials

- clear contact paper
- colored paper scraps
- rick rack
- lace
- ribbon
- sequins
- magazine pictures

What to do

1. Cut a rectangular piece of contact paper for each child.
2. Peel off the backing and place the sticky side up.
3. Let the child choose what he wishes to "stick" on the sticky paper to create a design or pattern.
4. When the child's design is finished, place a second sheet of clear contact paper over it, trim the edges, and the child has a personal placemat to take home.

More to do

- Before covering the child's design, place a photograph of him on the contact paper to personalize it!

Rainbow Glue

Materials

- four small bottles of white school glue
- food coloring
- small paper plates

What to do

1. Put five drops of red food coloring in one bottle of glue. Repeat with the other colors and other glue.
2. Do not shake the glue. The color will diffuse overnight to create colored glue.
3. Give each child a paper plate and allow her to drizzle different-colored glue all over the plate.
4. Have the child tilt the plate slightly to allow the colors to run together.
5. Let dry overnight.

More to do

- Let the children sprinkle glitter on the glue before allowing it to dry.

Tape Tangle

Materials

- paper, cardboard or styrofoam trays
- assorted types of tape—duct, transparent, masking, first aid, colored, strapping, florist
- children's scissors

What to do

1. Let each child create a tape collage on his tray.
2. Ask the children to create a picture or shape using the assorted types of tape.

Eat It Up

Materials

- precut construction paper shapes of bread, cheese, meat, pickles, lettuce and tomato
- glue with yellow food coloring in an old mustard squeeze jar (or an old ketchup bottle and red glue)
- plastic wrap

What to do

1. Let the children construct their own "sandwiches" with the construction paper shapes, sticking it together with "mustard" or "ketchup."
2. When the children have completed their sandwiches, they can wrap it in plastic wrap to take home. Yummy!

Almost Good Enough to Eat

Materials

- gelatin mix (raspberry, black cherry, or blackberry)
- glossy fingerpaint paper
- water

What to do

1. Wet the fingerpaint paper on the glossy side.
2. Sprinkle two tablespoons of dry gelatin on each child's paper.
3. Let the children fingerpaint.

Goofy Glue

Materials

- white school glue
- pastel construction paper
- watercolors
- paintbrushes

What to do

1. Let each child drizzle a design with glue on a piece of construction paper.
2. Let dry overnight.
3. Have each child paint over her piece of paper with watercolors. The glue dries clear and forms a relief on the paper.

Lick 'Em and Stick 'Em

Materials

- colored construction paper or wallpaper pieces
- stickers, stick-on bows, band-aids
- junkmail stamps

What to do

1. Let each child stick on stickers, stamps and bows for a colorful sticker collage.

Sticky Surprise

3+

Materials

- masking tape
- glossy fingerpaint paper
- tempera paint (any color)
- paintbrushes

What to do

1. Let each child place masking tape strips on the glossy side of the paper.
2. Use the paintbrush to cover the entire paper with paint.
3. Let the paint dry. Remove the tape and watch the interesting designs appear.

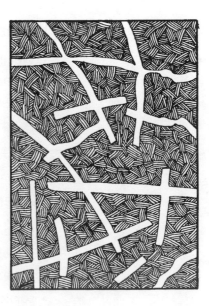

Catch a Ray

Materials

- small plastic margarine tub lid, one per child
- white school glue
- seeds, beans, shells, beads, buttons, glitter
- needle and thread

What to do

1. Let each child squeeze a puddle of glue into her plastic lid.
2. Each child may choose from a variety of beans, seeds, shells, buttons and glitter to put into the glue.
3. Let dry for several days. The glue will dry clear and the whole puddle will pop out of the plastic lid.
4. Insert a thread, using a needle, for hanging.
5. This makes a beautiful suncatcher to hang in the window!

More to do

- Try using "Rainbow Glue" to give your suncatcher a rainbow hue.

Stickers by Me

Materials

- white contact paper or plain white labels
- markers

What to do

1. Cut contact paper or labels into small shapes.
2. Let each child draw a design or picture on the non-sticky side.
3. When each child has finished his drawing, peel off the backing and let the child wear his own personalized sticker.

Magnetic Mounts

Materials

- magnetic strips
- springtype clothespins
- markers

What to do

1. Let each child draw a design on her clothespin.
2. Peel off the backing and stick the magnetic strip to the back of the clothespin.
3. The children can put these on their refrigerators to hold the papers they bring home.

More to do

- Prior to this activity, hot glue each child's clothespin to a tongue depressor to give the child more surface to decorate. Or the magnetic strip can be attached to the back of a tongue depressor.

Toothpick Stick

Materials

- box of toothpicks
- jelly beans
- marshmallows
- raisins

What to do

1. Have each child create a "sticky" sculpture using toothpicks and the "sticky" materials provided.
2. Eat the sculptures for snack! Watch out for toothpicks!
3. Add styrofoam pieces for inedible sculptures.

Music and Movement Activities

Bee Dance

What to do

1. Use the tune and actions to "London Bridge" with the following words:
   Bees are buzzing all around, all around, all around,
   Bees are buzzing all around, all around the hive.
   They caught one and they caught two and they caught you!

Jump the River

Materials

- masking tape

What to do

1. Make an imaginary river by placing two long strips of masking tape on the floor parallel to each other.
2. Invite the children to jump over the "river" or into the "river." Encourage them to swim in the river, sail boats or even fish!

Friendly Attraction

What to do

1. Have the children pretend they are magnets.
2. Have them choose partners and then link their arms or legs, stick their noses or their knees together. . . they are "attracted" to each other!

Human Web

Materials

- three or four chairs
- yarn or string

What to do

1. Place three or four chairs in a circle with the seats facing out.
2. Attach a piece of yarn or string on one leg of a chair.
3. Give a child an end of the string and have her "weave" from chair to chair.
4. Let each child have a turn, creating a "sticky" spider web.
5. Children can crawl under the web on their bellies or on their backs.

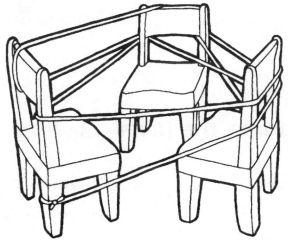

Three-Leggedness

Materials

- rope or long piece of cloth

What to do

1. "Stick" two children together by tying the right leg of one and the left leg of the other together.
2. Let them try to walk this way.

More to do

- Older children might want to run relay races with their legs "stuck" together.

Human Sandwich

Materials

- a small blanket

What to do

1. Have three children lie down on their stomachs next to each other.
2. Lay a blanket on top.
3. Have three more children lie on top to make a sandwich.
4. Ask the children what kind of sandwich they are.
5. This activity is a great follow-up to *The Giant Jam Sandwich*, by John Vernon Lord.

Weave-a-Web

Materials

- thumbtacks
- string or yarn

What to do

1. Have the children weave a big web on the wall or bulletin board using the thumbtacks and string.

Math Activities

Calendar

Materials

- plain calendar or paper and markers

What to do

1. Make or purchase a plain calendar with only the days of the week marked on it.
2. Each month, make different paper patterns to fit your theme. For example: for the "sticky" theme you may want to use peanut butter and jelly jars; three or four dif-

ferent colors of lollipops; small, medium, or large bees; or two different kinds of gum wrappers such as regular gum and bubble gum.

3. The days of the week may be sung to the tune of "Frere Jacques." "Sunday, Monday, Tuesday, Wednesday, Thursday, Friday, Saturday. It's not Sunday, it's not Monday, it's not Tuesday, it is. . . " (Let the children fill in the blank for whatever day of the week it is.)

4. School Days Countdown—make an ongoing number line for the number of days the children have been at school. Follow the same pattern as your monthly calendar pattern. Place a star on the number ten, twenty and thirty. This enables the children to count by tens. For older children, a blue star or some other designation may be used for numbers ending in five.

Calendar Patterns
for Sticky

Bandaid Match

3+

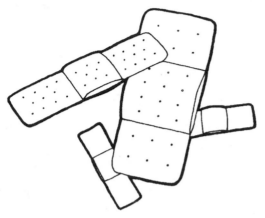

Materials

- one file folder
- one box of different-sized bandaids
- laminating film or clear contact paper

What to do

1. Stick one of each size of bandaid to the inside of the file folder. Laminate or cover with contact paper.
2. Laminate or cover with contact paper identical bandaids, and store them in a metal bandaid box.
3. Have the children match the bandaids in the box to the bandaids on the folder.

Bees Are Buzzing

3+

Materials

- one file folder
- markers
- construction paper
- scissors
- laminating film or clear contact paper

What to do

1. Draw a beehive inside the file folder.
2. Draw and cut out six pairs of bees, each with a different pattern.
3. Glue one bee from each pair of bees around the hive. Laminate or cover folder with clear contact paper.
4. Laminate the other pairs of bees or cover them with contact paper.
5. Have the children match the sets of bees to the ones near the hive.

Guessing Box

Materials

- box or paper bag
- bandaids
- pumpkins
- magnets
- marshmallows

What to do

1. Show a "sticky" item such as a jar of honey to the children and talk about its properties, such as its shape, color, container, size and uses.
2. Bring out the guessing box with another sticky item in it. Use the same box each time, no matter what size the item is. Storage boxes for clothing are the ideal size.

3. Say:

> "There is something in my guessing box.
>
> Would you like to guess?
>
> First you ask a question and
>
> I'll answer no or yes."

4. Children then ask questions. Encourage them to ask in the form of a question. "Is it. . . ?"
5. After a brief time, if you notice they aren't asking questions that pertain to the item in the box, give broad hints.

> "It's something small." Wait for guesses.
>
> "It's something round." Wait for guesses.
>
> "It's something with many colors." Wait.
>
> "It's something you chew." Wait for guesses.
>
> ("Yes, it's gumballs!")

More to do

- If you choose gumballs, estimate the number, sort and classify by color, count the number of each color, graph the favorite color, chew the gum and blow bubbles! If you choose watermelon, estimate its weight by asking, "Is it lighter than. . . ?" "Is it heavier than. . . ?" Estimate its circumference by letting the children cut strips of yarn to fit around the melon. Ask if there will be more white seeds or black seeds inside the melon. Cut the melon and eat it. Wipe off the "sticky" juice!

Count and Clink

Materials

- 10"-12" long styrofoam sheet
- pennies in a storage box
- marker

What to do

1. Divide the styrofoam sheet into ten sections.
2. Number each section consecutively from one to ten.
3. Draw dots in each section corresponding to the number in that box.
4. Let the children place the corresponding number of pennies in each section.

Sticky Feet

Materials

- paper and pencil

What to do

1. Have the children observe their shoes and how they are fastened.
2. Tally the number of velcro shoes, tied shoes, buckle shoes and slip-on shoes.
3. Discuss which ones are easiest to get on and off.

Sticky Guesses

Materials

- bandaids
- bandaid box
- paper and pen

What to do

1. Let the children look in the bandaid box and estimate how many bandaids are in it.
2. Record each guess.
3. Count the number of bandaids in the box as a group and congratulate those who guessed the closest.

Sticky Tally

4+

Materials

- three or four packs of gum, assorted flavors
- posterboard
- marker
- tape

What to do

1. Allow each child to choose a stick of gum.
2. Unwrap the gum and save the wrapper. Tape each wrapper to the posterboard and draw columns under each wrapper.
3. While the children are chewing, have them tape their wrappers on the posterboard according to the type of gum. (Match the wrappers.)
4. Decide which gum was the favorite.

More to do

- This activity can be done with snack-sized candy bars.

Language Activities

Sticky Stuff

3+

Materials

- paper
- markers

What to do

1. On a large piece of paper record a list of "sticky" things suggested by the children.
2. Add to the list as the children discover more "sticky" things while experiencing the "sticky" activities in this chapter.

It Hurts!

3+

Materials

- oblong pieces of paper, 8 1/2" by 14"
- markers and crayons
- stapler

What to do

1. Have each child describe how and where he has gotten a "boo-boo" (a scrape or cut).
2. Record their injuries on separate oblong sheets of paper, rounded at the edges to give the appearance of a large bandaid.
3. Let each child illustrate his injury.
4. Bind into "A Book of Boo-Boos."

More to do

- This activity is a good extension for *The Prince Has a Boo-Boo* by Harriet Zeifert.

Catch a _____

Materials

- paper
- crayons and markers
- stapler

What to do

1. Draw a partial spider web on a piece of paper for each child.
2. Ask each child to finish the picture by drawing what got caught in her sticky web.
3. Bind the children's creations into a book.

More to do

- This activity is an excellent extension for *The Very Busy Spider* by Eric Carle.

Transition Activities

Sit On It

What to do

1. Have the children blow up a bubble with pretend bubble gum.
2. Tell them to stick them to their bottoms and sit down.
3. They are stuck to that spot!

Blow It Up

What to do

1. Have the children follow your actions as you blow up a pretend bubble.
2. Hold your breath for a couple of seconds and let air out slowly.

Songs and Chants

- "Eensy Weensy Spider" (traditional)

  "The eensy weensy spider went up the water spout.

  Down came the rain and washed the spider out.

  Out came the sun and dried up all the rain.

  And the eensy weensy spider went up the spout again."

- Variation:

  "Three little spiders went up the water spout.

  Down came the rain and washed one spider out.

  Out came the sun and dried up all the rain.

  And two little spiders went up the spout again."

- Repeat with two little spiders and one little spider.

- Instead of the word "little" you may want to substitute words such as "black," "red," "big," "scary."

- "Little Miss Muffet"

  Little Miss Muffet sat on a tuffet

  Eating her curds and whey.

  Along came a spider

  Who sat down beside her

  And frightened Miss Muffet away

- "Five Sticky Doughnuts"

  Five sticky doughnuts in the bakery shop

  Shining so bright with the icing on top.

  Along came (child's name) with a penny to pay

  He/she picked this sticky doughnut and went away.

- Repeat verse with four, three, two, one until. . .

  No sticky doughnuts in the bakery shop

  Shining so bright with the icing on top.

  The baker closed the shop up for today

  But come back tomorrow with a penny to pay!

- "Lollipop, Lollipop"

  Let's all go to the candy shop

  Licorice, bubble gum, and soda pop.

  (Child's name) had some money for a lollipop.

  Which color lollipop did she choose?

- Put a colored lollipop up on the flannel board. Let the children name the color. Repeat the poem using different names and colors until all the lollipops are gone.

- Use a pattern for "Lollipop, Lollipop." Make a variety of colored lollipops. Brown flannel or a popsicle stick can be used for the lollipop stick.
- "Bubble Gum, Bubble Gum"

   Bubble gum, bubble bum in a dish,

   How many pieces do you wish?

   1-2-3-4-5!

- "Sticky, Icky"

   Sticky, icky,

   Gooey, ooey,

   Yucky, ucky,

   SMACK! (smack lips)

Theme Extensions and Variations

Field Trips

- If possible, take a trip to a bee farm (apiary). See where honey comes from.
- If you live in an area where there is maple tree tapping, this would be a wonderful "sticky" experience.

Variations

- Call the theme "Sticky and Icky" to add some interesting tactile activities to this unit.
- Try doing the theme in different seasons or months. For instance, during October you can bring in the aspect of pumpkins, spiders, and "sticky" candy.
- In the spring, you can focus on bees and honey, making maple syrup or exploring related ideas from our chapter entitled "Muddy Puddles, Soap and Bubbles."

Bibliography

- *Bartholomew and the Oobleck*, Dr. Seuss. NY: Random House, 1949. The king orders Oobleck from the sky, which is green and sticky on everyone. The Oobleck has to say "I'm sorry" to save the kingdom.
- *Bread and Jam for Frances*, Russell Hoban. NY: HarperCollins, 1965. Frances wants to eat bread and jam for breakfast, lunch, and supper until she finally gets tired of having the same thing!

- *Giant Jam Sandwich, The*, John Vernon Lord. Boston, MA: Houghton Mifflin Co., 1987. A town is plagued by wasps and the townspeople devise an ingenious plan to capture them in a sticky giant jam sandwich.

- *Mouse Paint*, Ellen Stoll Walsh. San Diego, CA: Harcourt Brace Jovanovich Publications, 1989. Three white mice find some paint (in primary colors) and mix them and discover secondary colors.

- *Oh, Were They Ever Happy!* Peter Spier. NY: Doubleday, 1978. Three children decide to help out and paint their house while their parents are out.

- *Pancakes for Breakfast*, Tomie de Paola. NY: Harcourt Bract Jovanovich Inc., 1978. A wonderful wordless picture book that follows a little old lady through all her troubles in making a stack of pancakes.

- *Peanut Butter and Jelly*, Nadine Bernard Westcott. NY: Dutton Children's Books, 1987. A book about the popular play rhyme describing how to make a peanut butter and jelly sandwich.

- *Prince Has a Boo-Boo, The*, Harriet Ziefert. NY: Random House, 1989. The prince bumps his head and everyone rushes to his aid.

- *Strega Nona*, Tomie de Paola. NY: Simon & Schuster, 1979. Strega Nona has a magic pot that makes pasta, and while she is gone Big Anthony gets carried away with his magic and can't stop the pot!

- *The Very Busy Spider*, Eric Carle. NY: Putnam Publishing Group, 1989. As the very busy spider spins its web, children can feel the raised lines of the web. Also, reinforces various animal sounds.

Recordings

- "Bubble Gum," *Abracadabra*, Joe Scruggs, (Shadow Play Records & Video) Educational Graphics Press, Inc. 1986.

- "School Glue," *Abracadabra*. Joe Scruggs, (Shadow Play Records & Video) Educational Graphics Press, Inc. 1986.

- "Peanut Butter," *Following Directions*. MacMillan. 1987.

- "Grape Jelly Cure," *Late Last Night*. Joe Scruggs, (Shadow Play Records & Video) Educational Graphics Press, Inc. 1984.

- "Flight of the Bumblebee"

Crash, Bang, Boom

Mondays

Start Weather or Not
Do Swat Team

Field trip to High School Band Room
Do Homemade Band

Field trip to Fire Station
Sing "fire" songs

Do Muddy Pig, Muddy Pig, what Do You Hear?
Read Polar Bear, Polar Bear, What Do You Hear?

Tuesdays

Read The Listening Walk
Play Guess What?

Read Ben's Trumpet
Play Leader of the Band

Bring something noisy for Guessing Box ~ Make a Noisy Graph

Do Our Favorite Songs & Puff-n-Paint

Wednesdays

Read Crash! Bang! Boom!
Do Shout or Whisper

Read Gobble Growl Grunt
Fizzy Juice for Snack

Read Noisy Nora
Play Musical Chairs

Read Angry Arthur
Make Stormy Weather

Thursdays

Play Balloon Race
Play Name That Tune

Play Windy Ping Pong
Read Night Noises

Do Shake an Egg
Play Shout It Out

Do Blow Your Top!
Do Crumpled Paper Painting

Fridays

Read I Hear a Noise
Play Tell-A-Phone

Do Corny Counting
Do Have You Lost Your Marbles?

Read Where the Wild Things Are
Do Wild Rumpus

Do Whistling Steam
Read Flash Crash Rumble & Roll

Crash, Bang, Boom

Theme Objectives

- To experience various sounds in and around the environment
- To observe loud, soft and in-between sounds
- To discover different instruments and their sounds

Learning Centers

Dramatic Play

- various instruments: drums, harmonica, cymbals, bongos, autoharp, electric piano or maracas
- band uniform and hat
- office: typewriter, calculator, phones, adding machine
- rain gear: coats, boots, umbrella
- pots and pans
- alarm clock

Library

- tape player and earphones
- various tapes and storybooks
- storybooks with sound

Writing

- squiggle pen writer
- typewriter

Science

- Tornado Tube (see activity in Discovery section)
- sandblocks
- plastic sandwich bags to fill with air and pop
- Ocean Waves (see activity in Discovery section)
- crickets
- piece of sheet metal (supervise closely)
- megaphone
- whistles

- gavel

Blocks

- hammer, nails and other tools (supervise closely)
- carpenter's bench
- assorted sizes and types of cars and trucks
- PVC Pipe Phone (see activity in Discovery section)
- plastic bowling set
- walkie-talkies

Snacks

- crunchy chips and quiet dip
- pretzels
- nacho chips and cheese
- popcorn
- crispy rice cereal
- carrot sticks
- celery sticks
- peanut butter
- apples
- slurping soup
- crackers
- Fruit Smoothie (see activity in Discovery section)
- Fizzy Juice (see activity in Discovery section)

Discovery Activities

Fruit Smoothie

Materials

- frozen yogurt
- juice
- blender
- cups
- straws

What to do

1. Fill the blender 2/3 full with frozen yogurt.
2. Add juice to top.
3. Blend, pour into cups and slurp the smoothies through straws.

Fizzy Juice

Materials

- juice
- seltzer water
- cups

What to do

1. Fill a cup or glass half full of juice.
2. Add a small amount seltzer water until the drink becomes bubbly.
3. Pour a cup for each child, listening to the fizzy sounds. Bottoms up!

PVC Pipe Phone

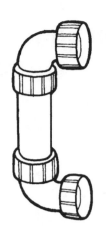

Materials

- two 1 1/2 inch PVC elbows
- one 2" PVC section

What to do

1. Place a 1 1/2 elbow over each end of the 2" section. Make several, for these will be popular.

Tornado Tube

Materials

- Tornado Tube, available from most teacher supply stores or catalogs or by writing to:

  Tornado Tube
  26 Dearborn St.
  Salem, MA 01970

- two empty, clean soda bottles with their labels removed
- food coloring
- water

What to do

1. Fill one bottle 3/4 full of water and add a few drops of desired color of food coloring. Leave the second bottle empty.
2. Connect the two bottles with the Tornado Tube.
3. Make a tornado funnel by rotating the bottle in an upright position using a swirling motion.

Shake an Egg

Materials

- twelve colored plastic Easter eggs
- egg carton
- six sets of three small items that make noise, such as rice, rocks, paper clips, jingle bells, beans, sand, staples or marbles
- glue or tape

What to do

1. For each set of items, put two in individual eggs and glue or tape the third inside the lid of the egg carton.
2. Have the children try to match the eggs by shaking each egg and listening for the same sounds.
3. Have them put the eggs they think match inside the carton under the item they think is inside the egg.
4. Open the eggs to see if the match is correct and if the items correspond to the glued or stapled item above them in the carton.

Windy Ping Pong

Materials

- ping pong ball
- masking tape
- table

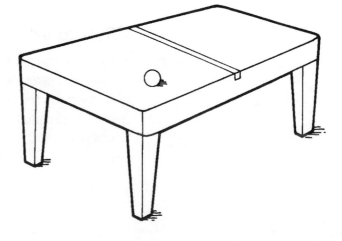

What to do

1. Place a strip of masking tape at the halfway mark across a table top. This is your net.
2. Two to four players are needed to either play singles or doubles.
3. Have the children blow the ping pong ball with their mouths.

4. A point is made each time the "server" blows it across the net and off the table on the opponent's side.

More to do

- Squeeze empty dish detergent bottles to make the ball move.

Guess Who?

Materials

- tape recorder
- blank cassette tape

What to do

1. During free play, tape the voices of as many students as possible. This may be a formal or informal taping.
2. Play the tape back at circle time, stopping after each voice to let the children guess whose voice they hear.

Guess What?

Materials

- several items that make an identifiable noise, such as a stapler, two spoons, a kitchen timer or an alarm clock
- a cardboard divider

What to do

1. Show the items to the children.
2. Hide the items behind the cardboard divider.
3. Make a noise with an item and let the children guess which one made the noise.

More to do

- Don't show the items beforehand and see if the children can guess them.

Blow Your Top!

Materials

- playdough or clay
- baking soda
- red food coloring
- vinegar
- tray with sides

What to do

1. Use playdough or clay to form a volcano shape on the tray. This is a good way to use up old playdough.
2. Make a hole in the top about 1" deep.
3. Mix a few drops of red food coloring with the vinegar.
4. Put a teaspoon of baking soda in the hole of the volcano.
5. Using a medicine cup, slowly pour the vinegar and food coloring mixture into the hole until it bubbles and overflows like lava.
6. Slowly pour the vinegar mixture again. Repeat until it no longer bubbles. Then add more baking soda and repeat procedure.

HINT: Make several playdough volcanoes. This will be a popular activity.

Whistling Steam

4+

Materials

- whistling teakettle
- water
- stove or hot plate

What to do

1. Fill the teakettle with water.
2. Heat it until it whistles. This is a good opportunity to talk about steam, water vapor and kitchen safety.

More to do

- Serve hot tea or instant cocoa.

Ocean Waves

Materials

- water
- blue food coloring
- rubbing alcohol
- mineral oil
- clear plastic two-liter bottle

What to do

1. In the clear plastic bottle, pour 1/3 of a bottle of rubbing alcohol.
2. Fill the rest of the way with two parts of water to one part mineral oil and add several drops of blue food coloring.
3. Show the children how waves roll in and out by gently tilting the bottle back and forth.
4. Seal on the lid of bottle with duct tape and allow the children to freely explore ocean waves.

More to do

- Small plastic fish can be added to ocean before sealing.

Art Activities

Place 'n Trace

Materials

- various musical instruments
- markers
- crayons
- large sheets of newsprint or other paper

What to do

1. Have each child choose an instrument to trace around.
2. Remove the instrument after tracing.
3. Draw and color in details.
4. Cut out and display the instruments on a wall mural or bulletin board.

More to do

● Match the drawings to the real instruments. Tally each type of instrument.

Have You Lost Your Marbles?

3+

Materials

● shoebox
● tempera paint
● colored construction paper
● marbles
● plastic spoons

What to do

1. Cut the paper to fit inside the shoebox and put the paint into small shallow containers.
2. Put a marble or two into several colors of paint.
3. Using a spoon, roll the marble around in the paint in order to cover the entire marble.
4. Lift the marble out of the paint and place it on the paper in the box.
5. Roll the marbles around using a side-to-side motion. The more marbles you use the noisier it is!

More to do

● Place the lid on the box and shake the marbles around.

Mix It Up

Materials

- electric hand mixer
- soap flakes
- water
- cardboard or styrofoam meat trays
- large bowl

What to do

1. Add water to the soap flakes in a large bowl and mix on high speed until fluffy. Add more water or flakes as needed.
2. Have the children use the fluff as fingerpaint.
3. Have them try to sculpt with it.

Crumpled Paper Painting

3+

Materials

- construction paper
- newspaper, one sheet per child
- tempera paint
- flat trays

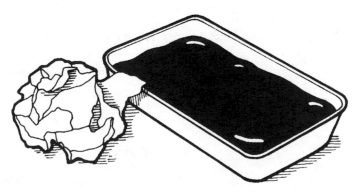

What to do

1. Have each child crumple a piece of newspaper into a ball.
2. Have him dip the newspaper ball into the tempera paint and dab it on a piece of construction paper.

Swat Team

3+

Materials

- several flyswatters
- large box
- several colors of tempera paint
- white paper
- paint shirts

What to do

1. Place the white paper in the box with the top removed.
2. Place plenty of newspaper around.
3. Have the children dip the flyswatters into the paint and swat the paper inside the box.

NOTE: This activity splatters paint everywhere! It is a good activity to do outside in the spring or fall.

At the Races

3+

Materials

- several miniature race cars
- brown tempera paint
- large paper

What to do

1. Have the children dip the wheels of the car into brown paint and run them over the large paper to make tracks.
2. They can make race car sounds while painting.

Puff 'n Paint

Materials

- straws
- thinned tempera paint
- paper
- eyedropper

What to do

1. Water down the tempera paint so it can be blown easily.
2. Using an eyedropper, place a little tempera on the paper.
3. Have the children blow through a straw and try to spread the paint around on the paper.

Music and Movement Activities

Sit on It

Materials

- balloons, one per child

What to do

1. Blow up and tie each balloon.
2. Count to three and have each child sit on her balloon and pop it!

Pop Goes the Weasel

What to do

1. Sing "Pop Goes the Weasel" and "pop up" when you sing it.
2. Whisper the song and "pop up."
3. Hum the song and "pop up."

Song Can

Materials

- small can with a lid, such as an empty can of lemonade or iced tea mix
- contact paper
- small cardboard pieces, about 2" x 4"
- markers

What to do

1. Draw picture clues to songs on the cards. For example, a school bus could be used for "The Wheels on the Bus," a spider for "Eensy Weensy Spider," or a star for "Twinkle, Twinkle Little Star." Put the name of the song on the back of the picture.
2. Cover each card with contact paper and store them in the empty can.
3. Use this song can during a regular music period or as a minute filler by letting a child draw a card, guess the song title and lead the class in the song.

Name That Tune

Materials

- electric piano or piano

What to do

1. Hum or pick out a familiar tune on the piano, such as "Old MacDonald," "Jingle Bells" or "Happy Birthday."
2. Have the children guess the name of the song.
3. Sing the entire song after it has been guessed.

Crash, Bang, Boom

Homemade Band

4+

Materials

- two metal spoons
- two wooden spoons
- two dowel rods
- two pan lids
- pan lid and a spoon
- pot and a wooden spoon
- milk jugs to blow in
- Christmas bells

What to do

1. Use the materials listed as instruments, or the children can make their own instruments or use non-traditional items to make music in their own classroom band. The following are suggestions:

   Kazoo: Take one toilet paper tube, and using a paper punch, punch a hole about 1" from the bottom. Place about a 4" square of wax paper over the bottom hole and gather closed with a rubber band. Blow in the other end.

   Bongos: Cover a round oatmeal box with contact paper or decorated construction paper. Beat on the lid with your hand or a wooden spoon.

   Shakers: Fill yogurt cups or small margarine tubs with beans, rice or pebbles and put the lid on. Decorate as desired. Experiment with different items to get varying sounds.

   Tambourines: Place two paper plates together facing each other and staple their edges together, leaving a small opening. Fill them with beans, rice, or pebbles and staple the hole shut. Children can decorate them with markers or colorful crepe paper streamers.

   Bell Bracelets: Have children string jingle bells on a piece of yarn or string. Tie the ends together to make a bracelet. Shake your wrists to make music!

Tinkle Tunes

Materials

- five drinking glasses
- water
- metal spoon

What to do

1. Fill the glasses with water to varying levels, and order them from most to least full.
2. Demonstrate for the children how they can gently tap the side of a glass to make music.
3. Which glass has the highest sound? Which has the lowest?
4. Let the children try to make their own music.

NOTE: Teacher supervision on this project is strongly suggested.

Tell-a-Phone

4+

What to do

1. Seat the children in a circle.
2. Start the telephone by whispering a word or phrase in the first child's ear.
3. Tell him to pass it on.
4. The last child gets to say the word aloud. (Words like underwear and supercalifragilisticexpialidocious work great!)

More to do

- Let the children think of words to pass on. With older children, you could have the last child say the word backwards!

Balloon Race

Materials

- balloons, one per child

What to do

1. Write each child's name on a balloon with permanent marker.
2. Give each child a balloon and let her inflate it.
3. Let the balloons go and watch them race around the room. Listen to the sound!

Stormy Weather

Materials

- large trash bags
- cymbals
- flashlight

What to do

1. Tell the children that they are going to be a storm.
2. Some children can use their fingers to tap their fingers on a table for rain.
3. Fill a couple of trash bags with air and have the children shake them for a wind noise.
4. Have other children crash the cymbals for thunder.
5. Use a flashlight for lightning.
6. Begin softly—it's just a light drizzle. Build the storm up to a hurricane (you might even want to have some children stomping to accent the thunder sounds), and then slowly bring it down to a shower, then a light patter, until finally the storm is gone and everyone is quiet.

Leader of the Band

4+

Materials

- marching songs, such as "76 Trombones" or John Philip Sousa marches
- baton

What to do

1. Choose a child to be the leader and hand him the baton.
2. The leader chooses a motion and moves to the marching music. All the other children follow in a line behind the leader.
3. Stop the music.
4. Have the leader pass his baton to a new leader.
5. Make available the following at special movement times:

> punch balls
>
> paddle balls
>
> Klackers
>
> kinetic steel balls
>
> beanbags
>
> balloons for balloon volleyball
>
> bubble packing material

Math Activities

Our Favorite Songs

3+

Materials

- posterboard or large piece of paper
- musical note stamp or sticker

What to do

1. Prepare a graph by drawing in a grid.
2. Recall at least three favorite songs. The children can nominate them, or you may choose them if the children are too young.

3. Write the song titles in each of the three squares on the grid. If possible, draw a picture by the title so that it is easily identified by the children.

4. Sing all three songs with the children.

5. Have the children vote for their favorite song by using a musical note stamp or sticker.

Calendar

Materials

- plain calendar or paper and markers

What to do

1. Make or purchase a plain calendar with only the days of the week marked on it.

2. Each month, make different paper patterns to fit your theme. For example: for the "crash bang boom" theme you may want to use cymbals (crash), a snare drum (bang) and a kettle drum (boom). (See the illustration for calendar patterns.)

3. The days of the week may be sung to the tune of "Frere Jacques." "Sunday, Monday, Tuesday, Wednesday, Thursday, Friday, Saturday. It's not Sunday, it's not Monday, it's not Tuesday, it is. . . " (Let the children fill in the blank for whatever day of the week it is.)

4. School Days Countdown   make an ongoing number line for the number of days the children have been at school. Follow the same pattern as your monthly calendar pattern.

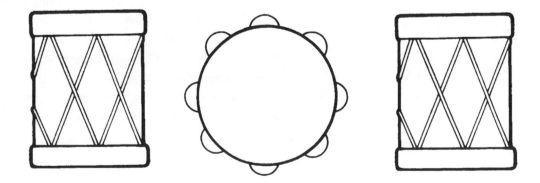

Guessing Box

4+

Materials

- box or paper bag
- musical instrument
- unpopped popcorn
- potato chips
- tape recorder
- telephone
- alarm clock
- punch ball

What to do

1. Show a "crash bang boom" item such as an alarm clock to the children and talk about its properties: its shape, color, container, size, and uses.

2. Bring out the guessing box with another "crash bang boom" item in it. Use the same box each time, no matter what size the item is. Storage boxes for clothing are the ideal size.

3. Say:

    "There is something in my guessing box.

    Would you like to guess?

    First you ask a question and

    I'll answer no or yes."

4. Children then ask questions. Encourage them to ask in the form of a question. "Is it. . . ?"

5. After a brief time, if you notice they aren't asking questions that pertain to the item in the box, give broad hints.

    "It's something small." Wait for guesses.

    "It's something round." Wait for guesses.

    "It's something hard." Wait.

    "It's something that pops." Wait for guesses.

    ("Yes, it's a kernel of unpopped popcorn!")

Corny Counting

Materials

- two baby food jars
- unpopped corn
- popped popcorn

What to do

1. Fill one baby food jar with popped corn. Count the corn as you put it in the jar.
2. Place the same amount of unpopped corn in the other jar.
3. Show the two jars of popcorn to the children.
4. Have the children guess which one has more.
5. Tell the children that the jars have the same amount and ask them why one jar is filled and the other one isn't.
6. Count the contents of both jars with the children. Supervise closely.

Weather or Not

Materials

- weather graph
- crayons

What to do

1. Prepare a weather graph to use throughout the month. Keep it simple.
2. Everyday at calendar time, let the children take turns graphing the day's weather.
3. To graph, the child colors in the appropriate square for that day's weather.
4. At the end of the month, ask how many sunny days, cloudy days or rainy days you had. Ask, "Did we have more cloudy days or snowy days?"

Pop Up

Materials

- air popper
- popcorn
- clean sheet
- dot stickers, one per child

What to do

1. Spread a clean sheet out on the floor.
2. Have the children sit around the perimeter of the sheet.
3. Place the air popper in the center of the sheet. Talk about how far the popcorn will pop out.
4. Let the children place a sticker where they think the furthest-popping kernel will land.
5. Add the popcorn and plug in the popper. Leave the lid on the popper until it gets hot. When the kernels start to pop, remove lid.
6. Listen to the sounds of popping corn.
7. Did anybody place their sticker correctly?
8. Eat the popcorn right off the sheet!

Noisy Graph

4+

Materials

- plain-colored shower curtain
- permanent marker
- noisy items brought from home

What to do

1. Make a floor graph by marking off 12"-14" squares with a permanent marker on a vinyl shower curtain. (For this activity only two columns are needed, but for future use make the graph at least four columns wide and several rows long.)
2. Label one column loud and one soft, or one high and the other low. Start with only two comparing columns. The more you use the floor graph, the better the children will get at comparing!
3. The day before the activity, send a note home requesting children to bring in an item from home that makes either a loud or soft noise.

4. Spread the floor graph out on the floor. Have the children sit around the perimeter of the graph.

5. Ask a child what kind of noise her item makes, and have her place it in the appropriate column. Choose one or two more children with an item in the same category to get the graph going.

6. After two or three children have participated, ask a child who has an opposite noise to begin the next column.

7. Repeat the procedure until every child has placed her item in a square.

8. Ask the children, "Which has more, the loud column or the soft? Which has less?"

More to do

- Ask the children, "Can you remember who brought each item?"

Language Activities

Fire Drill

3+

Materials

- *The Fire Station* by Robert Munsch

What to do

1. Arrange to have the fire alarm go off at a designated time.
2. Read and discuss *The Fire Station*.
3. Ask the children if they have ever seen or been in a fire.
4. Have they ever heard the fire alarm?
5. Prepare the children for the school fire alarm by telling them to expect a loud noise. Give them directions on what to do and where to go.
6. When the fire alarm sounds, carry out a fire drill.

More to do

- Incorporate other safety activities, and visit a fire station.

Wild Rumpus

3+

Materials

- pots
- pans
- tambourines
- drums
- any noisemakers
- *Where the Wild Things Are* by Maurice Sendak

What to do

1. Read *Where the Wild Things Are.*
2. Have your own wild rumpus using noisy instruments.

Shout It Out

3+

Materials

- chart paper or other large paper
- markers
- megaphone (optional)

What to do

1. Make up a cheer about the school or use the following cheer. Write it out on chart paper with pictures or photographs to show motions.
2. Teach the class the cheer by following along with words and motions on the chart.
3. Start by whispering the cheer and gradually get louder until you are shouting.

More to do

- Let older children work in groups or as a class to make up an original school cheer.

School Cheer

> We're in preschool, couldn't be prouder.
> If you can't hear us we'll yell a little louder.

- Repeat even louder. Instead of saying, "We're in preschool" you might say, "We're from (school name)."

My Noisy Family

Materials

- *Noisy Nora* by Rosemary Wells
- drawing paper
- markers
- crayons

What to do

1. Read *Noisy Nora*.
2. Discuss Nora's family.
3. Ask the children, "Who lives at your house?" Have them draw pictures of their families.

More to do

- Draw pictures of family members doing something noisy. For example: a sister practicing saxophone, a mother mowing the lawn or the dad vacuuming.

Angry Pictures

Materials

- drawing paper
- markers
- crayons
- *Angry Arthur*, by Hiawyn Oram

What to do

1. Read *Angry Arthur* and discuss it with the children.

2. Let the children draw a picture of themselves or someone else looking like they are angry.

Shout or Whisper

Materials

- two charts or large pieces of paper
- marker

What to do

1. Tell the children that they are going to make a list of things that make a loud noise.
2. Start by giving them an example such as "thunder."
3. Write down their responses.
4. Keep adding to the list throughout the theme.

More to do

- A few days later, start a "soft" list. This may be more difficult for them.

Muddy Pig, Muddy Pig, What Do You Hear?

Materials

- *Polar Bear, Polar Bear, What Do You Hear?* by Bill Martin, Jr.
- drawing paper
- markers
- crayons
- book binder or rings

What to do

1. Read *Polar Bear, Polar Bear, What Do You Hear?* aloud to the children.
2. Let each child draw a farm animal. Follow the pattern of the text of the polar bear book. Example: waddly duck, lazy dog, milking cow, fast horse or little chick.

Parading Around

4+

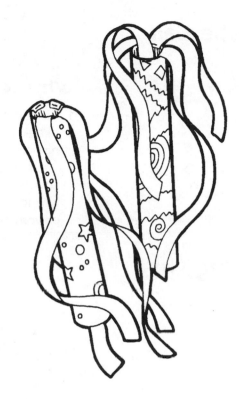

Materials

- chart or large paper
- paper towel tubes, one per child
- colored crepe paper streamers
- stickers and markers or crayons
- *Parade* by Donald Crews
- marching music

What to do

1. Let the children color and decorate their paper towel rolls with stickers and crayons or markers.
2. Attach three or four 12" streamers by stapling them to one end of the paper towel tube.
3. Read *Parade*.
4. Have your own school or classroom parade by lining up and parading through the room with streamers to the marching music.

More to do

- Discuss parades. Have they ever seen a parade? What did they see? Make a list of their responses.

Transition Activities

Read My Lips

What to do

1. If you want to dismiss children from a group in a quiet and orderly fashion, whisper each child's name. Children have to be quiet and watch your lips to know when their name has been called.

Cattle Call

What to do

1. Dismiss children one or two at a time by calling their names and telling them to make a cow sound, a cat sound or a dog sound all the way to the bathroom, gym or playground.

Acting Up

What to do

1. Choose a child and whisper what he should act out without talking. Some examples are: going to bed, playing golf, catching a ball, climbing stairs, sleeping, driving a car, playing drums, playing a flute, painting or taking a bath.
2. Let other children guess what the actor is doing.
3. Choose three or four children to be actors while taking turns going to the bathroom or washing up.

Songs and Chants

- "Little Raindrops," "Clap, Clap, Clap," "Hear the Wind Blow," and "Mr. Wind is a Mischief," *I Have a Song for You.* (About People and Nature), Janeen Brady, Vol. 1. USA: Brite Music Enterprises, Inc., 1979. (songbook)
- Sing the following additional verses of "Two Little Blackbirds."

  Two little blackbirds sitting on a cloud.
  One named soft (soft voice), one named LOUD (shout).
  Fly away soft, Fly away LOUD.
  Come back soft, Come back LOUD.
  Two little blackbirds sitting on a cloud.
  One named soft, one named LOUD!
  Two little blackbirds sitting on some snow.
  One named fast, one named slow.
  Fly away fast, fly away slow.

Come back fast, come back slow.

Two little blackbirds sitting on some snow.

One named fast, one named slow.

- Or substitute high and low instead of fast and slow.
- "Going on a Bear Hunt"—traditional
- "Five Noisy Children"

Five noisy children jumping on the bed.

One fell off and bumped his head.

"Shhh!" said the mother.

"Quiet!" said the dad.

"Any more noise and I'll be mad!"

- Repeat with four, three, two and one.

Theme Extensions and Variations

Field Trips

- Local factory
- High school band room and band practice
- School office
- Bowling alley
- Handbell choir
- Airport
- Fire station
- Church—organ

Variations

- Incorporate some of the noisier activities and stories from the "Meanies, Monsters and Make Believe" chapter.
- For older children, emphasize more of earth's geological features such as earthquakes, typhoons and hurricanes.

Bibliography

- *Angry Arthur*, Hiawyn Oram. NY: Dutton Books, Inc., 1989. When Arthur's mother won't let him have his way, he becomes angry enough to create a thunderstorm, a hurricane and an earthquake!

- *Ben's Trumpet*, Rachel Isadora. NY: Greenwillow Books, 1979. Ben loves playing his imaginary trumpet, but he wants a real one. Maybe the musician from the Zig Zag Club can help!

- *Crash! Bang! Boom!* Peter Spier. NY: Doubleday and Co., 1990. Pictures of things that make sounds with the sound word it makes.

- *Flash Crash Rumble & Roll*, Franklyn M. Branley. NY: Trophy, 1987. Explains how and why a thunderstorm occurs and gives safety tips to follow when it is lightening.

- *Fire Station*, The, Robert Munsch. Toronto, Canada: Annick Press, Ltd., 1986. Michael and Sheila are accidently on the fire truck when suddenly there is a fire.

- *Gobble Growl Grunt*, Peter Spier. NY: Doubleday and Co., 1988. Six hundred animals are portrayed along with the sound each one makes.

- *I Hear a Noise*, Diane Goode. NY: E.P. Dutton, 1992. A little boy, hearing noises at his window at bedtime, calls for his mother. His worst fears are realized, but he learns that monsters have mothers too.

- *Listening Walk, The*, Paul Showers. NY: Harper Collins Publishers, 1991. A little girl and her father take a quiet walk and identify the sounds around them.

- *Night Noises*, Mem Fox. NY: Harcourt Brace Jovanovich Publishers, 1989. Old Lily Laceby dozes by the fire with her faithful dog at her feet as strange night noises herald a surprise awakening.

- *Noisy Nora*, Rosemary Wells. NY: Dial Books, 1973. Crash! Nora wants some attention, but everybody's too busy. When she decides to hide, and it becomes so quiet, everyone comes to see what's the matter.

- *Polar Bear, Polar Bear, What Do You Hear?* Bill Martin, Jr. NY: Henry Holt and Co., 1991. Zoo animals from polar bear to walrus make their distinctive sounds for each other, while children imitate the sounds for the zookeeper.

- *Parade*, Donald Crews. NY: Greenwillow, 1983. Illustrations and brief text present the various elements of a parade.

- *Where the Wild Things Are*, Maurice Sendak. NY: Harper and Row Publishers, 1988. Max goes to "where the wild things are" becomes king and has a wild rumpus!

Poems

- "Clatter," *Kids Pick the Funniest Poems*. Joyce Armour. NY: Meadowbrook Press, 1991, p. 3.

- "Snap!" *A Light in the Attic*. Shel Silverstein. NY: Harper and Row, 1981, p. 64.

- "I Know All the Sounds That Animals Make," *Something Big Has Been Here*. Jack Prelutsky. NY: Greenwillow Books, 1990, p. 9.

Crash, Bang, Boom

- "Ourchestra," *Where the Sidewalk Ends*. Shel Silverstein. NY: Harper and Row, 1974, p. 23.

Recordings

- "Play Your Instrument," *Play Your Instrument and Make a Pretty Sound*, Ella Jenkins, Folkways Records and Service Corp. 1968.
- "Tap Your Sticks," *Rhythms on Parade*, Hap Palmer, Hap-Pal Music, Inc. 1989.
- "The Hammer Song," *Tickly Toddle*, Hap Palmer, Educational Activities, Inc. 1981.
- "Shout and Whisper," *Tickly Toddle*, Hap Palmer, Educational Activities, Inc. 1981.
- "So Much to Hear," *Tickly Toddle*, Hap Palmer, Educational Activities, Inc. 1981.

Giant, Teeny, Tiny

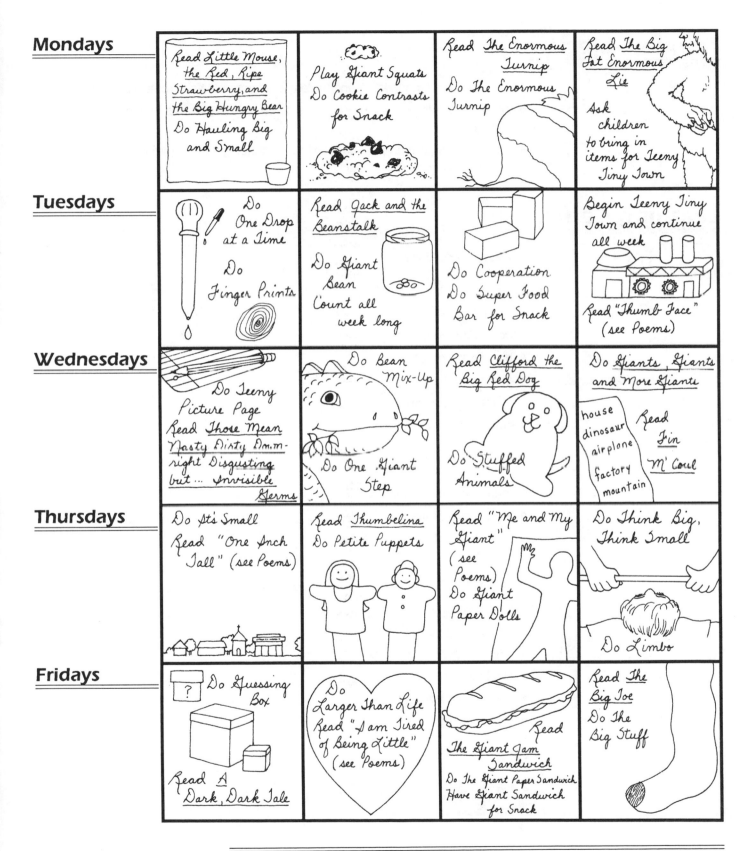

Mondays

Read _Little Mouse, the Red, Ripe Strawberry, and the Big Hungry Bear_
Do _Hauling Big and Small_

Play _Giant Squats_
Do _Cookie Contrasts_ for Snack

Read _The Enormous Turnip_
Do _The Enormous Turnip_

Read _The Big Fat Enormous Lie_
Ask children to bring in items for Teeny Tiny Town

Tuesdays

Do _One Drop at a Time_
Do _Finger Prints_

Read _Jack and the Beanstalk_
Do _Giant Bean Count_ all week long

Do _Cooperation_
Do _Super Food Bar_ for Snack

Begin _Teeny Tiny Town_ and continue all week
Read "Thumb Face" (see Poems)

Wednesdays

Do _Teeny Picture Page_
Read _Those Mean Nasty Dirty Downright Disgusting but ... Invisible Germs_

Do _Bean Mix-Up_
Do _One Giant Step_

Read _Clifford the Big Red Dog_
Do _Stuffed Animals_

Do _Giants, Giants and More Giants_
house, dinosaur, airplane, factory, mountain
Read _Fin M'Coul_

Thursdays

Do _It's Small_
Read "One Inch Tall" (see Poems)

Read _Thumbelina_
Do _Petite Puppets_

Read "Me and My Giant" (see Poems)
Do _Giant Paper Dolls_

Do _Think Big, Think Small_
Do _Limbo_

Fridays

Do _Guessing Box_
Read _A Dark, Dark Tale_

Do _Larger Than Life_
Read "I am Tired of Being Little" (see Poems)

Read _The Giant Jam Sandwich_
Do _The Giant Paper Sandwich_
Have _Giant Sandwich_ for Snack

Read _The Big Toe_
Do _The Big Stuff_

Giant, Teeny, Tiny

Theme Objectives

- To learn about the folklore and fantasy of giants and tiny creatures
- To become aware of size differences, to be able to label sizes and to order sizes in sequence
- To create larger-than-life and small-scale projects that require perception, concentration and attention to detail

Learning Centers

Dramatic Play

- small dolls and accessories
- adult-sized clothes
- doll house and props
- big plates
- super-sized cups
- tiny tea sets, spoons
- small table and chairs
- assorted sizes of dolls and doll clothes
- three sizes of bowls
- three sizes of serving utensils
- three sizes of lids
- three sizes of pots and pans

Manipulatives

- miniature dolls/figures
- interlocking plastic miniblocks
- seriation props (counters)
- stacking cups
- miniature puzzles
- giant floor puzzles

Library

- big books
- tiny books

- finger and arm puppets
- big pillows for sitting on

Blocks

- big hollow blocks
- small blocks
- big waffle blocks
- plastic dinosaurs
- giant tumble ball
- large and small cars and trucks

Writing

- blank books, both tiny and big
- big and small pencils
- large and small templates
- shape paper punchers, i.e., heart, foot, duck, tree
- yard stick and rulers
- sand mold letters and small magnetic letters

Science

- three-legged magnifying glass
- small plastic magnifying glass
- ant farm
- turkey baster and eyedroppers at the water table
- huge horseshoe magnet and small magnets
- tape measure
- microscope

Art

- jumbo chalk and regular chalk
- big paintbrushes and small artist's brushes
- big poster-sized paper and small scraps of paper
- big crayons
- cotton swabs
- large and small scissors

- roll of wide, clear packing tape and regular transparent tape
- giant markers and regular markers

Snacks

- small and large version of the same cookie
- marshmallows—jumbo and mini
- pretzels—Bavarian and small twists
- muffins—jumbo and mini
- hot dogs—foot long and cocktail
- pasta shells—jumbo and small
- tacos—salad shell and mini shells
- small and large versions of the same cracker
- Giant Sandwich (see activity in Discovery section)
- Cookie Contrasts (see activity in Discovery section)
- Super Food Bar (see activity in Discovery section)

Discovery Activities

Giant Sandwich

Materials

- large loaf of French bread
- jar of jam
- bread knife for the teacher
- small, dull knives for the children

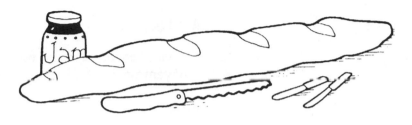

- *The Giant Jam Sandwich* by John Vernon Lord and Jane Burroway

What to do

1. Slice the loaf of bread lengthwise.
2. Spread jam thickly on bottom half.
3. Cover with top half.
4. Read *The Giant Jam Sandwich* to the children.
5. Serve your own giant sandwich for snack! You can even drop it from above as in the story.

Cookie Contrasts

Materials

- two packages of slice-and-bake cookie dough, or a double batch of your own cookie recipe
- cookie sheet

What to do

1. To make a Giant Cookie, cut open one package of cookie dough and spread it onto large, lightly greased cookie sheet.
2. Bake a bit longer than directions.
3. To make Mini Cookies, cut open one package of cookie dough, and using a teaspoon, drop cookie dough on prepared cookie sheet.

4. Bake for less time than package directions indicate.

5. Discuss the cookies with the children. Which is bigger? Which are smaller? Is the bigger one more than all of the smaller ones combined? Is it less? Or is it the same?

Mouse Hunt

Materials

- small paper or felt mouse with a 6" yarn tail

What to do

1. Hide the mouse in a new place in the classroom each day.

2. Each day when the children arrive, have them look for the mouse. At first, have the mouse in full view. As the theme progresses, hide the mouse so only the tail shows.

Wrap It Up

Materials

- large and small sizes of everyday items such as laundry soaps, diapers, shampoos, cereal boxes and novelty items such as big erasers, pencils or glasses, brought from home

What to do

1. Ask the children if they can match up the large and small size of each item.

2. Read the labels and talk about some of the descriptive words—trial size, extra large, giant.

3. Ask the children to group the items into different classifications: sizes, uses, colors.

4. Explore, examine and add to this activity as the theme progresses.

Giant, Teeny, Tiny

Stuff It

Materials

- a pair of giant bib overalls (We borrowed a size 54 pair from a local store.)

What to do

1. Tell the children that you have something to show them. Hold up the bib overalls.
2. Ask them how many children they think can fit in the overalls.
3. Help the children climb into the bib overalls, one at a time, until the bibs are "stuffed."
4. Repeat until all of the children have had a turn.

More to do

- Have an overall-shaped piece of chart paper ready. Record the words they use to describe the overalls, or record guesses about the number of children who can fill them. Send a copy of your overall chart to the store as a thank you for the use of the overalls.

Hauling Big and Small

Materials

- garbage bags
- small cups (medicine cups work well)

What to do

1. Give each child a garbage bag or a cup. Tell her that you are going on a trash hunt.
2. Instruct the children that they can fill their bags with "big" trash, but not any bigger than their bags. The cups can be filled with "tiny" trash; it must fit into the cup.
3. Go around the neighborhood and pick up all the "big" and "tiny" trash you see.
4. Return to school and compare notes on the "big" and "tiny" things you found.
5. Put your findings in a trash can when you are finished.

Big-Little Surprise!

Materials

- package of Big Boy tomato seeds
- package of cherry tomato seeds
- potting soil
- cups or small pots

What to do

1. Show the children both packages of seeds and talk about the names and sizes of the tomatoes.
2. Mix the seeds in a bowl.
3. Have the children plant the mixed seeds in soil.
4. Guess whether the plants will be Big Boys or cherry tomatoes.
5. Wait and see!

More to do

- Plant any tiny seed and observe the size of the plant that grows from that tiny seed.

Teeny Tiny Town

Materials

- a tabletop or large piece of cardboard
- tiny items brought from home to be used in making a town: bottlecaps, spools, lace scraps, washers, corks, pillboxes, buttons, empty paper towel and toilet paper tubes, margarine tubs
- aluminum foil

What to do

1. Ask the children to bring in any small items that can be used to make a town.
2. Place the cardboard tubes and margarine tubs in random spots on the table.
3. Cover the table, tubs, and tubes with foil to create a landscape.

4. Using small props, develop a town. Items may be glued together, clustered or otherwise constructed to create any prop for the town.

5. Plan on developing this tiny village over several days time. It can be as elaborate or as simple as the children want it to be.

More to do

• Instead of a town, try designing a house, forest or castle.

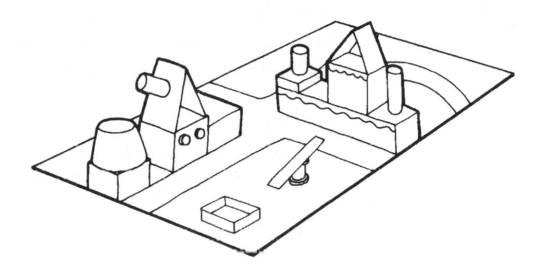

Flower Power

Materials

• string
• thumbtacks
• giant sunflower, harvested in the fall
• pie tin

What to do

1. Examine the sunflower for several days, noticing all the seeds and how they are tightly packed.
2. Hang the sunflower upside down by a string and place the pie tin underneath.
3. Watch the seeds fall from the flower as the sunflower dries out.
4. This process can take months. To speed up the process, periodically pull some seeds out by hand.

More to do

- Older children can estimate the number of seeds to fall in a day or a week. Record the estimates. When the seeds have fallen, count and see whose estimate is the closest. Roast and eat the seeds!

Super Food Bar

Materials

- large and small snacks—crackers, cheese, graham crackers, olives and fruit
- serving utensils
- napkins

What to do

1. Arrange the foods in a serving line with serving utensils.
2. Invite the children to choose a snack as they move through the food line.
3. Enjoy!

More to do

- "Tiny" snacks can be eaten using tiny bathroom sized paper cups, cocktail napkins, small paper plates. Lower the tables to lowest level. With "giant" snacks, raise the table to its highest level, use big folding chairs, super-sized fast food cups, large paper plates and large dinner napkins.

Blow-Up

Materials

- microscope
- slides, prepared or made by you

What to do

1. Discuss how some tiny things are hard to see, such as germs or fleas.
2. Using the microscope, let the children have the experience of seeing these tiny things up close.

Cooperation

4+

Materials

- interlocking miniblocks
- basic building blocks
- large hollow blocks or boxes
- parquetry blocks
- paper
- pencils

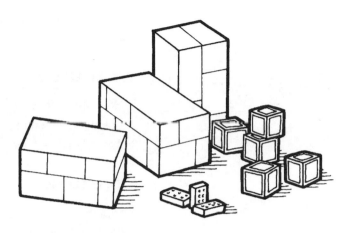

What to do

1. Divide the children into four groups.
2. Assign each group to one of the four sets of blocks.
3. Instruct the children to work together to design a structure using their blocks. They can discuss the design or use drawings to plan it out.
4. Encourage the children to assign a job to each person in the group.
5. Give the groups a time limit (five to ten minutes) to construct their plan.
6. Call all the children together. Go from one set of blocks to another, observing the structures and asking questions of the builders.
7. Ask the children, "Which set is the smallest? Which is the largest? Which is the next-to-smallest or next-to-largest?"
8. Have the children order the four constructions with numbers one to four, one being the smallest.

More to do

- Take photos of the constructions for display. Order the photos by the size of their subject.

Let's Pretend

Materials

- box
- props collected from around the room such as a bowl, a book or a block, one per child

What to do

1. Have each child pick one object out of the box.
2. Ask the children to imagine themselves teeny tiny.
3. Ask them how they would use the objects if they were tiny.

More to do

- Use the opposite concept and ask the children how they would use the objects if they were giants.

One Drop at a Time

4+

Materials

- plastic meat baster
- plastic eyedropper
- tubs with water
- paper towels
- small cups

What to do

1. Let the children experiment with the baster and the eyedropper.
2. Ask the children which one will become empty first. Why? Try it.
3. Ask the children which one will make a bigger drop of water. Test results on paper towels.
4. Ask the children which one will fill the cup faster. Why? Experiment.
5. Ask the children which one would be better for giving medicine. Why?
6. Ask the children which one is easier to squeeze. Which one is more fun to squeeze?

Oh Say, Can You See?

4+

Materials

- pictures with lots of detail and small features
- magnifying glasses
- paper
- crayons

What to do

1. Have the children look at the pictures. Encourage them to look at the details.
2. Record some of the small things they notice.
3. Have them write a few words or a story about the picture.

More to do

- Children can work in teams of two and play "I Spy." One child says, " I spy a small . . ." and the other child looks for it, using the magnifying glass if needed. They take turns asking and spying.

Art Activities

Giant Collage

3+

Materials

- roll of large paper
- glue or tape
- collage materials

What to do

1. Cut a sheet of paper to cover the table.
2. Let the children cover the paper with scraps and other collage materials.
3. Let dry and hang.

The Enormous Turnip

3+

Materials

- large inflatable ball or very large balloon
- newspaper
- scissors
- paint
- flour
- water
- bowl
- *The Enormous Turnip* by Kathy Parkinson

What to do

1. Mix the flour and water until the solution has a soupy consistency.
2. Have the children tear or cut strips of newspaper.
3. Let them dip the newspaper into the flour mixture and then wrap it around the balloon.
4. Cover the balloon with wet newspaper strips.
5. Let it dry overnight.
6. Have the children repeat the layering with newspaper dipped in the flour and water mixture.
7. Let dry overnight.
8. Paint the creation to resemble a turnip.
9. Use as a prop when reading *The Enormous Turnip* and then display.

Chalk Maze

Materials

- jumbo chalk and regular chalk
- spray bottle with water
- paper

What to do

1. Spray the water on the paper.
2. Using the jumbo chalk, have each child draw a line that snakes around his paper.
3. Let him switch to a new color and repeat as often as he desires.
4. When the picture is dry, have him trace the path of one color with his finger.

More to do

- On the same paper, mix both jumbo and regular chalk. Notice the thickness of the lines.

The Giant Paper Sandwich

Materials

- two paper bags cut so they open full length
- construction paper
- scissors
- glue
- any collage supplies such as Easter grass, cotton balls or felt pieces

What to do

1. Cut the brown bags into two large ovals to resemble French bread.
2. Place one bag on the table as the bottom piece of bread.
3. Have the children add the sandwich fillings by gluing on collage materials. Easter grass could be lettuce, and round, red pieces of felt could be tomatoes.
4. Glue the layers together.
5. Cover with the other piece of "bread."
6. The children will love showing this to their parents.

More to do

- Make up a story about who would eat this sandwich. After the sandwich is dry and has been on display, cut into "slices" to take home. For fun, put a few drops of yellow food coloring in the glue and pour it into an empty mustard squeeze bottle. Then children can glue their sandwich together with "mustard." If you can get large circular cardboard from businesses who use rolls of paper, use it as the crust for a giant pizza and use some of the ideas above.

Finger Prints

Materials

- stamp pad
- paper
- markers, pencils, pens

What to do

1. Have each child press her thumb or fingers on the stamp pad and then on the paper.
2. Use markers, pencils or pens to turn fingerprints into tiny creatures by adding eyes, arms, legs and hair.

Larger Than Life

Materials

- roll of large paper
- scissors
- paint
- paintbrushes
- glue
- crayons

What to do

1. Cut very large shapes out of paper: giant Easter eggs, Christmas trees or hearts.
2. Let the children paint, glue, or decorate them in any fashion.

Giant Canvas

Materials

- jumbo chalk
- sidewalk or patio

What to do

1. Give the children the chalk and let them use the patio as their canvas for a giant picture.

It's Small

Materials

- large sheet of paper to cover table
- paints
- glue or tape
- scissors
- assorted colored paper

What to do

1. Talk about what a tiny scene would look like. Choose a theme for the mural, such as a farm, a snow scene, a zoo or the ocean.
2. Using paints, have children design the background.
3. Have children cut out the miniature houses, people, cars and other figures to be included in the scene.
4. Arrange the miniatures on the mural and glue or tape them down.
5. Hang when dry.

More to do

- Children may want to write a descriptive story about their mural or make labels to identify different areas. Mount the story near the mural. Reverse the mural theme and draw giant ants and spiders.

Teeny Picture Page

Materials

- one piece of paper
- pens and pencils

What to do

1. Ask the children to take turns drawing a tiny picture on the same sheet of paper.
2. Copy the sheet, one for each child, to take home.

More to do

- Use the tiny drawings in your newsletter. Have each child distinguish his drawing from the others. Cut out all the drawings and use them as characters in a class book.

Giant Paper Dolls

4+

Materials

- roll of large paper
- markers
- paint
- scissors

What to do

1. Roll out the paper and let one child lie on the paper.
2. Trace around the child.
3. Have the child cut out her shape.
4. Have the child use markers and paint to make her cutout resemble her and what she is wearing that day.
5. Mount the "children" on the ceiling and walls.

More to do

- Have the children trace around dolls or tiny figures found in the classroom. Cut them out and mount them on the walls and ceiling. Compare these to the giant paper dolls.

Little People

Materials

- clothespins
- corks
- fabric and yarn scraps
- markers
- glue
- scissors

What to do

1. Using corks or clothespins as bodies, glue on scraps of fabric and yarn to resemble a person.
2. Draw on a face with markers.

Stuffed Animals

Materials

- roll of large paper
- newspaper
- paint
- markers
- string
- hooks
- stapler
- tape
- scissors

What to do

1. Have the children decide on a giant animal to make.
2. Assign children different tasks: rolling out the paper and drawing the animal, cutting out the animal, tracing around the first animal, cutting out the second identical animal, wadding newspaper into stuffing and painting the animal halves.
3. Help the children staple or tape the two animal pieces together, but leave openings for the stuffing.

4. Stuff the animal.
5. Staple the openings.
6. Hang the animal from the ceiling.

More to do

- Repeat this activity with several animals so that you have a mini-zoo!

Giant Crayons

Materials

- old crayons with paper peeled off
- pot pie tins

What to do

1. Put the crayon pieces into the pie tin, making sure to put all of one color in the same tin. This makes a good sorting activity.
2. Heat in the oven on low heat until the pieces melt together.
3. Let the crayons cool.
4. Pop them out of the tin and let the children color with giant crayons.

More to do

- Repeat the activity using muffin tins.

Petite Puppets

Materials

- strips of paper about 2" wide and 2 1/2" long
- markers
- tape

What to do

1. Have the children draw a face and other features in the middle of their piece of paper.
2. Roll the strip into a cylindrical shape, face side out, and secure with tape.
3. Place on the child's finger and use as a finger puppet.

More to do

- Use a familiar fingerplay such as "Where Is Thumbkin?" and make a series of finger puppets to use while reciting rhyme.

Colorful Confetti

Materials

- paper punches: holes and shapes
- glue
- colored paper cut into fourths

What to do

1. Have the children punch out lots of small shapes and dots.
2. Have the children glue them onto the small paper, either randomly or in a specific design.
3. Hang them out on display after they are dry.

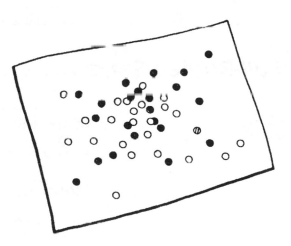

More to do

- For younger children, prepunch confetti.

Music and Movement Activities

Giant Squats

What to do

1. Reach high in the air on the word "giant."
2. Bend to a middle level when "teeny" is called.
3. Squat low for the word "tiny."
4. Have children take turns being the director and calling out those three words in any order they wish.

Moving From Here to There

What to do

1. Have the children stand at one end of the room.
2. Have them take giant steps to the other side.
3. Have them come back using tiny steps.
4. Give them directions to the other side again by saying: "Take four giant steps, stop. Take three tiny steps, stop. Take one giant step, stop." (Repeat until they are across the room.)

Full-Bodied Sandwich

Materials

- sheet or small blanket

What to do

1. Have three children lie down side by side on their stomachs on the floor with their heads all at the same end. This is the bottom "bread."
2. Spread the blanket across their bodies as the "filling."
3. Have three more children lie across the "filling," with their heads at the same end. This is the top "bread."
4. Giggle and enjoy.

Step Aerobics—Dinosaur Style

Materials

- big hollow blocks, one per child
- recording, "Dinosaurs," from *Circle Around*, Tickle Tune Typhoon

What to do

1. Have each child step up on his block with his right foot, then his left foot, and then down with his right and down with his left.
2. Have them step up and down with only their right feet, and then just their left feet.
3. Use basic step moves, but keep it very simple.

More to do

- Use any music with a strong beat and pretend to be giants making thunder. Use carpet squares and step on and off carpets rather than up and down.

Limbo

Materials

- broom handle or pole

What to do

1. Have two volunteers hold the pole at an even height.
2. Show the children how to go under the limbo pole, or go under in any fashion.
3. When you call out "giant," have them raise the pole high.
4. When you call out "teeny," lower it a bit.
5. When you call out "tiny," it should be lowered enough that you must crawl under it.
6. Vary the cues each time a child goes under.

More to do

- Go over the limbo pole instead of under. Let the group decide what to do on the "giant" call.

Math Activities

Calendar

Materials

- plain calendar or paper and markers
- three sizes of toy mice
- a giant and two elves
- a dinosaur and two ants

What to do

1. Make or purchase a plain calendar with only the days of the week marked on it.

2. Each month, make different paper patterns to fit your theme. For example: for the "giant teeny tiny" theme you may want to use a giant and two elves, or a dinosaur and two ants (giant, teeny, tiny).

3. The days of the week may be sung to the tune of "Frere Jacques." "Sunday, Monday, Tuesday, Wednesday, Thursday, Friday, Saturday. It's not Sunday, it's not Monday, it's not Tuesday, it is. . ." (Let the children fill in the blank for whatever day of the week it is.)

4. School Days Countdown—make an ongoing number line for the number of days the children have been at school. Follow the same pattern as your monthly calendar pattern.

More to do

● Ask children to decide on actions to do with words. For example, reaching up high (giant), pressing palms down towards floor (teeny), and pressing palm closer to the floor (tiny).

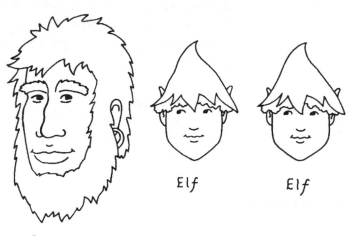

Elf   Elf

Giant

Calendar Patterns for
Giant, and Teeny Tiny

Giant   Teeny   Tiny

Mice

Giant, Teeny, Tiny

Guessing Box

Materials

- small cubical box. Ideas for a small box include:
    - tiny book
    - elf figure
    - mouse
    - piece of bite-sized candy
- big box. Ideas for large box include:
    - giant rubber bugs
    - giant eyeglasses
    - large candy bar
    - extra large bib overalls
    - jumbo box of detergent

What to do

1. Show a "giant teeny tiny" item such as a tiny book to the children and talk about its properties: its shape, color, size and uses.
2. Bring out the guessing box with another tiny item in it. Use the same box for the teeny tiny items, and the larger box for the giant items. Storage boxes for clothing are the ideal size.
3. Say:

    "There is something in my guessing box.

    Would you like to guess?

    First you ask a question and

    I'll answer no or yes."
4. Children then ask questions. Encourage them to ask in the form of a question. "Is it. . . ?"
5. After a brief time, if you notice they aren't asking questions that pertain to the item in the box, give broad hints.

    "It's something small." Wait for guesses.

    "It's something round." Wait for guesses.

    "It's something with chocolate." Wait.

    "It's something you chew." Wait for guesses.

    ("Yes, it's a bite-sized piece of candy!")

Giant Bean Count

Materials

- jar
- beans, any kind
- paper
- pen

What to do

1. Show the children the jar with about eight beans in it.
2. Have them estimate and record guesses.
3. Count the beans and see who was closest.
4. Add more beans the next day and record guesses.
5. Continue all week and give the children practice at estimating amounts.

Bean Mix-Up

Materials

- bag of mixed beans
- sorting tins
- storage container

What to do

1. Have the children sort the beans according to kind, color, or size.
   HINT: Carefully supervise this activity.

More to do

- Estimate which kind has the most beans. Use tweezers to pick up and sort beans.

Can You Believe Your Eyes?

Materials

- one jar with a few tiny beans
- one jar with the same number of large beans

What to do

1. Show both jars to the children.
2. Ask them which jar has the most.
3. Count the beans in both jars.
4. Ask the children what they think happened and why they guessed the way they did.

Order This!

Materials

- three different-sized sets of dishes, utensils, lids, cups

What to do

1. Ask the children to set the table for a small, a medium, and a large eater.
2. See if the children can seriate each different setting piece correctly.
3. Tell the children that someone else is coming for dinner, and introduce a new set of dishes.
4. Observe where the children insert this new set.

More to do

- Refer to the eaters as, "small, medium and large," or "giant, average and tiny," or whatever vocabulary works best.

One Giant Step

4+

Materials

- string or adding machine tape
- scissors
- tape measure

What to do

1. Show the children the tape measure. Measure off one inch and cut a piece of string or paper that long.
2. Measure ten feet of string or paper. Repeat seven times before cutting to make a 70-foot long piece.
3. Talk about inchworms and show the children the one-inch piece.
4. Talk about dinosaurs and explain that some were 70 feet long. Hold up the 70-foot piece rolled up.
5. Find a clear area either inside or out. Unroll the 70-foot section and walk it.
6. Listen to the words the children use to describe the length of the dinosaur.
7. See if anything else in the school is either one inch long or seventy feet long, using these two strings as measuring tapes.

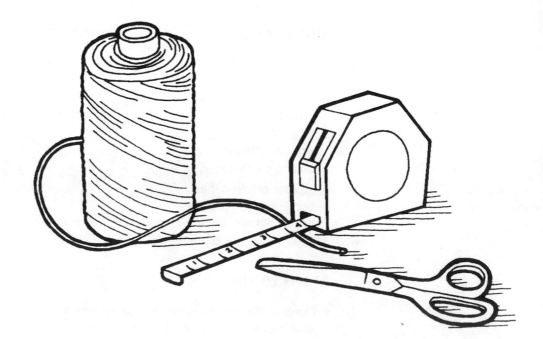

Language Activities

The Big Stuff

3+

Materials

- fiberfill
- bright red paint
- pantyhose legs (cut off) or knee-high stockings
- *The Big Toe*, by June Meiser and Joy Cowley

What to do

1. Read *The Big Toe* aloud to the children.
2. Follow up the story by stuffing the pantyhose foot with fiberfill.
3. Tie off the pantyhose.
4. Give the big toe on the foot a big red toenail with bright red paint.
5. Reread the story and use this as a prop.

Germ Warfare

4+

Materials

- paper
- markers or crayons
- *Those Mean Nasty Dirty Downright Disgusting But. . . Invisible Germs* by Judith Rice

What to do

1. Read *Those Mean Nasty Dirty Downright Disgusting But. . . Invisible Germs* aloud to the children.
2. Have each child draw a picture of a new kind of germ and dictate how that germ makes people sick.
3. Make the creations into a class book.

Other Words for Tiny

Materials

- tiny chart (about 5" x 7")
- small pen or pencil

What to do

1. Ask the children what "tiny" means.
2. Ask the children if they know any other words that mean the same thing.
3. Write those words on the tiny chart.
4. Add more words as the children think of them throughout the theme.

More to do

- Repeat this activity, using a large sheet of paper and a jumbo marker to record synonyms for giant.

Giants, Giants and More Giants

Materials

- long sheet of paper with a giant drawn in one corner
- markers

What to do

1. Ask the children to think of things they consider "giant."
2. Record their words on the sheet of paper.
3. Add to the sheet as the theme progresses.

More to do

- Use a sheet of paper with a tiny figure in one corner. Repeat steps 1, 2, and 3 above using "tiny" as the descriptive term.

Think Big, Think Small

Materials

- posterboard
- markers
- children's name tags
- tape

What to do

1. With a marker, divide one side of the posterboard into as many learning centers as there are in your classroom.
2. Label each area and draw an identifying symbol.
3. On the other side of the posterboard make a similar diagram, but very small.
4. As the children make their first plans each day, have them stick their name in the box that symbolizes their choice. Change the sides from one day to the next, or even before lunch and after.

More to do

- A more advanced child may move his name tag from area to area as he changes his plan.

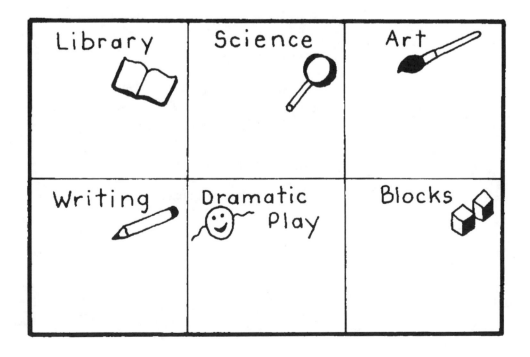

Inching Along

Materials

- paper, one sheet per child
- crayons or markers

What to do

1. Print "If I were one inch tall, I could. . ." on the top of each paper.
2. Ask the children to finish the sentence.
3. Have them draw and dictate their response.

More to do

- Make into a class book. Repeat the above process using the phrase, "When I get bigger I can. . ."

Sketch Pad

4+

Materials

- large and small paper
- pens and pencils

What to do

1. Talk about giants and what they might look like.
2. Have the children draw their ideas of giants on large paper.
3. Repeat with leprechauns using the small paper.

More to do

- Bind both into class books.

Giant, Teeny, Tiny

Songs and Chants

- Traditional "Eensy Weensy Spider." Repeat chant but substitute "The great big spider. . ," using a great big voice.

- "Giant, Teeny, Tiny" (tune: "Farmer in the Dell")

    "Giant, teeny, tiny

    Giant, teeny, tiny

    Reach up high and reach down low.

    Giant, teeny, tiny."

- "Pass the Elf Round and Round" (tune: "London Bridge")

    "Pass the elf round and round,

    round and round, round and round.

    Pass the elf round and round,

    All around the circle."

- Have the children stand in a circle with one child in the middle. The middle child closes his eyes while the others pass a small elf figure around the circle. When the chant ends, the child holding the elf hides it behind her back. All the children in the circle put their hands behind their backs. The child in the middle opens his eyes and tries to guess who has the elf. If he guesses correctly, the child holding the elf becomes the one in the middle. Repeat until everyone has had a turn in the middle.

- "Two Little Blackbirds" (a rhyming chant)

    "Two little blackbirds sitting on a hill,

    One named Jack, the other named Jill.

    Fly away Jack. Fly away Jill.

    Come back Jack. Come back Jill.

    Two little blackbirds sitting on a hill,

    One named Jack, one named Jill."

- Substitute the following lines:

    "Two little blackbirds going to the mall,

    One named short, the other named tall."

    "Two little blackbirds swimming at the pool,

    One named hot, the other named cool."

    "Two little blackbirds sitting on a cloud,

    One named soft, the other named loud."

    "Two little blackbirds playing in the snow,

    One named high, the other named low."

    "Two little blackbirds sitting on their dad,

    One named happy, the other named sad."

    "Two little blackbirds sounding kind of whiny,

One named giant, the other named tiny."
"Two little blackbirds shooting arrows with a bow,
One named fast, the other named slow."

Theme Extensions and Variations

Field trips

- Shoe Store—Visit a shoe store and look for the biggest shoe made as well as the smallest shoe. Compare sizes. Trace around both and bring outlines back to school for comparisons.

Variations

- Incorporate dinosaurs in more detail.
- Use this theme as a springboard to expand on opposites.
- Call this unit "It's a Very Small World" and concentrate on tiny things such as bugs.

Bibliography

- *Big Fat Enormous Lie, A*, Marjorie Weinman Sharmat. NY: E.P. Dutton, 1978. A boy's little lie comes alive in the form of a monster who grows and grows until the boy finds the only way to make it go away—by telling the truth.
- *Big Toe, The*, June Meiser and Joy Cowley. New Zealand: Shortland Publications Limited, 1980. A big book about an old woman who finds a big toe and is followed home by the owner.
- *Clifford the Big Red Dog*, Norman Bridwell. NY: Scholastic, 1988. Emily Elizabeth describes the activities she enjoys with her very big, very red dog.
- *Dark, Dark Tale, A*, Ruth Brown. NY: Dial Books for Young Readers, 1981. Story of a dark, dark house and a tiny secret hiding in the cupboard.
- *Enormous Turnip, The*, Kathy Parkinson. Niles, IL: Albert Whitman and Co., 1985. One of Grandfather's turnips grows to such an enormous size that the whole family including the dog, cat, and mouse try in vain to pull it up.
- *Fin M'Coul*, Tomie dePaola. NY: Holiday, 1981. A delightful version of the popular Irish giant, Fin M'Coul and his encounter with another giant, Cucullin.
- *Giant Jam Sandwich, The*, John Vernon Lord and Jane Burroway. Boston: Houghton Mifflin Company, 1987. Four million wasps come to the town of Itching Down. The townspeople devise a plan to make a giant jam sandwich to trap the wasps to get rid of them.

Giant, Teeny, Tiny

- *Jack and the Beanstalk*, Stella Williams Nathan. NY: Western Publishing Co., Inc., 1973. The traditional story of a little boy named Jack who gets revenge on the giant at the top of the beanstalk.

- *Little Mouse, The Red Ripe Strawberry, and the Big Hungry Bear, The*, Don and Audrey Wood. Singapore: Child's Play (International) Ltd., 1990. The little mouse will do anything to save his strawberry from the big, hungry bear.

- *Those Mean Nasty Dirty Downright Disgusting but. . . Invisible Germs*, Judith A Rice. St. Paul, MN: Redleaf Press, 1989. A little girl who accumulates germs on her hands during her busy day defeats them by washing and drying her hands.

- *Thumbelina*, Hans Christian Andersen. NY: Picture Book Studio, 1992. The adventure of a tiny girl no bigger than a thumb and her many animal friends.

Poems

- "Thumb Face," *A Light in the Attic*, Shel Siverstein. NY: Evil Eye Music, Inc., Harper and Row Publishers, 1981, p. 55.

- "I Am Tired of Being Little," *Something Big Has Been Here*, Jack Prelutsky. NY: Greenwillow Books, 1990, p. 24.

- "Something Big Has Been Here," *Something Big Has Been Here*, Jack Prelutsky. NY: Greenwillow Books, 1990, p. 7.

- "Me and My Giant," *Where the Sidewalk Ends*, Shel Silverstein. NY: Evil Eye Music, Inc., Harper and Row Publishers, 1974, p. 39.

- "Melinda Mae," *Where the Sidewalk Ends*, Shel Silverstein. NY: Evil Eye Music, Inc., Harper and Row Publishers, 1974, p. 154.

- "No Difference," *Where the Sidewalk Ends*, Shel Silverstein. NY: Evil Eye Music, Inc., Harper and Row Publishers, 1974, p. 81.

- "One Inch Tall," *Where the Sidewalk Ends*, Shel Silverstein. NY: Evil Eye Music, Inc., Harper and Row Publishers, 1974, p. 55.

Recordings

- "Dinosaurs," *Circle Around.* Tickle Tune Typhoon Recording Co., 1983.

- "I'm a Little Teapot," "This Little Light of Mine," "The Incey Wincey Spider," and "Where Is Thumbkin?" *If You're Happy and You Know It.* Bob McGrath, Kids' Records, 1985.

- "Please Don't Bring a Tyrannosaurus Rex to Show and Tell," *Late Last Night.* Joe Scruggs, (Shadow Play Records & Video) Educational Graphics Press, Inc., 1984.

- "If I Had a Dinosaur," *More Singable Songs For the Very Young.* Raffi, Hap-Pal Music, 1988.

Giant, Teeny, Tiny

- "Little Ants," "Little Elf," and "The Friendly Giant," *Pretend*. Hap Palmer, Educational Activities, Inc., 1975.

- "The Mice Go Marching," *Rhythms on Parade*. Hap Palmer, Troubadour Records, Ltd., 1977.

Muddy Puddles, Soap & Bubbles

Mondays	Read <u>Peter Spier's Rain</u> Do Muddy Footprints Snack—Muddy Brew I	Read <u>A Walk in the Rain</u> Do Rain Painting Muddy Sandwiches (peanut butter) for Snack	Read <u>Baby's Boat</u> Do Sail Away Do Robin Red-Breast's Nest	Read <u>Bringing the Rain to Kapiti Plain</u> Do Rain or Shine
Tuesdays	Do Evaporation Investigation Begin Catch That Drop!	Do Muddy Brew II Do Soapy Mud Sandy Cups or Muddy Cups for Snack	Do Bubbling Raisins Do Effervescent Eggs Have Hot Mud for Snack	Do Dig That Soap Do Rub-a-Dub Classroom Do Veggie Scrub for Snack
Wednesdays	Hot Mud for Snack Read <u>Cloudy with a Chance of Meatballs</u> Do It's Raining Pizza!	Field Trip to a Car Wash Do Dirt, Dirt and More Dirt	Read <u>Time of Wonder</u> Do Splish, Splash Do Slippery Soap Paint	Read <u>Hurricane</u> Read <u>Storm in the Night</u> Do Stormy Weather
Thursdays	Read "Shadow Wash" (see Poems) Do This is the Way We Wash _____	Read "Quack, Quack, Quack" (see Poems) Do Car Wash Have Chocolate Pudding for Snack	Do Catch the Bubbles Do Catch a Bubble	Field Trip to a Laundromat Do Magic Drawings
Fridays	Read <u>No Bath Tonight</u> Do More to Wash Root Beer floats for Snack	Read <u>Miss Rumphius</u> Do Pick a Seed Do Plant Pudding	Read <u>The Mud Pony</u> Do Michelangelo	Do Cake, Slime, or Pie, Please Do A Can of Worms

Muddy Puddles, Soap & Bubbles

Theme Objectives

- To explore the physical properties of mud, puddles, soap, and bubbles
- To discover and explore the uses, functions and sources of mud, puddles, soap, and bubbles

Learning Centers

Dramatic Play

- washing machine/dryer (make with cardboard boxes)
- clothesline
- clothespins
- baby bathtub
- empty detergent and shampoo bottles
- sponges
- plastic scrubbers
- dishtowels
- dishcloths
- dishes
- washcloths
- bath towels
- bars of soap
- fingernail brush
- scrub brush
- dishpans
- dish drainer and drainboard

Science

- vinegar (supervise closely)
- baking soda (supervise closely)
- detergent
- cups/straws
- bubble wands
- food coloring (supervise closely)
- birds' nests

Muddy Puddles, Soap & Bubbles

- materials for making mud
- molds for making bricks
- bars of soap
- jars of soap for smelling
- pond water samples
- filter for cleaning water
- tadpoles
- duck egg incubator
- turtles

Art

- playdough
- clay
- clay sculpting tools: table knives, forks, spoons, toothpicks, craft sticks
- food coloring (supervise closely)

Writing

- a collage of soap labels and coupons
- ink pads and animal stamps: frogs, pigs, ducks
- bubble and soap-shaped paper/tablets
- bar-shaped paper
- bars of soap for making rubbings

Library

- pig puppets
- duck puppet
- frog puppet
- turtle puppet
- flannel board
- flannel board stories
- tape recorder

Manipulatives

- collection of small farm animals
- barn and fences

Muddy Puddles, Soap & Bubbles

Blocks

- farm animals
- barn and fences
- boats

Snacks

- Muddy Brew I (hot chocolate)
- Muddy Brew II (see activity in Discovery section)
- Hot Mud (oatmeal with cocoa mix)
- goldfish crackers
- Plant Pudding (see activity in Discovery section)
- Sandy Cups (see activity in Discovery section)
- chocolate pudding
- muddy sandwiches (peanut butter)
- Veggie Scrub (see activity in Discovery section)
- root beer floats
- puddle juice (chocolate milk)

Discovery Activities

Bury It!

Materials

- seeds
- potting soil
- small pots or outdoor planting area
- water
- spoons or digging tools

What to do

1. Prepare an outdoor planting area, if necessary. If planting is to be done indoors, prepare a place for the pots where they will receive sunlight.
2. Ask the children to recall all the things they've seen mud and dirt used for.

Muddy Puddles, Soap & Bubbles

3. Show them the seeds and discuss what seeds need to grow.
4. Give each child a seed to plant. Discuss and establish a routine for regular watering.

More to do

- Observe and record germination time and plant growth.

Water on the Glass

Materials

- ice water
- large glass
- paper towels, preferably brown

What to do

1. Dry the outside of the glass with a paper towel. Brown paper towels are best, as they dramatically illustrate the absence of moisture. Show to all the children.
2. Pour ice water into the glass. Discuss for a minute or two what the children think will happen.
3. Look at the glass. What is happening to the outside of the glass? Does it have holes in it? Where did that water come from? What's it called?

Water Under the Glass

Materials

- a grassy area
- warm sunny day
- a clear plastic glass

Muddy Puddles, Soap & Bubbles

What to do

1. Invert the glass or container in the grass in a sunny location.
2. Have the children make note of the fact that the glass is dry—no water.
3. Leave the glass undisturbed. Check the glass in 15-20 minutes. What's in it? Where did that water come from?
4. Introduce the term, "condensation."

Muddy Footprints

Materials

- brown paint
- large shallow pan
- paper on a roll
- dishpan with soapy water
- old towels

What to do

1. In an area of the classroom that is not a part of the main traffic pattern, set up a chair with the shallow pan on the floor in front of it.
2. Three feet away, set up another chair facing the first, with the dishpan with soapy water in front of it.
3. Unroll a three-foot length of paper in between the shallow pan and the dishpan with soapy water.
4. Pour a small amount of brown paint into the shallow pan.
5. Have the children remove their shoes and socks when it is their turn. Roll up their pant legs.
6. Hold their hands and have them step into the shallow pan and then out onto the paper. Have them walk the length of the paper to the dishpan and step into it.
7. Have the child sit down on the chair by the dishpan and assist the child in washing and drying his feet. Talk about how his footprints look on the paper.

NOTE: If possible, arrange for a parent to help with this project.

Muddy Puddles, Soap & Bubbles

Rub-a-Dub Classroom

Materials

- sponges
- pails
- soapy water

What to do

1. This is an excellent activity to do at the end of the year. Remove items from shelves before beginning this activity.
2. Provide each child with a pail, soapy water and a sponge.
3. Direct each child to a piece of equipment or shelf.
4. Be sure to demonstrate how to squeeze out the sponge.
5. Wash cubbies, shelves, tables and chairs. The children love to help clean.

Car Wash

Materials

- sponges
- pails
- soapy water
- outdoor faucet and hose
- cars

What to do

1. Ask several parents to participate by bringing their cars to school for washing—assign times. This can be done only if the cars can be washed away from the street.
2. Provide a sponge and a pail of soapy water for each child to use.
3. Supervise the children as they help wash the car. Talk about each part that must be washed as the children work.
4. Rinse.

Muddy Puddles, Soap & Bubbles

Blowing Bubbles

Materials

- glycerine, liquid detergent and water, or purchased bubble solution
- cups
- bubble wands

What to do

1. Mix glycerine, liquid detergent, and water together or use purchased bubble solution.
2. Provide the children with cups of bubble solution and bubble wands.
3. Let them blow bubbles. Ask them how big a bubble they can blow. Can they catch any bubbles?

More to do

- Giant bubbles can be made with hula hoops, large plastic lids with the middle cut out or a length of string or cord tied on both ends to a stick.

Bubbling Raisins

3+

Materials

- vinegar
- baking soda
- clear jar
- raisins

What to do

1. Put a few raisins in the jar.
2. Add vinegar, filling the jar about three-quarters full.
3. Add two to three teaspoons of baking soda.
4. Watch the raisins bounce up and down. Watch all the bubbles.
5. Add more soda if needed.

Muddy Puddles, Soap & Bubbles

Effervescent Eggs

Materials

- clear jar
- white vinegar
- raw egg in the shell

What to do

1. Place egg gently in the jar.
2. Add vinegar (enough to cover the egg entirely) and seal the jar.
3. Observe what happens to the egg. Where do the bubbles come from? What does the egg look like?
4. After five days, remove the egg and feel how rubbery it is. Where did the shell go?

Splish, Splash

Materials

- plastic baby bathtub
- towels
- soap
- washcloth
- washable plastic dolls

What to do

1. Gather materials together and find a place in the dramatic play center or outside to set up this activity.
2. Have the children assist in filling the baby bathtub. Talk about the temperature of the water and the parts of the baby that need to be washed.
3. Allow the children to bathe the "babies" and dry them.

Muddy Puddles, Soap & Bubbles

A Can of Worms

3+

Materials

- earthworms
- transparent container with a lid
- dirt and coffee grounds
- digging tool

What to do

1. Scout out a good place to dig up earthworms. Take the children along to help dig and find them, or take the class to a bait shop to buy some earthworms.
2. Put the earthworms in the transparent container with the coffee grounds and moistened dirt.
3. Watch them for a few days before releasing them in a garden.

This Is The Way We Wash _____

3+

Materials

- laundry soap
- two dishpans
- clothesline
- clothespins
- doll clothes
- clothes basket

What to do

1. Find a place in the dramatic play center of the classroom to string a short clothesline.
2. Explain to the children that they are only to wash the doll clothes.
3. Have the children assist in filling the dishpans with warm water and adding laundry soap to one of them.
4. Let the children hand wash the doll clothes. Show them how to squeeze the water out of the clothing.
5. Rinse the clothes and hang them out to dry.

Muddy Puddles, Soap & Bubbles

More to Wash

3+

Materials

- dishpans
- drainboard
- drainer
- dishcloth
- dishes
- detergent
- dishtowels

What to do

1. Gather the materials together and set them up where other classroom equipment will not be damaged by water.
2. Have the children help fill the dishpans and squirt dish detergent into one of them.
3. Let the children wash, rinse and dry the plastic play dishes.

Muddy Brew II

4+

Materials

- large glass or plastic jar with lid (2 quart or larger)
- sunny day
- six to eight bags of herbal or decaffeinated tea

What to do

1. At the beginning of the class period, have the children help you fill the jar with cold water and hang the tea bags over the edge.
2. Screw the cover on with the tea bags inside the jar in the water.
3. Put the jar in a sunny place. Have the children check the jar once or twice throughout the class period. What's happening?
4. Serve Muddy Brew II for snack.

Muddy Puddles, Soap & Bubbles

Washing Water

Materials

- muddy water from a puddle or pond
- collection jars with lids
- several kinds of filters (aquarium, coffee)

What to do

1. If possible, have the children help collect muddy water from a puddle. Talk about how the water looks.
2. Using a different filter each time, have the children pour the water from the jar through the filter, letting it flow into a clean jar. Take a look at the water after it has been through a filter.
3. Ask the children, "Which filter seemed to work best?"

More to do

- Visit your city's water treatment plant.

Plant Pudding

Materials

- one 20 oz. package of chocolate sandwich cookies
- three boxes of vanilla instant pudding
- 6 cups milk
- two 8 oz. packages of cream cheese
- whipped cream
- rolling pin
- wax paper
- clean flower pot

3. Layer the cookies, pudding-and-cheese mixture and whipped cream in the flower pot and let cool.

4. Sprinkle some more cookies on top! Add silk flowers growing out of your "dirt" for the finishing touch! A yummy snack treat!

Sandy Cups

Materials

- 4 cups cold milk
- two packages of vanilla instant pudding
- 8 oz. whipped cream
- one package of vanilla wafers, crushed
- clear plastic cups

What to do

1. Pour the milk into a large bowl. Add the pudding mix and beat the mixture until well blended.

2. Stir in whipped cream and half of the crushed cookies.

3. Place one tablespoon full of crushed cookies into each cup.

4. Fill the cups 3/4 full with the pudding mixture.

5. Top with the remaining crushed cookies. Refrigerate for one hour.

More to do

- Make "Mud Cups" with chocolate pudding.

Muddy Puddles, Soap & Bubbles

Soapy Mud

Materials

- several bars of soap
- several rolls of toilet paper
- water
- vegetable peelers
- large plastic tub or water table

What to do

1. Have several children tear off sheets of toilet paper and put them into the tub.
2. Have other children use vegetable peelers to shave off bits of soap into the tub.
3. Add some water and have the children mix it all up with their hands.
4. Let the children play and explore this "clean mud!"

Dirt, Dirt and More Dirt

Materials

- large cups or small pails
- digging tools or spoons
- styrofoam trays

What to do

1. Take a walk around the neighborhood or playground with the children.
2. Use the spoons and cups to collect dirt samples at different locations.
3. After returning to the classroom, dump the dirt samples out on a separate styrofoam tray and examine each sample.
4. Make a list of the things in each dirt sample. Ask why the dirt is different in different locations.

Muddy Puddles, Soap & Bubbles

Cake, Slime or Pie, Please

4+

Materials

- large tub of dirt
- pitcher of water
- spoons
- small clear cups
- newspaper

What to do

1. Cover the work area with newspaper.
2. Give each child a cup and a spoon.
3. Let them experiment mixing dirt and water to make mud pies.
4. What happens if there is not enough water added? The mixture is thick, like cake.
5. What happens if too much water is added? The mixture is runny, like slime.

Robin Red-Breast's Nest

4+

Materials

- deserted bird's nest
- tub of dirt
- bowlful of grass or twigs
- two or three large mixing bowls
- water
- spoons
- aluminum pie tins
- newspaper

Muddy Puddles, Soap & Bubbles

What to do

1. Cover the table with newspaper and display the bird's nest.
2. Have the children examine the bird's nest. Ask them what kind of animal made this nest.
3. Show them the dirt, twigs, grass, and water.
4. Using the foil pie tin as a place to work, ask the children to fashion a nest using the materials on the table.

Bubble Mountains

Materials

- vinegar
- baking soda
- small cups
- teaspoon
- measuring cups
- newspaper and/or paper towels

What to do

1. Put one teaspoon of baking soda into a cup. Add 1/3 cup of vinegar. Watch!
2. Ask the children, "What makes all the bubbles?" Record their responses.
3. After presenting this activity to the group, make it available for further exploration during choice time.

More to do

- Fill a clear jar half way with white vinegar. (A sixteen ounce soda bottle works well.) Put several teaspoons of baking soda into the balloon. Pull the balloon over the bottle and watch what happens! Ask the children what they think happened. How long will the ballon stay inflated?

Muddy Puddles, Soap & Bubbles

Veggie Scrub

Materials

- potatoes
- celery
- milk
- salt
- margarine
- measuring cup
- cooking pot
- vegetable brushes
- knives
- cutting board
- bowl of water

What to do

1. Have the children scrub the potatoes and celery with the water and brushes. Talk about the necessity to wash food like we wash other things.
2. Assist the children in cutting up the potatoes and celery.
3. Place the potatoes and celery in the pot and add 1/3 to 1/2 cup of milk and 3 tablespoons of margarine. Salt to taste.
4. Cook until potatoes and celery are soft. You have potato soup for snack!

Bubble Gum Chew

Materials

- bubble gum, one piece per child

What to do

1. Tell the children that you have bubble gum and that you would like to see how many children know how to blow bubbles with it.
2. Give a piece to each child. Explain the bubble-blowing technique to those who have difficulty.
3. Remind the children to throw their gum in the trash when they are finished chewing.

Muddy Puddles, Soap & Bubbles

Art Activities

Rain Painting

Materials

- shaker filled with powdered tempera paint
- heavy paper
- permanent marker
- sprinkler can (or a rainy day!)

What to do

1. Write each child's name on her paper with the permanent marker.
2. Have the children sprinkle powdered tempera on their papers.
3. Carefully hold each paper out a doorway in the rain, or hold over a tub and sprinkle water from the sprinkling can onto the paper.
4. Let them dry, and shake off any dry tempera over a wastebasket.

Muddy Tire Tracks

Materials

- several small washable cars or trucks (preferably with different kinds of tire markings)
- brown paint
- styrofoam trays
- paper

What to do

1. Pour a small amount of brown paint onto two or three styrofoam trays.
2. Have the children run the cars and trucks through the paint to coat the wheels.
3. Let them run the cars and trucks on their papers to make muddy tracks.

Muddy Puddles, Soap & Bubbles

Squish Painting

Materials

- small pieces of sponge
- spring-type clothespins
- paint
- styrofoam trays
- paper

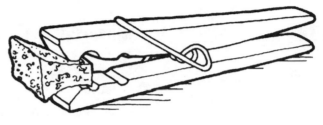

What to do

1. Clip a small piece of sponge in each clothespin and pour a small amount of paint into the styrofoam trays.
2. Have the children use the clothespins with sponges as paintbrushes.
3. Have them dip the sponges in the paint and squish it down on their paper.
4. Use several different colors of paint.

More to do

- Cut the sponges into the shapes of ducks, frogs, or fish.

Muddy Playdough

Materials

- any playdough recipe or:
    - 4 cups flour
    - 4 cups water
    - 1/2 cup salt
    - 4 tablespoons vegetable oil
    - 4 tablespoons cream of tartar
    - electic frying pan or pot and hot plate
- dry, brown tempera or vanilla extract

What to do

1. Mix flour, cream of tartar and salt. Add water and stir until dry ingredients have dissolved. Add oil and heat until mixture thickens.
2. Add brown tempera to playdough and knead to mix. Use a mud dough.
3. Or add vanilla extract to give the playdough a clean fragrance like soap.

Slippery Soap Paint

3+

Materials

- soap flakes
- water
- measuring cup
- bowl
- electric hand mixer
- tempera paint
- paper
- vinyl placemats

What to do

1. Have the children help measure equal amounts of soap flakes and water into the bowl. Using the mixer, whip the mixture until it is the consistency of soft whipped cream.
2. Spoon a portion of the whipped soap out onto a vinyl placemat and add a few drops of food coloring or tempera.
3. Let each child mix this on the mat with his fingers and use as fingerpaint.
4. Let the child explore and experience the feel of the whipped soap. Encourage him to make a pattern or design on his mat.
5. When the child is finished, place a clean piece of paper down on his placemat and make a print of his design. Let dry.

More to do

- Instead of whipping soap, you can get the same results using shaving cream from a can. Sprinkle glitter onto the soap print.

Muddy Puddles, Soap & Bubbles

Catch the Bubbles

Materials

- bubble solution
- food coloring
- straws
- small bowls
- paper

What to do

1. Pour a small amount of bubble solution into the bowls and add a generous amount of food coloring, making each bowl a different color.
2. Have the child choose a color and blow bubbles with the straw until they reach its brim. NOTE: Be sure to instruct the child to blow out only.
3. "Catch" the bubbles by placing a piece of paper on top of the bowl. Do this with several different colors.

Pack a Bubble

Materials

- colored construction paper
- several colors of liquid tempera
- bubble packing materials
- paintbrushes

What to do

1. Use paintbrushes to paint the bubble side of the packing plastic.
2. Place the paint side down on the construction paper and press.
3. Lift to see colored "bubbles" on the paper.

Muddy Puddles, Soap & Bubbles

Clean Collage

Materials

- soap bar wrappers

What to do

1. Send a note home to parents several weeks prior to this activity asking them to save and send to class their empty soap wrappers and boxes.
2. When enough wrappers have accumulated, set them out in the art area with glue and heavy paper to use in making a collage.

Magic Drawings

Materials

- small soaps
- white or light-colored paper
- watercolor paints
- paintbrushes
- water
- newspaper

What to do

1. Cover work area with newspaper.
2. Let the children draw on their paper with the small soaps. It is difficult to see the soap on the paper because it is so light.
3. Have the children paint over their paper with watercolors. Watch what happens!

Michelangelo

5+

Materials

- pictures of sculptures or a real piece of sculpture
- clay
- carving instruments: plastic knives, spoons, craft sticks

Muddy Puddles, Soap & Bubbles

- styrofoam trays

What to do

1. Show the pictures of sculptures and explain that many begin as clay.
2. Give each child a styrofoam tray with a portion of clay on it.
3. Using the carving instruments, let each child make her own sculpture.
4. When they are finished, let them air dry to harden.

More to do

- Children may want to add decorations to their sculptures, such as beads, buttons or pipe cleaners.

Catch That Muddy Track

5+

Materials

- plaster of Paris
- water
- styrofoam tray
- bowl and spoon
- a good footprint in the mud

What to do

1. After it has rained, look outside for a good footprint in the mud.
2. Mix the plaster of Paris according to the directions on the box.
3. Take the liquid plaster outside and pour into the footprint. Let it harden until the mold can be lifted out.
4. You should have a perfect mold of the footprint to take inside your classroom.

More to do

- Compare each child's foot next to the plaster footprint to see if you can guess whose footprint it is.

Dig That Soap

Materials

- soap, one bar per child
- carving tools: plastic knives, spoons, craft sticks and vegetable peelers
- newspapers

What to do

1. Over newspaper, let each child carve on her bar of soap. Supervise closely.
2. Talk to each child about what she is trying to carve.
3. Let them take their carvings home to use in the bathtub!

Math Activities

Bath/Shower Line-Up

3+

Materials

- pictures or sketches of a bathtub and a shower

What to do

1. At group time ask the children to remember whether they took a shower or a bath yesterday.
2. Have them line up behind the pictures accordingly. Count how many are in each line.

More to do

- Attach the pictures to a piece of posterboard. Give each child a sticker dot to put under the corresponding picture. Count the sticker dots under each picture.

Muddy Puddles, Soap & Bubbles

Calendar

3+

Materials

- plain calendar or paper and markers

What to do

1. Make or purchase a plain calendar with only the days of the week marked on it.
2. Each month, make different paper patterns to fit your theme. For example: for the "Muddy Puddles, Soap and Bubbles" theme you may want to use soap wrappers (two the same and one different); bubble, bubble, puddle, puddle and repeat (use white or pale pink or blue to make round bubbles and then use brown to make irregular shaped puddles); or muddy, puddle, soap, bubble. Use a brown irregular circle to represent a puddle for muddy and puddle. Use a pastel rectangle with the word "soap" on it for soap, and use a white circle to represent the bubble.
3. The days of the week may be sung to the tune of "Frere Jacques." "Sunday, Monday, Tuesday, Wednesday, Thursday, Friday, Saturday. It's not Sunday, it's not Monday, it's not Tuesday, it is. . . " (Let the children fill in the blank for whatever day of the week it is.)
4. School Days Countdown—make an ongoing number line for the number of days the children have been at school. Follow the same pattern as your monthly calendar pattern.

Calendar Patterns
for Muddy Puddles,
Soap and Bubbles

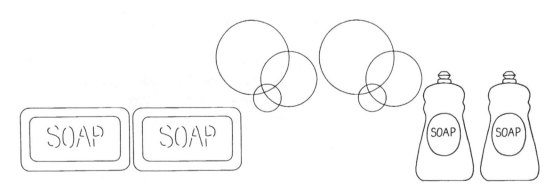

Muddy Puddles, Soap & Bubbles

Guessing Box

4+

Materials

- box or paper bag
- bar of soap
- dish detergent
- bubble solution
- bubble gum
- box of laundry detergent
- watering can
- water gun

What to do

1. Show a "Muddy Puddles, Soap and Bubbles" item such as a bar of soap to the children and talk about its properties: shape, color, container, size and uses.

2. Bring out the guessing box with another "Muddy Puddles, Soap and Bubbles" item in it. Use the same box each time, no matter what size the item is. Storage boxes for clothing are the ideal size.

3. Say:

> "There is something in my guessing box.
> Would you like to guess?
> First you ask a question and
> I'll answer no or yes."

4. Children then ask questions. Encourage them to ask in the form of a question. "Is it. . . ?"

5. After a brief time, if you notice they aren't asking questions that pertain to the item in the box, give broad hints.

> "It's something small." Wait for guesses.
> "It's something flat." Wait for guesses.
> "It's something sweet." Wait.
> "It's something you chew." Wait for guesses.
> ("Yes, it's gum!")

Muddy Puddles, Soap & Bubbles

Catch That Drop!

Materials

- large rain gauge
- posterboard
- marker

What to do

1. Fasten the rain gauge in an open outdoor area.
2. Prepare a chart with columns to record the amount of rain.
3. After a rain, take the children outside to observe how much rain fell.
4. Record the amount on the chart.
5. Keep a record for an entire month. This is an excellent activity to do during the spring.

Rain or Shine

Materials

- posterboard
- markers

What to do

1. Divide the poster-board into three columns, labeled Sunny, Rainy and Cloudy. Draw symbols to represent these: a sun, raindrops, and a gray cloud.
2. Select one child each day to look outside and decide what kind of a day it is.
3. Have that child come forward and put an X under the column that represents the weather for that day.
4. At the end of the month, tally the number in each column and make comparisons.

Muddy Puddles, Soap & Bubbles

Bubble Gum Tally

4+

Materials

- jar of different types of bubble gum
- posterboard
- tape
- paper
- marker

What to do

1. Have the children estimate how many pieces of bubble gum are in the jar. Record their guesses on a piece of paper.
2. Open the jar and count the pieces of bubble gum together.
3. Let each child choose a piece of bubble gum to chew. Ask them to save their wrapper after they open it.
4. Ask the children to bring their wrappers up and tape them on the posterboard in rows according to the style of wrapper.
5. Count how many in each row and write the tally at the bottom of each row. Which had the most? Which had the least?

Soap Sort

4+

Materials

- empty hand soap containers
- empty dish detergent bottles
- empty laundry detergent boxes
- empty shampoo bottles

What to do

1. Send a note home to parents asking them to save empty soap containers and send them to the classroom. Wait until you've accumulated at least enough containers so that each child has one.
2. At group time set out the soap containers. Talk about the types, shapes, colors and sizes.
3. Have the children sort the containers according to their size, color, type of container or type of contents.

Muddy Puddles, Soap & Bubbles

More to do

- Try to sort the containers several different ways and compare.

Evaporation Investigation

Materials

- several transparent plastic containers such as a carry-out salad container, a peanut butter jar or a soda bottle
- a measuring cup
- water
- posterboard
- markers
- permanent marker
- ruler

What to do

1. Make a record-keeping chart with a picture of each container on it.
2. Have the children help measure the water and pour the same amount in each container.
3. Mark the water line on each container with a permanent marker.
4. Check the water line each day and measure with a ruler how far the water has gone down. Where does the water go?

Where Did It Go?

Materials

- a large puddle
- measuring tape
- chalk
- paper and pencil

Muddy Puddles, Soap & Bubbles

What to do

1. Find a large puddle to measure. Measure its length and width with the measuring tape, and record the measurements.
2. Draw around the outer edge of the puddle with chalk.
3. Follow the same procedure the next day. Why is the puddle smaller? Where did the water go?

More to do

- Follow this procedure each day until the puddle is totally gone!

Language Activities

It's Raining Pizza!

Materials

- paper
- crayons
- markers
- *Cloudy with a Chance of Meatballs* by Judi Barrett

What to do

1. Read *Cloudy with a Chance of Meatballs* aloud to the children.
2. Ask the children to list what they wish would rain from the sky.
3. Record the children's responses.

More to do

- Have the children draw a picture of their favorite food raining from the sky. This could be made into a class book.

Muddy Puddles, Soap & Bubbles

Stormy Weather

Materials

- paper
- markers
- crayons
- collage materials
- watercolors
- paintbrushes
- *Hurricane* by David Wiesner, *Time of Wonder* by Robert McCloskey and *Storm in the Night* by Mary Stolz

What to do

1. Read several of the books from the bibliography about storms.
2. Ask the children if they remember a storm. Ask them to list what they remember about the storm. Record the responses.
3. Ask them to draw the storm—how did the sky look? Record any dictation on their drawing.

Sail Away

Materials

- paper
- colored pencils
- markers
- crayons
- *Baby's Boat* by Jean Titherington

What to do

1. Read *Baby's Boat* aloud to the class.
2. Talk about the imaginary aspect of the story.
3. Ask the children to use their imaginations and think about where they would sail to if they could sail anywhere they wanted to go.
4. Let the children draw the type of boat they would sail away in or the place to which they would sail. Record dictation at the bottom of their drawings.

Pick a Seed

Materials

- garden catalogs
- scissors
- glue
- paper
- *Miss Rumphius* by Barbara Cooney

What to do

1. Read *Miss Rumphius* to the children.
2. After reading, have the children look through the garden catalogs and cut out pictures of two or three flowers or vegetables that they would like to plant.
3. Let the children glue their cuttings onto a piece of paper.

More to do

- Take a trip to a nursery to find and buy seeds. Have the children bring their catalog pictures along so that they can make their selections, or fill out an order and mail away for the seeds they like.

Transition Ideas

Bath or Shower

- Those who took a shower today may go wash your hands first.
- Those who took a bath today may go wash their hands.
- Those who did not take a bath or a shower may go wash their hands.

Nighttime or Morning

- If you shower or bathe in the morning, you may get your coat.
- If you shower or bathe at night, you may get your coat.

Muddy Puddles, Soap & Bubbles

Getting from one activity to another:

- Row your boat to. . .
- Pull on your boots and splash through the puddles to. . .
- Jump over the puddles to. . .
- Hop like a frog to. . .
- Crawl like a turtle to. . .
- Swim like a fish to. . .
- Walk through the mud,
- Pretend your feet are getting stuck in it.
- Waddle like a duck to. . .

On a rainy day:

- Those who wore rain coats may. . .
- Those who wore boots may. . .
- Those who used an umbrella today may. . .

Theme Extensions and Variations

Authors' Note

- The dictionary defines a pond as a still body of water—much like a giant puddle. Expand the theme to include the exploration of ponds and pond life, allowing many science-rich opportunities. Hatch a duck egg or chicken egg, bring turtles in the room at the science table, or have a fish aquarium in your classroom. The theme is also easily adapted to include the unique characteristics of a coastal environment.

Field Trips

- Visit a carwash.
- Watch a potter throw a pot on a potter's wheel.
- Visit a laundromat.
- Visit a farm with a pond.
- Visit a water treatment plant.
- Visit a plant nursery.

Muddy Puddles, Soap & Bubbles

Bibliography

- *Baby's Boat*, Jean Titherington. NY: Greenwillow, 1992.

- *Bringing the Rain to Kapiti Plain*, Verna Aardema. NY: Puffin Books, Inc., 1992. Ki-pat, a herder of cattle, finds a way to end the drought on Kapiti Plain using his bow and the feather from an eagle. This is an African tale told in cumulative verse.

- *Cloudy With a Chance of Meatballs*, Judi Barrett. NY: Macmillan, 1978. Life is delicious in the town of Chewandswallow where it rains soup and juice, snows mashed potatoes, and blows a storm of hamburger—until the weather takes a turn for the worst.

- *Growing Colors*, Bruce McMillan. NY: Lothrop, Lee, and Shephard, 1988. Photographs of green peas, yellow corn, red potatoes, purple beans, and other fruits and vegetables.

- *Hurricane*, David Wiesner. NY: Houghton Mifflin, 1990. The morning after a hurricane, two brothers find an uprooted tree which becomes a magical place, transporting them on adventures limited only by their imaginations.

- *Listen to the Rain*, Bill Martin, Jr. and John Archambault. NY: Henry Holt and Co., 1988. Describes the changing sounds of rain, the slow soft sprinkle, the dry-drop tinkle, the sounds of pounding roaring rain and the fresh wet after-time of rain.

- *Miss Rumphius*, Barbara Cooney. NY: Viking Books, Inc., 1985.

- *Mud Pony, The*, retold by Caron Lee Cohen. NY: Scholastic, 1988. A poor boy becomes a powerful leader when Mother Earth turns his mud pony into a real one, but after the pony turns back to mud, he must find his own strength.

- *No Bath Tonight*, Jane Yolen. NY: Harper and Row, 1978. A small boy refuses to take a bath until his grandmother shows him how to make "kid tea."

- *Peter Spier's Rain*, Peter Spier. NY: Doubleday, 1982. In this wordless book, a brother and sister explore a neighborhood in their rain coats and galoshes during a rain storm.

- *Storm in the Night*, Mary Stolz. NY: HarperCollins Publishers, 1988.

- *Time of Wonder*, Robert McCloskey. NY: Viking Penguin, Inc., 1957. Describes the coming of a storm, its gale force and subsequent destruction that a family experiences at their summer home on the islands of Penobscot Bay.

- *Walk in the Rain, A*, Ursel Scheffler. NY: Putnam Publishing Group, 1986. Josh goes for a walk in the rain with his grandmother and wears his new rain gear.

Muddy Puddles, Soap & Bubbles

Poems

- *Hand Rhymes*, Marc Brown. NY: E.P. Dutton, 1985. "Quack! Quack! Quack!" p. 22-23.
- *Light in the Attic, A*, Shel Silverstein. NY: Harper and Row Publishers, 1981. "Messy Room," p. 35. "Snap," p. 64. "Crowded Tub," p. 86. "Arrows," p. 127.
- *Sing a Song of Popcorn*, selected by Beatrice Schenk deRegniers, Eva Moore, Mary Michaels White, and Jan Carr. NY: Scholastic, Inc., 1988. "Clouds," p. 17. "Rain," p. 17. "Rain, Rain, Go Away," p. 18. "Galoshes," p. 18. "The Duck," p. 74. "The Little Turtle," p. 74.
- *Where the Sidewalk Ends*, Shel Silverstein. NY: Harper and Row Publishers, 1974. "The Dirtiest Man in the World," p. 96-97. "Shadow Wash," p. 113. "Instructions," p. 129. "Skinny," p. 143.

Recordings

- "Bathtime," and "Little White Duck," *Everything Grows*. Raffi, (Shoreline Records) Troubadour Records, 1987.
- "Don't Drink the Water," "Don't Step on the Rain," *The One and Only Me*. Lisa Atkinson, A Gentle Wind, 1989.
- "In My Garden," *One Light, One Sun*. Raffi, (Shoreline Records) Troubador Records, 1985.
- "Ain't Gonna Rain No More," "Rain, Rain Go Away," and "Down By the Bay," *Playing Favorites*. Greg and Steve, Youngheart Music Inc., 1991.
- "Five Little Ducks," and "Ducks Like Rain," *Rise and Shine*. Raffi, (Shoreline Records) Troubadour Records, 1982.
- "Muddy Water Puddle," *Sally the Swinging Snake*. Hap Palmer, Educational Activities, Inc., 1987.
- "Robin in the Rain," and "5 Little Frogs," *Singable Songs for the Very Young*. Raffi, (Shoreline Records) Troubadour Records, 1976.

Meanies, Monsters & Make-Believe

Mondays	Read *It Didn't Frighten Me!* Do *It Didn't Frighten Us!*	Read *There's A Nightmare In My Closet* Do *What's a Monster Look Like?*	Do *Cooperative Castle Building* Do *Castle Caricature*	Read *Eyes of the Dragon* Do *Touch of Gold* Dragon Eggs for Snack
Tuesdays	Do *Monster Crayon Mess* Do *Nasty Faces* Monster Toast for Snack	Begin *Monster Maché* Read *"Monsters I've Met* (see Poems) Dragon Burgers for Snack	Read *Simon's Book* Do *Penned-Up Monster* Do *Getting a Head*	Read *The Princess and the Pea* Do *Princess' Nightmare Collage* Princess Pea Soup for Snack
Wednesdays	Read *My Mama Says There Aren't Any Zombies, etc.* Do *Making Meanie Bathwater*	Read *Where the Wild Things Are* Continue *Monster Maché* Do *Wild Rumpus*	Read *Those Mean Nasty Dirty etc.* Do *Mean, Nasty, Down-right Disgusting Germs* Do *Beastly Bubble Bath*	Do *How High Will They Go?* Do *Who Is the Best Guesser?*
Thursdays	Read *The Knight and the Dragon* Do *A Dragon's Fare* Begin *The Dragon's Lair* Do *Coat of Arms*	Do *Guessing Box* Do *King (or Queen) For A Day* Dragon Soup for Snack	Read *A Lion for Lewis* Do *Magic Carpet Ride* Do *Me and My Shadow*	Read *Jack and the Beanstalk* Do *Growing a Beanstalk* Jack's Beans for Snack
Fridays	Do *The Fifth Dragon Story* Do *Dragon Burgers* for Snack	Read *The Hungry Thing* Hungry Thing Foodles for Snack	Read *"Sockmonster"* (see Poems) Do *Hocus Pocus*	Do *Once Upon a Time* Do *If I Were a King / Queen*

Meanies, Monsters & Make-Believe

Theme Objectives

- To explore and experiment with the concept of make-believe and fantasy
- To facilitate the discrimination between reality and fantasy
- To discover the source and content of children's fears
- To facilitate the discovery of healthy and effective methods of coping with children's fears

Learning Centers

Dramatic Play

- Costumes:
    - knights
    - princess
    - dragon
    - monster
    - lion
    - bear
- crowns, tiaras
- magic wands
- princess hats
- big chair as a throne
- soft swords
- jewelry
- large refrigerator box made into a dragon's cave or king's castle

Blocks

- wooden castle blocks
- waffle castle blocks
- horses and knights
- large hollow wooden blocks
- knights' helmets
- wooden rocking horse

Meanies, Monsters & Make-Believe

Manipulatives

- castle sets
- deck of cards

Library

- flannel board and stories
- turtle, dragonfly, dragon and snake puppets
- tape recorder and stories
- make-a-monster flip book
- velcro puppet with assorted body part attachments

Science

- dried dragonflies
- pictures of the Loch Ness Monster
- shadow box
- sand table with sand castle molds
- crystal growing kit (supervise closely)

Art

- feathers
- felt
- fake fur
- glitter
- beads
- gems
- green playdough
- fingerpaint
- shaving cream (supervise closely)
- paper grocery bags
- lunch sacks
- paper plates
- buttons

Meanies, Monsters & Make-Believe

Writing

- stamp pads and dragon stamp
- fairy tale stamp-a-story
- make-a-face stamp set
- castle, dragon, crown and banner stencils
- strip maps

Snacks

- Monster Toast (see activity in Discovery section)
- Dragon Burgers (see activity in Discovery section)
- Jack's Beans (see activity in Discovery section)
- Princess Pea Soup (see activity in Discovery section)
- Dragon Eggs (see activity in Discovery section)
- Hungry Thing Foodles (see activity in Discovery section)

Discovery Activities

Jack's Beans

Materials

- fresh, unsnapped green beans
- large pot
- water
- butter
- salt
- *Jack and the Beanstalk* retold by Steven Kellogg

What to do

1. Read *Jack and the Beanstalk* aloud to the children.
2. Have the children help snap the beans. They will love doing this!
3. Wash the beans.
4. Place the clean, snapped beans into a large pot of water and cook them.
5. When the beans are done, drain them and add a little butter and salt and eat!

Meanies, Monsters & Make-Believe

Monster Toast

Materials

- bread
- toaster
- milk
- food coloring
- cotton swabs
- butter or margarine
- four small cups

What to do

1. Pour a small amount of milk into each of the four cups.
2. Color each cup of milk with three or four drops of food coloring.
3. Let the children dip a cotton swab into the colored milk and draw faces on their bread.
4. When the drawing is done, toast, butter, and eat!

Princess Pea Soup

Materials

- dried split peas
- water
- salt
- large pot
- carrots and celery (optional)
- ham bone
- *The Princess and the Pea* by Hans Christian Andersen

What to do

1. Read *The Princess and the Pea* to the children.
2. Boil the peas in about two quarts of water for five minutes.
3. Remove them from the heat, cover, and let them stand for about one hour.
4. Add the ham bone, salt, celery and carrots. Let the soup simmer for three to four hours or until the peas are very soft.
5. Remove the bone and thin the soup with milk or water if necessary.

Meanies, Monsters & Make-Believe

Dragon Eggs

3+

Materials

- hard-boiled eggs, one per child
- food coloring
- vinegar
- four small cups
- white crayons

What to do

1. Boil the eggs and let them cool.
2. Fill each cup with 1/2 cup of hot water, one tablespoon of vinegar and a few drops of food coloring.
3. Have the children decorate the eggs with the crayons. Have them draw dragons or monster faces on them.
4. Dip each egg in a cup for at least two minutes.
5. The crayon on the egg resists the color, making the child's drawing appear.
6. Allow the eggs to dry, and then peel and eat them for snack.

Hungry Thing Foodles

3+

Materials

- curly pasta noodles
- cheese, Cheddar or American
- large pot
- water
- strainer
- milk
- *The Hungry Thing* by Jan Slepian and Ann Seidler

What to do

1. Bring a large pot of water to boil. Caution children that the pot is hot.

2. Add curly noodles to the boiling water. Let them cook for five to seven minutes, and then strain.

3. Mix the pasta, cheese and milk in the large pot. Cook on low heat until the cheese melts.

4. Serve when reading *The Hungry Thing*.

Me and My Shadow

Materials

- bedsheet (white or light-colored) or a blank wall
- gooseneck lamp

What to do

1. If you do not have a blank wall, hang the sheet where there is space for the children to move.
2. Place the lamp on a small table or chair so that it is shining on the sheet or wall.
3. Ask a child if he knows what his shadow looks like.
4. Have him stand between the lamp and the wall so he can see his shadow.
5. Ask him if he can make his shadow move.
6. What else can you make your shadow do? Can you make it bigger? Smaller? How?

More to do

- Use the lamp and sheet at group time after the children have had a chance to experiment with it individually. Pick out some music and have the children shadow dance. Show shadows of simple objects for the children to guess.

Growing a Beanstalk

Materials

- large planting pot filled with potting soil
- an old broomstick or garden stake
- a package of navy beans
- *Jack and the Beanstalk* retold by Steven Kellogg

What to do

1. Read *Jack and the Beanstalk* to the children.
2. Discuss what plants need in order to grow.
3. Give each child a bean. Show her how to poke a hole in the dirt with her finger, drop the seed in and cover it up.
4. Have each child plant a seed in the large pot.
5. Water, watch and wait!

Magic Crayon Mixture

3+

Materials

- warming tray
- muffin tins
- small amount of cooking oil or foil muffin cups
- old crayons

What to do

1. If you will be using metal muffin tins, you will need to coat the cups lightly with oil. Oil is not needed when using "disposable" aluminum foil muffin tins or foil muffin cups.
2. Have the children help peel the paper off the old crayons.
3. Place the muffin tins or foil muffin cups on the warming tray.
4. Break the crayons into small pieces and drop them into the muffin cups.
5. Watch them melt. If desired, stir with a craft stick.
6. When the crayons have completely melted, remove the muffin tin from the warming tray or unplug the tray to allow cooling.
7. When the crayon mixtures have hardened, remove from the muffin tin. Presto change-o! You have chunky crayons.

CAUTION: The crayon mixture is hot! Supervision is needed for this activity.

More to do

- Discuss why the crayons melted and then hardened again. Experiment with mixing colors to make new colors, such as blue pieces and yellow pieces to make green, or red, blue and white pieces to make light purple.

Meanies, Monsters & Make-Believe

Watch It Grow!

3+

Materials

- package of navy beans
- clear plastic cups, one per child
- paper towels, one per child
- water

What to do

1. Wet the paper towels.
2. Recall and discuss the planting of the beans in the large pot.
3. Ask if they would like to see what the bean looks like when it's growing.
4. Explain that the cup will take the place of the pot and the paper towels will take the place of the dirt.
5. Have each child put his wet paper towel into his cup. Demonstrate how to push a bean in between the paper and the side of the cup.
6. Check the cups each day. These cups need not be kept in the sun.

More to do

- Graph how many beans sprout each day.

Monster Crayon Mess

3+

Materials

- warming tray
- old crayons or chunky crayons
- paper
- aluminum foil

What to do

1. Cover the warming tray with foil before plugging it in.
2. Cut paper to fit on warming tray.
3. If using old crayons, peel the paper from them.
4. Place one sheet of paper on the warming tray. Caution the child that the warming tray will feel hot to the touch.

5. Have the child slowly move the crayon across the paper to see how it melts. The colors will mix and melt together as the child uses more crayons on his paper.

NOTE: Instruct the children to use caution. Supervise closely, especially when this activity is first introduced.

Slime!

Materials

- cornstarch
- water
- green food coloring
- large bowls

What to do

1. Mix water and cornstarch in a bowl until they reach the consistency of mashed potatoes.
2. Add green food coloring.
3. Try to pick it up—it slips through your fingers!

Slime Two!

Materials

- school glue
- liquid starch
- airtight container
- green food coloring

What to do

1. Mix equal parts of school glue and liquid starch, and a few drops of green food coloring.
2. Let the mixture sit overnight. By morning it will stretch very thin and return to its original shape.
3. Stretch it, enjoy it!

Meanies, Monsters & Make-Believe

Making Meanie Bathwater

3+

Materials

- five small transparent containers
- water
- food coloring
- spoon for mixing

What to do

1. Fill four containers with water, leaving the fifth empty.
2. Tell this story as you proceed:

> "There were five meanies who lived together. At bedtime they all had to take a bath. The first meanie was playing in the dandelions. When he came in to clean up he turned the bathwater. . .(wait for a response) yellow! (Add three drops of yellow food coloring to a small container of water.) The second meanie had been picking blueberries. When he came in to take a bath, he turned the bathwater. . . blue! (Add three drops of blue food coloring to a separate small container of water.) The third meanie had been cutting the grass and had grass stains all over him. When he took a bath ho turned the water. . . green! (Add three drops of green food coloring to a separate small container of water.) The fourth meanie had been in the strawberry patch eating all the strawberries. When he took a bath he turned the bathwater. . . red! (Add three drops of red food coloring to a separate small container of water.)

> The fifth meanie was a lazy meanie. He poured all the bathwater into his tub and jumped in! Ugh! Meanie Bathwater!!!"

More to do

- If the children have had previous experience with food coloring you may want to allow them to add the drops of food coloring themselves. Set out water, clear cups and food coloring. The children can experiment making their own "meanie bathwater" by mixing colors.

Meanies, Monsters & Make-Believe

Cooperative Castle Building

Materials

- large hollow blocks
- unit blocks
- interlocking plastic blocks

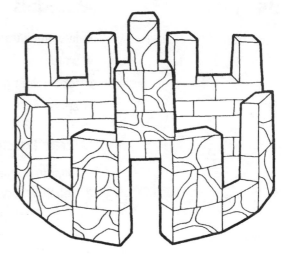

What to do

1. Divide the children into three groups. Give each group a different set of blocks. One groups gets unit blocks, one group gets plastic interlocking blocks, and so on.
2. Ask each group to build a castle using the materials they have.

More to do

- Use large chart paper and markers and let each group draw a picture when it is finished, or take a Polaroid snapshot of each castle to display for parents.

Dragon Burgers

Materials

- ground beef
- hamburger buns
- electric skillet or outdoor grill, charcoal and matches
- *The Knight and the Dragon* by Tomie dePaola
- paper plates

What to do

1. Give each child a small amount of ground beef and allow her to make a small hamburger patty.
2. Grill the hamburgers outside if weather is nice. Otherwise, you can grill them on the electric skillet in the classroom.
3. Serve the burgers and read *The Knight and the Dragon*.

Meanies, Monsters & Make-Believe

More to do

- You may want to make this into a family fun night and include moms, dads and siblings.

Monster Tracking Tool

Materials

- magnifying glasses
- paper
- markers and crayons
- masking tape

What to do

1. Cut out many large "monster" footprints. Tape them to the floor in the room or down the hall, leading to a table with paper, markers and crayons.
2. Divide the children into groups and give each group a magnifying glass. Tell them they are going for a walk to track a "monster."
3. Have the "monster tracks" lead to the table with paper, markers and crayons. Have the children draw what they think the "monster" might look like.

Art Activities

Princess' Nightmare Collage

Materials

- crayons and markers
- paper
- glue
- glitter or sequins
- *The Princess and the Pea* retold by Toni Bernahard
- *Jack and the Beanstalk* retold by Steven Kellogg

Meanies, Monsters & Make-Believe

What to do

1. Read the fairy tales *The Princess and the Pea* and *Jack and the Beanstalk* before doing this activity.
2. Ask the child to draw a picture about one of the stories.

More to do

- Add special materials to the drawings such as glitter and sequins.

Touch of Gold

Materials

- 8" x 10" cardboard
- gold tempera
- paintbrushes
- glue
- gold glitter
- collage material, such as buttons, corrugated cardboard, small beads or lids, and so on

What to do

1. Glue collage materials on cardboard. Let dry.
2. Brush on gold paint
3. Sprinkle glitter on while paint is still wet. You have the golden touch!

Meanies, Monsters & Make-Believe

Nasty Faces

Materials

- large paper plates, one per child
- collage materials—ribbon, Easter grass, styrofoam pieces, tissue paper scraps, construction paper scraps and glitter
- books about monsters or dragons

What to do

1. Have the books about monsters and dragons out for the children to look at.
2. Ask the children to create a monster face using the materials available.

Castle Caricature

Materials

- drawings and pictures of castles
- drawing paper
- markers or crayons

What to do

1. Display drawings and pictures of castles where children can see them.
2. Give each child a piece of paper and ask her to draw a castle.

The Dragon's Lair

Materials

- tape
- resource books about caves
- large box
- wrapping paper, brown paper sacks or paint

Meanies, Monsters & Make-Believe

What to do

1. Look at the books about caves and decide how the class could build one for the classroom using the large box.
2. Make paper or paint available to cover the cave. They may also want to decorate the walls of their cave with drawings or with collage materials.

Monster Mache

Materials

- assorted sizes of empty boxes
- newspaper
- flour
- water
- pail or bucket
- paper towel and toilet paper tubes
- paper
- yarn
- paint
- Easter grass
- jar and milk jug lids
- corrugated cardboard
- measuring cup
- mixing spoons
- a place for the "monster" to dry

What to do

1. Prepare your papier-mache using equal parts of flour and water. You might want to write your recipe in pictograph form so the children can "read" it with you.
2. Discuss with the children what they want their monster to look like. How many legs, horns or arms will it have? Where are you going to put its tail, mouth and eyes? Will it have fur, teeth, scales? Encourage all of the children to contribute.
3. Have the children look at the materials and talk about what material to use for eyes, hair, and so on.
4. Have the children help to assemble the monster's skeleton by taping on tubes for horns, lids for eyes or Easter grass for hair.
5. Have them cut or tear newspaper into 1" to 2"-wide strips.

6. Show them how to dip the newspaper strips into the papier-mache and apply to the "monster." **IMPORTANT**: Children should have their clothing covered by a smock or art shirt because this step is very messy.

7. When the skeleton of the creation has acquired a layer of papier-mache, find a place to set it to dry.

8. After the first layer is dry, apply a second layer of papier-mache and let that dry.

9. Apply paint, yarn, Easter grass and other materials.

More to do

- Use the "monster" in a dramatization of a story. Find a place in the community to display it such as the library or a parent's place of business.

It's a Dragon!

Materials

- dryer vent hose
- construction paper scraps
- tissue paper scraps
- tape
- a paper lunch bag
- rubber band
- newspaper

What to do

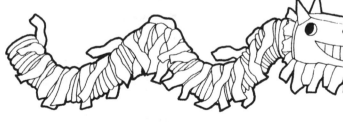

1. Ask the children how they could turn the hose into a dragon.

2. Have the children crumple newspaper and stuff it in the paper bag to make a head.

3. Fasten the head to one end of the hose with the rubber band.

4. Have the children cover the dragon with paper scraps and tape.

5. Have the children draw or glue eyes, a nose, ears, and a mouth to the dragon's head using pens and paper scraps or other collage material.

Meanies, Monsters & Make-Believe

Dragon Wigglers

Materials

- 1" wide strips of construction paper
- paper scraps
- glue
- scissors

What to do

1. Demonstrate to the children how to fold the strips accordion-style. Show them how it wiggles when unfolded.
2. Let each child fold his own. He can cut shorter strips, fold them, and glue them to the long strip as legs.
3. Allow the children to be creative in adding to their dragon.

Getting a Head

Materials

- large pieces of construction paper in many skin tones
- large pieces of construction paper as background
- markers
- scissors
- glue
- collage materials, such as cloth, beads, rickrack, braid trim, small lids, buttons, yarn, feathers, and so on

What to do

1. With the help of the older children, cut the contruction paper in the shape of a head and neck of a person.
2. Each child picks out a head shape to glue on a large sheet of construction paper.
3. Using collage materials, make the "person's" eyes, nose, mouth, hair, clothes (just shoulders), crown, and so on.
4. Or use markers for the facial features.

Meanies, Monsters & Make-Believe

Green Sculpture

Materials

- green playdough
- box of toothpicks
- *The Princess and the Pea* retold by Toni Bernahard

What to do

1. Roll the playdough into small pea-sized pieces.
2. Read *The Princess and the Pea* to the children.
3. Set out the playdough and toothpicks on small trays.
4. Demonstrate to the children how the toothpick can be used to connect two pieces of playdough.
5. Let the children create their own sculptures.

Beastly Bubble Bath

Materials

- four cups or small bowls
- water
- liquid detergent
- food coloring
- straws
- paper

What to do

1. In each cup, mix water, liquid detergent and four or five drops of food coloring.
2. Give a child a straw and a cup of the colored detergent water.
3. Direct her to blow into the cup with the straw to make bubbles. Remind her to blow, not suck!
4. As the bubbles come to the top of the cup and overflow, quickly put a piece of paper over the top of the cup to make a print.
5. The children will want to try all the colors. These prints look especially nice as the colored bubble prints overlap on the paper.

Meanies, Monsters & Make-Believe

King (or Queen) for a Day

Materials

- long cardboard strips, one per child
- jewels, beads, glitter, shiny ribbon and sequins
- glue
- stapler and staples

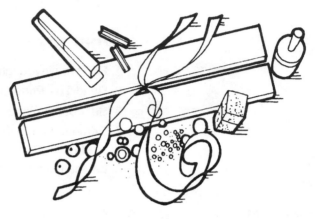

What to do

1. On one long edge of each cardboard strip cut a zigzag edge to make points like a crown.
2. Give each child a cardboard strip. Measure it around his head, allowing enough room for it to overlap slightly. Cut off any extra cardboard.
3. Lay the strip flat and let the child decorate his crown with the jewels, beads and glitter that are available.
4. When the glue has dried, staple the ends of the cardboard together to form a crown.

Coat of Arms

Materials

- rectangular pieces of construction paper, one per child
- glitter
- jewels, beads
- scraps of material, ribbon
- glue stick

What to do

1. Cut one of the ends of each piece of construction paper to a point. This will be the bottom of the banner.
2. Show the children pictures of families' coat of arms. Explain that when there were princesses, princes, kings and queens, every family had their own banner.
3. Allow the children to create their own banner using the materials provided.
4. Let the banners dry, and hang them around the classroom.

More to do

- If they can print their own names, show them how to do it with the glue stick on their banners. Sprinkle the glued areas with glitter. Their names will be in shiny letters on their own personalized banner or coat of arms!

Music and Movement Activities

Magic Carpet Ride

What to do

1. Pretend each child has a magic carpet. Glide along and tell about all the places your carpet goes and all the wonderful things you see.

Hocus Pocus

Materials

- a magic wand (a dowel with a cardboard star covered with glitter)

What to do

1. Wave the magic wand and say,
   "Hocus, pocus, alakazam,
   Turn into a frog if you can!"
2. The children hop around like frogs. This can be repeated using a variety of animals.

Meanies, Monsters & Make-Believe

Wild Rumpus

3+

Materials

- *Where the Wild Things Are* by Maurice Sendak

What to do

1. Read *Where the Wild Things Are*.
2. Have your own wild rumpus in your classroom. Put on music and dance or use noise makers and parade around the room.

Math Activities

Calendar

3+

Materials

- plain calendar or paper and markers

What to do

1. Make or purchase a plain calendar with only the days of the week marked on it.
2. Each month, make different paper patterns to fit your theme. For example: for the "meanies, monsters and make-believe" theme you may want to use three crowns. The first day the crown only has one jewel, the second day the crown has two jewels, and the third day the crown has three jewels. On the fourth day start over and repeat the pattern. We made our crowns out of shiny paper with a sequin for the jewel. Make crowns for your number line also.
3. The days of the week may be sung to the tune of "Frere Jacques." "Sunday, Monday, Tuesday, Wednesday, Thursday, Friday, Saturday. It's not Sunday, it's not Monday, it's not Tuesday, it is. . . " (Let the children fill in the blank for whatever day of the week it is.)
4. School Days Countdown—make an ongoing number line for the number of days the children have been at school. Follow the same pattern as your monthly calendar pattern.

More to do

- For actions to the calendar pattern, hold up one finger on the day there is one jewel, hold up two fingers on the day there are two jewels, and hold up three fingers on the day there are three jewels.

Meanies, Monsters & Make-Believe

Calendar Patterns for
Meanies, Monsters and
Make Believe

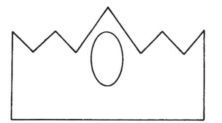

How High Will They Go?

3+

Materials

- large pieces of wallpaper or wrapping paper
- scissors
- tape

What to do

1. Read or tell the story of *The Princess and the Pea*.
2. Ask each child to pick the pattern of paper she likes.
3. Each child cuts a long, narrow rectangle out of the paper. Cut the rectangle as long as possible and about six inches wide.
4. Tape this "mattress" to the wall.
5. Tape each "mattress" on top of each other, in a stack.
6. Count the mattresses.
7. Place a small round green circle under the mattress to represent the pea that the princess slept on.

Meanies, Monsters & Make-Believe

Guessing Box

4+

Materials

- box or paper bag
- monster masks
- crown
- jewels
- swords
- monster bubble wand
- beans

What to do

1. Show a "meanies, monsters and make-believe" item such as a pea to the children and talk about its properties, such as its shape, color, size, and uses.

2. Bring out the guessing box with another "meanies, monsters and make-believe" item in it. Use the same box each time, no matter what size the item is. Storage boxes for clothing are the ideal size.

3. Say:

    "There is something in my guessing box.

    Would you like to guess?

    First you ask a question and

    I'll answer no or yes."

4. Children then ask questions. Encourage them to ask in the form of a question. "Is it. . . ?"

5. After a brief time, if you notice they aren't asking questions that pertain to the item in the box, give broad hints.

    "It's something medium-sized." Wait for guesses.

    "It's something round." Wait for guesses.

    "It's something with many colors." Wait.

    "It's something you wear on your head." Wait for guesses.

    ("Yes, it's a crown!")

Meanies, Monsters & Make-Believe

Bean Sort

Materials

- mixture of dried beans and peas
- muffin tin or sorting tray

What to do

1. Give each child a small portion of the beans and peas and a sorting tray.
2. Start by saying, "Find all the beans that look like this one and put them in this section."
3. Have the children sort the beans in this way. Allow the children to have time to experiment with this activity on their own. Supervise closely.
4. Cook the peas or beans for a snack

Who's the Best Guesser?

Materials

- jar
- dried beans
- marker
- paper

What to do

1. Place the beans in the jar and allow the children to examine the jar.
2. Ask each child to guess how many beans are in the jar. Record each guess next to the child's name on the paper.
3. Open the jar and count the beans with the children.

More to do

- Use fewer beans for younger children. Older children could make piles of ten beans and count by tens. Cook the beans for a snack.

Meanies, Monsters & Make-Believe

Language Activities

What's a Monster Look Like?

Materials

- marker
- easel and paper

What to do

1. At small group time say, "Tell me what a monster looks like."
2. Record all responses.

More to do

- Draw a monster according to the directions given by the children. Have the children draw their own idea of what a monster looks like.

Penned-Up Monster

Materials

- paper
- assorted colored pens and pencils
- *Simon's Book* by Henrik Drescher

What to do

1. Read *Simon's Book* to the children.
2. Ask the children to make their own monsters using pens and pencils.

Meanies, Monsters & Make-Believe

Mean, Nasty, Downright Disgusting Germs

Materials

- paper
- colored markers and pencils
- *Those Mean, Nasty Downright Disgusting But...Invisible Germs* by Judith Rice

What to do

1. Read *Those Mean, Nasty Downright Disgusting But. . . Invisible Germs* to the children.
2. Ask the children to draw pictures of what they think a germ would look like and name their germ.

The Fifth Dragon Story

Materials

- chart paper
- markers
- tape

What to do

1. Before telling the story, stress that it involves five dragons. As you mention each dragon draw a sketch of it, or draw each one ahead of time and tape the drawings up as you tell the story.

   "Once there were five dragons who were brothers. They all helped out around the neighborhood. The first dragon was a green, greasy, grimy dragon who ate grass. The second dragon was a silver, slimy, snakelike dragon who ate mice out of basements. The third dragon was a funny, fat, frog-like dragon who ate flies in a restaurant. The fourth dragon was a big, black, box-like dragon who ate dirt and dead leaves out of the gutters."

2. Pause after the fourth dragon as though you are finished. If the children haven't caught on to the fact there are only four dragons, remind them there should be five dragons.

3. Ask the children to describe the fifth dragon and a useful job he could do. Draw a sketch as the children describe him.

Meanies, Monsters & Make-Believe

More to do

- Older children could draw their own picture of the fifth dragon.

If I Were a King/Queen

Materials

- chart paper
- markers

What to do

1. This activity is best attempted after several fairy tales have been read about kings and queens. Ask the children to imagine they are a king or a queen. What's one of the first things they would do?
2. Record all responses on chart paper.
3. As the theme progresses children may want to add more ideas to this list.

Once Upon a Time

Materials

- chart paper
- drawing paper
- markers or crayons
- bookbinding materials
- laminating film or clear contact paper

What to do

1. Tell the children that they are going to write a group fairy tale.
2. Start them off by writing on the chart paper, "Once upon a time there lived a. . ." Write the story as children contribute their ideas for the plot. Some prompting may be necessary. (You may want to jot a student's name by their sentence, to make sure everyone gets some input.)

3. During free choice time, call one or two students over at a time to illustrate their sentence(s). One student can make the book cover.
4. Laminate, if possible, or cover with contact paper, and bind.
5. Place in the library.

More to do

- Copy the book for each student and send home.

A Dragon's Fare

Materials

- paper
- markers or crayons
- binding materials
- *The Knight and the Dragon by Tomie dePaola*

What to do

1. Read *The Knight and the Dragon* to the children.
2. With the children, make a list of dishes dragons might like to eat.
3. Ask the children to dictate some dragon recipes. They may even want to illustrate their recipes.
4. Bind into a Dragon Cookbook.

More to do

- Children could bring their favorite recipe from home to make a classroom cookbook.

How to Catch a Dragon

Materials

- paper
- pencils, pens, markers or crayons
- binding materials

Meanies, Monsters & Make-Believe

What to do

1. Ask the children what steps they would take to catch a dragon. Tell them they must list each step.
2. Have them illustrate each step so that someone reading their book would know just how to catch a dragon.
3. Put the steps in order and bind.
4. Place in library.

Make-Believe

Materials

- *Where the Wild Things Are* by Maurice Sendak
- paper
- markers or crayons
- construction paper
- binding materials: hole punch and brads, stapler, binder and rings
- laminating film or clear contact paper

What to do

1. Talk about the "wild things" in the book.
2. Ask the children to draw one thing the "wild thing" might do if they came to your school.
3. Record what they say at the bottom of each page.
4. Make a cover out of construction paper.
5. Laminate or cover the pages with clear contact paper, and bind into a book.

More to do

- Older children can design the cover for the book.

Meanies, Monsters & Make-Believe

It Didn't Frighten Us!

4+

Materials

- *It Didn't Frighten Me!* by Janet Goss and Jerome Harste
- paper
- construction paper
- markers or crayons
- binding materials: hole punch and brads, stapler, binder and rings

What to do

1. Read *It Didn't Frighten Me!* to the children.
2. Make a list of scary things. Record these as the children list them.
3. Ask the children to draw a picture of something scary that they are not afraid of.
4. Record the descriptions of the scary drawings at the bottom of their papers.
5. Bind into a book.
6. Make a cover for the book out of construction paper.

More to do

- Add a library pocket and make the book available to check out.

Transition Activities

Dragon Walk

- Walk like a dragon when it is time to go outside. Be sure to huff and puff and roar like a dragon.

Monster Steps

- Have the children get to another area by taking big monster steps.

Meanies, Monsters & Make-Believe

Songs and Chants

- "The King in the Castle" sung to the tune of "The Farmer in the Dell"

The king in the castle,
The king in the castle,
Hi ho the castle oh,
The king in the castle.

The king takes a queen,
The king takes a queen,
Hi ho the castle oh,
The king takes a queen.

The queen takes a prince,
The queen takes a prince,
Hi ho the castle oh,
The queen takes a prince.

The prince takes a princess,
The prince takes a princess,
Hi ho the castle oh,
The prince takes a princess.

The princess takes a knight,
The princess takes a knight,
Hi ho the castle oh,
The princess takes a knight.

The knight takes a dragon,
The knight takes a dragon,
Hi ho the castle oh,
The knight takes a dragon.

The dragon stands alone,
The dragon stands alone,
Hi ho the castle oh,
The dragon stands alone.

Meanies, Monsters & Make-Believe

Theme Extensions and Variations

- Call this unit "Once Upon a Time" and concentrate only on fairy tales.
- Take a field trip to a costume shop.
- Have a costume party during this unit.
- Ask a clown to visit the classroom and show how he or she puts on make-up and a costume to become a clown.

Bibliography

- *Eyes of the Dragon*, Margaret Leaf. NY: Lothrop, Lee and Shepard Books, 1987. A Chinese proverb of a painter commissioned to paint dragons on the city walls. When the city magistrate insisted that the painter add eyes to the dragon, the painter complied against his better judgment. The two dragons came alive and broke loose from the wall.
- *Hungry Thing, The*, Jan Slepian and Ann Seidler. NY: Scholastic, Inc., 1988. A monster comes to town wearing a sign that says "Feed," but his requests come out in a puzzling jumble of words.
- *It Didn't Frighten Me!* Janet L. Goss and Jerome C. Harste. Worthington, Ohio: Willowisp Press, Inc., 1985. A predictable book about what a boy imagines in the tree outside his window.
- *Jack and the Beanstalk*, retold by Steven Kellogg. NY: William Morrow and Company, Inc., 1991. A boy climbs to the top of a giant beanstalk where he uses his quick wit to make his and his mother's fortune.
- *Knight and the Dragon, The*, Tomie dePaola. NY: Putnam Publishing Group, 1980. A knight who has never fought a dragon and an equally inexperienced dragon prepare to meet each other in battle.
- *Lion for Lewis, A*, Rosemary Wells. NY: Puffin Books, 1984. When Lewis plays make believe with his older siblings, he always gets the least desirable role until a lion suit in a corner turns him into a King.
- *My Mama says There Aren't Any Zombies, Ghosts, Vampires, Creatures, Demons, Monster, Fiends, Goblins or Things*, Judith Viorst. NY: Macmillan, 1973. If mother has made other important mistakes, can Nick trust her word that there are no goblins and such lurking around in the night?
- *Princess and the Pea, The*, Hans Christian Andersen, illus. by Paul Galdone. NY: Houghton Mifflin, 1979.
- *Simon's Book*, Henrik Drescher. NY: Lothrop, Lee and Shepard Books, 1983. Simon flees from a friendly monster with the aid of his drawing pens.
- *There's a Nightmare in My Closet*, Mercer Mayer. NY: Dial Books, 1985. A young boy conquers and then befriends the nightmare that's been lurking in his closet.

Meanies, Monsters & Make-Believe

- *Those Mean Nasty Dirty Downright Disgusting But. . . Invisible Germs*, Judith Rice. St. Paul, Minn: Redleaf Press, 1989. A little girl who accumulates germs on her hands during her busy day defeats them by washing and drying her hands.

- *Where the Wild Things Are*, Maurice Sendak. Harper and Row Publishers, 1988. Max is sent to his room without supper and sets sail for the land of the Wild Things who crown him king.

Poems

- "Sockmonster," *Kids Pick the Funniest Poems*. Bruce Lansky, NY: Meadowbrook Press, Simon Schuster, 1991, p. 75.

- "Magic Carpet," *A Light in the Attic*. Shel Silverstein, NY: Evil Eye Music, Inc., Harper and Row Publishers, 1981, p. 106.

- "Monsters I've Met," *A Light in the Attic*. Shel Silverstein, NY: Evil Eye Music, Inc., Harper and Row Publishers, 1981, p. 23.

- "I Lost My Invisible Puppy," *Something Big Has Been Here*. Jack Prelutsky, NY: Greenwillow, 1990, p. 132.

- "Magical Eraser," *Where the Sidewalk Ends*. Shel Silverstein, NY: Evil Eye Music, Inc., Harper and Row Publishers, 1974, p. 99.

Recordings

- "Puff the Magic Dragon," *Happiness Cake*. Linda Arnold, Ariel Records, 1988.

- "Monsters Never Comb Their Hair," *The One and Only Me*. Lisa Atkinson, A Gentle Wind, 1989.

- "Mice Go Marching," *Rhythms on Parade*. Hap Palmer, Hap-Pal Music, Inc., 1989.

Surprises & Celebrations

Mondays	Read *Birthday for Frances* Do Unbirthday Day	Do Weird Week Marvelous Monday Do Party on a Plate Popcorn for Snack	Pajama Day Read *Pajamas*	Do Wedding Week Field Trip to Bridal Shop
Tuesdays	Do Flower Power Do How Old Are You?	Terrific Tuesday: Show and Tell Do Gift Wrap Collage	Do Filter Fantasy Do Guessing Box Read "Surprise!" (see Poems)	Hat Day Read *Ruby Mae Has Something To Say*
Wednesdays	Read *Wacky Wednesday* Do Wacky! Wacky! Wacky!	Read *The Gift* Do Match the Gifts Wacky Wednesday: Eat Pickles and Ice Cream for Snack	Read *Wednesday Surprise* Do Surprise Pictures Surprise Pudding for Snack	Read *The Surprise Party* Do Salty Surprise Do Tilt-a-Swirl
Thursdays	Do Lace Rubbing Do Let's Celebrate! Marshmallow Surprise for Snack	Read *I Spy* Do Surprise! One, Two Drawings	Read *The Wolf's Chicken Stew* 100 Day Do 100th Day Do Eating Big	Field trip to Bakery Do Decorate the Cake
Fridays	Read *Night Noises* Surprise Muffins for Snack Do Secret Surprise Messages	Read *The Secret Birthday Message* Do Make a Wish Class Book Read "The Birthday Child" (see Poems)	Do How Many is 100? Picnic Day	Tea Party Day Read *Imogene's Antlers*

Surprises & Celebrations

Theme Objectives

- To explore and experience celebrations
- To help young children understand what a surprise is
- To practice good manners

Learning Centers

Dramatic Play

- party clothes
- wedding clothes
- veils
- hats of all types
- jewelry
- plastic pretend food, especially cakes and party food
- party napkins
- party plates and cups
- silk flower bouquets
- party hats

Manipulatives

- feature a new "surprise" game each week such as Candyland, Memory or Chutes and Ladders

Writing

- greeting cards and envelopes
- invitations
- hole punchers—dots and shapes
- stickers
- holiday stamps and stamp pads
- holiday shaped paper pads

Art

- colored glue
- construction paper

- tissue paper
- colored confetti
- glitter
- stickers
- neon paints
- neon paper
- watercolors
- salt
- tempera paint
- crayons
- foil and other shiny material
- doilies
- cupcake liners

Library

- bridal magazines

Snacks

- Marshmallow Surprise (see activity in Discovery section)
- Surprise Muffins (see activity in Discovery section)
- Surprise Pudding (see activity in discovery section)
- popcorn
- pizza
- ice cream and pickles

Discovery Activities

Surprise Pudding

3+

Materials

- two packages of instant vanilla pudding or ready-to-eat vanilla pudding
- food coloring
- spoons

What to do

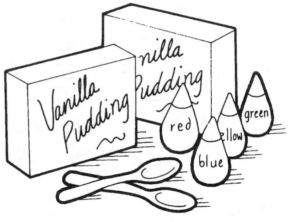

1. Since this is a surprise for the children, they do not help make the surprise pudding.
2. Spoon a small amount of pudding into each child's cup. Then place two drops of one color of food coloring on each child's pudding. Make some red, some blue, some green, and some yellow.
3. On top of the food coloring, place another spoonful of pudding.
4. Serve each child a cup of pudding at snack time.
5. Have each child stir his pudding before he starts eating it to find the surprise.
6. Each child is surprised to find his pudding turns a different color. It is fun to listen to the children asking each other what color pudding they have!

Racing Colors

3+

Materials

- coffee filters
- black water soluble markers
- water
- small clear cups

What to do

1. Cut each coffee filter into three parts. On each part draw a black horizontal line.
2. Dip one end into the water.
3. Have the children watch as the water slowly seeps up the paper filter.
4. Watch the colors separate as the water reaches the black line.
5. Surprise! You didn't know all those colors were in that black line!

Filter Fantasy

Materials

- coffee filters
- markers
- spray bottle
- water
- construction paper

What to do

1. Let each child use the markers to draw on a coffee filter.
2. Allow each child to spray her filter with the water in the spray bottle.
3. Watch the colors run together.
4. Let dry and mount on construction paper.

Marshmallow Surprise

Materials

- two rolls of biscuits
- large marshmallows
- melted butter
- cinnamon
- sugar
- baking sheet
- oven
- measuring cup and spoon
- small bowl

What to do

1. Mix 1/4 cup sugar with one teaspoon of cinnamon in a small bowl.
2. Have each child flatten a biscuit.
3. Have him then dip one marshmallow in melted butter and roll it in the cinnamon/sugar mixture.
4. Have him place the marshmallow in the middle of the flattened biscuit and fold up the sides to cover the marshmallow. Some children will need a little help.
5. Place the biscuit on a greased baking sheet, folded side down.
6. Bake at 350 degrees for about ten minutes or until brown.
7. Cool slightly and serve for snack. Surprise! Where's the marshmallow?

Surprise Muffins

4+

Materials

- cupcake liners
- muffin pan
- two mixes of any kind of muffins
- jelly or jam
- spoons
- bowl

What to do

1. Let the children help put a cupcake liner in each muffin cup.
2. Let the children help prepare the muffin mixes according to the directions on the package.
3. Fill each muffin cup about half full of muffin mix.
4. Have each child drop about half a teaspoon of jelly or jam into the middle of the muffin batter in each muffin cup.
5. Bake according to the package directions.
6. Cool and serve for snack. One bite will reveal the surprise—your muffin already has jelly inside!

How Many Are 100?

Materials

- children's collections

What to do

1. Send a note home asking each child to bring 100 pieces of a collection, such as 100 seashells, 100 pennies, 100 buttons or 100 bottle caps.
2. Let each child show the class her collection at group time.

More to do

- Let the children explore the collections using sorting trays. Add collections to math area, if children are willing to donate them to the class.

Special Days for Surprises and Celebrations

Weird Week

Materials

- popcorn
- *Wacky Wednesday* by Theo Le Sieg
- scary, thrilling books or stories

What to do

1. Name each day of the week: Marvelous Monday, Terrific Tuesday, Wacky Wednesday, Thrilling Thursday, and Funny Friday.
2. On "Marvelous Monday," begin your celebrations with a popcorn day.
3. On "Terrific Tuesday," take a field trip, serve a special snack, or have show and tell.
4. There are numerous things to do for "Wacky Wednesday." Be sure to read the book, *Wacky Wednesday* to the children. Have pickles and ice cream as a wacky snack. Instead of your regular classroom schedule, do everything backwards. For

example, have choice time last instead of first. Dress wacky: wear clothes that don't match, or wear shorts in the middle of winter.

5. For "Thrilling Thursday," read a scary, thrilling story or ask a special guest to come to class.

6. On "Funny Friday," change places with a child. Let one of the children do the calendar time or give directions about the art project.

Hat Day

Materials

- lots of hats
- *Ruby Mae Has Something to Say* by David Small
- paper cut into hat shapes
- glue
- flowers, ribbon, rickrack
- paper and markers

What to do

1. Give everyone a hat to wear.
2. Read *Ruby Mae Has Something to Say* to the children.
3. Decorate hat shapes or small styrofoam hats with flowers, ribbons and rickrack.
4. Graph the different types of hats: ball caps, colorful hats, hats with flowers.

Pajama Day

Materials

- pajamas
- recorded lullabies
- hot chocolate and cookies or cereal and milk
- *Pajamas* by Livingston and Maggie Taylor
- paper and markers

What to do

1. All children and teachers wear pajamas to school.
2. Play lullabies during choice time.
3. Serve hot chocolate and cookies or cereal and milk for snack.
4. Read the book *Pajamas* to the children.
5. Graph the different kinds of pajamas: with feet, without feet, long sleeves, short sleeves, nightgowns, robes, slippers.

Picnic Day

Materials

- blanket
- snack
- paper and markers or crayons

What to do

1. If the weather is nice take your snack outside as a picnic. If it is not nice have an indoor picnic.
2. Have the children draw a picture of their favorite food they like to eat on a picnic.

100th Day

Materials

- large cake with 100 candles
- balloons
- *The Wolf's Chicken Stew* by Keiko Kasza
- paper and markers

What to do

1. If you keep a countdown of how many days you have been at school, be sure to make the 100th day a big celebration.
2. Have a large cake with 100 candles on it.

3. Pop 100 balloons (if you can blow up that many!)
4. Clap, hop or stomp to 100.
5. Read *The Wolf's Chicken Stew* to the class.
6. Make a "100" book such as: "If I ate 100 _____, I'd look like this." "This is how I'll look when I'm 100 years old."
7. If possible, involve your whole school in this celebration. Hang banners and make the day very festive.

Unbirthday Day

Materials

- party hats and napkins
- party tablecloth
- cupcakes and ice cream
- toppings
- cups and plates
- spoons
- party games
- balloons
- optional, party favors

What to do

1. Since some children celebrate their birthdays during the school year and others are in the summer, we have an "unbirthday" day on which we celebrate everybody's birthday.
2. Sing "Happy Birthday to Us!"
3. Have everybody wear a party hat and have a birthday napkin at snack time. Cover the tables with paper birthday table covers.
4. Have cupcakes and ice cream for snack, or have a sundae bar. Each child gets a scoop of vanilla ice cream. Sundae toppings are set out so the child can make her own sundae. Toppings: nuts, chocolate syrup, whipped topping, chocolate sprinkles, and caramel or strawberry topping.
5. Play birthday type games such as Pin the Tail on the Donkey.
6. Decorate with balloons, and if possible, give each child a small party favor or trinket.

Tea Party Day

Materials

- paper and markers or crayons
- tablecloths
- optional, flowers and candles
- cookies
- "tea" (juice)
- plates and cups

What to do

1. Have each child design his own invitation to a tea party to take home to his parents inviting them to tea.
2. Invite the support staff to your tea party.
3. Use tablecloths on the tables and a floral centerpiece or candles in candlesticks.
4. Teachers and children all dress up for school and bring their guests.
5. Children "serve" tea and cookies to their guests.
6. We have had a tea party for several years and it is one of the most enjoyable activities of this theme.

Wedding Week

Materials

- dress-up wedding clothes
- paper and marker
- optional, personal wedding albums and dresses

What to do

1. The last week of this theme is usually Wedding Week.
2. Dress-up wedding clothes are available.
3. Take a field trip to a bakery to see wedding cakes.
4. Take a field trip to a bridal shop, a jewelry store, or a florist shop.
5. Make a list of how many children have been to a wedding or have been in a wedding.
6. The teachers might want to bring in their wedding albums and wedding dresses for children to see (and laugh at!).

Art Activities

Surprise Pictures

Materials

- white paper
- white crayon
- watercolors
- stencils (optional)
- paintbrushes

What to do

1. Draw simple shapes or drawings in white crayon on the white paper.
2. Give each child a drawing and have him paint over the entire paper with watercolors.
3. A surprise picture appears because the white crayon resists the watercolor.

More to do

- Older children can do their own white crayon drawings and paint over them.

Lace Rubbing

Materials

- paper
- doilies
- crayons or chalk

What to do

1. Peel the paper off the crayon so that you can lay the crayon on its side and rub with it.
2. Place a doily under each child's piece of paper.
3. Have the child hold the paper firmly with one hand while rubbing over the surface of the paper with her crayon or chalk.
4. The rubbings will look very lacy.

Flower Power

Materials

- cupcake liners, pastel or printed
- glue
- colored construction paper
- scissors
- markers

What to do

1. Let the children pick out the colors of cupcake liners they would like to use.
2. With scissors, each child makes cuts on the cupcake liners to form petals.
3. Glue the cupcake liner flowers on the colored construction paper.
4. Children may draw stems onto their flowers.
5. You can use party things in a new way!

Where Did the Color Go?

3+

Materials

- dark-colored construction paper: blue, purple, black, green
- bleach
- water
- small containers
- cotton swabs

What to do

1. In the small containers, mix three parts water with one part bleach.
2. Have the children use cotton swabs dipped in the bleach solution to paint on dark-colored construction paper. Supervise closely.

More to do

- Construction paper can be cut into shapes such as Christmas trees, hearts or eggs.

Gift Wrap Collage

Materials

- colored construction paper
- gift wrap scraps
- glue
- scissors

What to do

1. Place the materials out on the table so children can choose their materials.
2. Let each child cut and glue gift wrap pieces on her colored construction paper.

More to do

- Cut the construction paper into holiday or theme shapes.

Tilt-a-Swirl

3+

Materials

- paper plates
- white glue in four small bottles
- food coloring
- popsicle sticks

What to do

1. Prepare the colored glue by putting about five drops of food coloring in each bottle. Put red in one bottle, blue in another, green in the third and yellow in the last. Stir each bottle with a clean popsicle stick.
2. Give each child a paper plate.
3. Let each child squeeze some colored glue onto the surface of his paper plate. Encourage the child to use two or three different colors.

4. Have the child tilt the plate and let the colors run together.

5. These may take several days to dry, depending on how much glue was used on the plate.

More to do

- Add streamers to the paper plates and hang them up in your classroom.

Salty Surprise

Materials

- paper
- watercolors
- paintbrushes
- salt shaker
- water

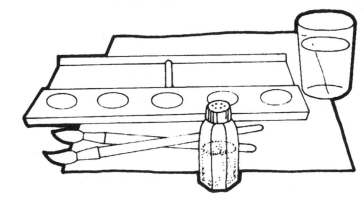

What to do

1. Let the child paint a picture using regular watercolors.

2. Allow the child to shake salt on his painting while it is still wet.

3. When the painting dries it will sparkle!

Party on a Plate

3+

Materials

- glue
- glitter
- paintbrushes
- confetti (premade or homemade with hole puncher & colored paper)
- bright-colored ribbon
- shiny paper
- shiny star stickers
- paper plates
- crepe paper streamers

What to do

1. Have the children spread glue on their paper plates with a paintbrush.
2. Let each child sprinkle glitter or confetti on her plate. She can also attach colored ribbon, stickers, or shiny paper—anything that makes it look festive.
3. Let them dry and add streamers of crepe paper and ribbon.
4. Hang them up in your classroom during a surprise or celebration.

Decorate the Cake

Materials

- thick tempera paint—add very little water
- food coloring
- paper
- cake decorators (at least four)
- glitter

What to do

1. Mix the paint so that it is very thick.
2. Cut the paper into tiered cake shapes.
3. Put the thick paint into the cake decorator and allow each child to squeeze the paint onto her cake in a squiggly design.
4. Let the child add glitter to her "frosting" if she desires.

More to do

- Another way to decorate a cake is simply to use squeeze bottles of colored glue to "frost" the cake. Glitter is optional, but always popular.

Secret Surprise Messages

Materials

- paper
- lemon juice
- iron
- newspapers
- cotton swabs

What to do

1. Each child may dip his cotton swab into the lemon juice and write a message or draw a picture on a white piece of paper.
2. Let dry.
3. Place the child's paper face down on a stack of newspapers and iron the back of the paper. His message or drawing will appear.

Surprise! One, Two Drawings

Materials

- paper
- carbon paper
- paperclips
- pencils or pens

What to do

1. Prepare two pieces of paper with a carbon in between. Use paper clips to hold the papers together.
2. Give each child a set of prepared papers.
3. Have her draw a picture on the top sheet.
4. Surprise her by showing her the copy when she is done drawing her picture.

Math Activities

Calendar

Materials

- plain calendar or paper and markers

What to do

1. Make or purchase a plain calendar with only the days of the week marked on it.
2. Each month, make different paper patterns to fit your theme. For example: for the "surprise" theme you may want to use a paper gift with bows of different colors: red bow, red bow, blue bow, red bow, red bow, blue bow, repeat throughout the month.
3. The days of the week may be sung to the tune of "Frere Jacques." "Sunday, Monday, Tuesday, Wednesday, Thursday, Friday, Saturday. It's not Sunday, it's not Monday, it's not Tuesday, it is. . . " (Let the children fill in the blank for whatever day of the week it is.)
4. School Days Countdown—make an ongoing number line for the number of days the children have been at school. Follow the same pattern as your monthly calendar pattern.

Calendar Patterns for Surprises and Celebrations

Large Medium Small

How Old Are You?

Materials

- paper
- stickers, any kind

What to do

1. Divide the paper into three columns. Write "3" at the top of one column, "4" at the top of the next and "5" atop the last.
2. Have each child place a sticker under the column that represents his age.
3. Count each column. Which one has the most stickers?

Match the Gifts

Materials

- old Christmas catalog
- scissors
- glue
- file folder
- contact paper or laminating film (optional)
- envelope

What to do

1. Cut pairs of "gifts" out of the catalog: bikes, dolls, trucks, sets of toy dishes, and so on.
2. Glue one from each pair of toys to the file folder and laminate the entire folder if possible, or cover it with contact paper.
3. Laminate or cover with contact paper the remaining toys and place them in the envelope.
4. Let the children match the sets of toys.

Surprises & Celebrations

Match the Bows

3+

Materials

- gift wrap
- wallpaper
- glue
- scissors
- file folder
- lamination film or contact paper
- envelope

What to do

1. Cut pairs of bow shapes out of gift wrap and wallpaper of different patterns.
2. Glue one bow from each pair to the file folder and laminate or cover with contact paper.
3. Laminate or cover with contact paper the remaining bows and place them in an envelope.
4. Have the children match the bows according to their patterns.

Guessing Box

4+

Materials

- box or paper bag
- gift wrap
- bows
- a wrapped gift
- candles
- flowers or bouquet
- a plastic cake
- veil

What to do

1. Show a "surprise" item such as gift wrap to the children and talk about its properties, such as its shape, color, size and uses.

2. Bring out the guessing box with another "surprise" item in it. Use the same box each time, no matter what size the item is. Storage boxes for clothing are the ideal size.

3. Say:

   > "There is something in my guessing box.
   >
   > Would you like to guess?
   >
   > First you ask a question and
   >
   > I'll answer no or yes."

4. Children then ask questions. Encourage them to ask in the form of a question. "Is it. . . ?"

5. After a brief time, if you notice they aren't asking questions that pertain to the item in the box, give broad hints.

   > "It's something small." Wait for guesses.
   >
   > "It's something pretty." Wait for guesses.
   >
   > "It's something you tie." Wait.
   >
   > "It's something you find on presents." Wait for guesses.
   >
   > ("Yes, it's a bow!")

Language Activities

Wacky! Wacky! Wacky!

Materials

- chart paper
- marker
- *Wacky Wednesday* by Theo Le Sieg

What to do

1. Do this activity on Wacky Wednesday.
2. Read *Wacky Wednesday* to the class.
3. Have the children dictate a list of all the "wacky" things they remember from the story.

Let's Celebrate!

Materials

- chart paper
- marker

What to do

1. Discuss with the children what a celebration is. What does it mean to celebrate?
2. Ask the children to list some of the celebrations they have been to. Add to the list as you explore the theme of surprises and celebrations.

Eating Big

Materials

- paper
- markers or crayons

What to do

1. Do this activity when celebrating the 100th day.
2. Give each child a piece of paper and say, "Draw what you would look like if you ate 100 _____." (The child fills in the blank with his favorite food.)

More to do

- Draw a vertical line in the middle of the paper. On one side have the child draw what he looks like and on the other side have him draw what he looked like after he ate 100. . . .
- This could be made into a "100" book for the classroom.

Make a Wish

Materials

- paper
- markers or crayons

What to do

1. Talk about what is supposed to happen when you blow out all the candles on your birthday cake.
2. Have each child draw what she would wish for if she blew out all of the candles on her birthday cake.

More to do

- Bind together and make into a class book.

Songs and Chants

- On the day you celebrate "Unbirthday Day," sing the following song to the tune of "Happy Birthday to You."

      Happy unbirthday to us,
      Happy unbirthday to us,
      Happy unbirthday to us,
      Happy unbirthday to us.

Theme Extensions and Variations

Field trips

Visit a bridal shop to see wedding gowns and tuxedos.

Visit a floral shop to see bouquets.

Visit a hat shop to see all the different types of hats.

Visit a grocery store and shop for items to take on a picnic.

Visit a bakery to see a wedding cake.

Visit a jewelry store to look at wedding rings.

Visit a photography studio and look at the wedding pictures.

Surprises & Celebrations

Bibliography

- *Birthday for Francis, A*, Russell Hoban. NY: HarperCollins, 1968. Francis is worried about getting a birthday gift for her sister, Gloria.
- *Gift, The*, John Prater. NY: Viking, 1985. A wordless book about a gift sent to two children. The gift comes in a big box which the children use to transport them on an imaginary trip.
- *I Spy*, Jean Marzollo. NY: Scholastic, Inc., 1992. A picture riddle book. You will be surprised at what you find in the pictures if you look carefully.
- *Imogene's Antlers*, David Small. NY: Random House, 1988. Imogene and her family get a big surprise one morning when Imogene wakes up!
- *Night Noises*, Mem Fox. NY: Harcourt Brace Javonovich, 1989. Lily Laceby is dreaming by the fire in her easy chair while her entire family plan a big surprise for her.
- *Pajamas*, Livingston and Maggie Taylor. San Diego, CA: Harcourt Brace Jovanovich, 1988. An illustrated version of the lyrics to the song "Pajamas" presents a child's view of getting ready for bed.
- *Ruby Mae Has Something to Say*, David Small. NY: Crown Publishers, Inc., 1992. Tongue-tied Ruby Mae Foote fulfills her dream of speaking for world peace at the United Nations when her nephew Billy Bob creates hats that solve her speech problem.
- *Secret Birthday Message, The*, Eric Carle. NY: HarperCollins, 1972. It is Tim's birthday. Instead of a package, Tim gets a mysterious letter—written in code!
- *Surprise Party, The*, Pat Hutchins. NY: Macmillan, 1986. Rabbit is having a surprise party, but the message gets misinterpreted by the other animals.
- *Wacky Wednesday*, Theo Le Sieg. NY: Random House, 1974. A small boy wakes up to find everything is "wacky," but no one else seems to notice but him.
- *Wednesday Surprise, The*, Eve Bunting. NY: Houghton Mifflin, 1989. On Wednesday nights when Grandma stays with Anna everyone thinks she is teaching Anna to read.
- *Wolf's Chicken Stew, The*, Keiko Kasza. NY: Putnam Publishing Group, 1987. A hungry wolf's attempts to fatten a chicken for his stewpot have unexpected results. A great book to use for the 100th day because the number one hundred is used several times.

Poems

- *A Light in the Attic*, Shel Silverstein. NY: Evil Eye Music, Inc., Harper and Row Publishers, 1981. "Backward Bill," p. 40. "Surprise!" p. 96.

Surprises & Celebrations

- "A Party," "The Birthday Child," "Five Years Old," *Poems to Read to the Very Young*. Josette Frank. NY: Random House, Inc., 1982.
- "Happy Birthday, Mother Dearest," *Something Big Has Been Here*. Jack Prelutsky. NY: Greenwillow Books, 1990, p. 10.

Recordings

- "Popcorn," *The Corner Grocery Store*. Raffi, (Shoreline Records) Troubadour Records, 1979.
- "Happiness Cake," *Happiness Cake*. Linda Arnold, (A & M Records) Ariel Records, 1988.
- "Popcorn," *Make Believe*. Linda Arnold, (A & M Records) Ariel Records, 1986.
- "Skin and Bones," *More Singable Songs for the Very Young*. Raffi, (Shoreline Records) Troubadour Records, 1977.
- "The Teddy's Bear's Picnic," *The One and Only Me*. Lisa Atkinson, A Gentle Wind, 1989.

All Tied Up

Mondays	Read *The Bear's Toothache* Do Don't Forget the ___ Do Floaters	Do Darn It Do Weave a Nest Shoestring Potatoes with dip for a Snack	Read "Jumping Rope" (see Poems) Do Jump the River String cheese and crackers for Snack	Ask someone who spins wool into yarn to come and demonstrate (see Field trips) Do Spin Me a Home
Tuesdays	Do Race to the Top Do Cut It Out Fresh string beans for Snack	Read *Curious George Flies a Kite* Begin Merrily We Roll Along	Do Gee! Oh! Board Do All Tied Up Wear any kind of tie or bow tomorrow	Read *Nathan's Fishing Trip* Have a fisherman/woman come to class with equipment and explain use
Wednesdays	Do Over and Under and Under and Over Do Stringing Along Licorice strings for Snack	Read "How to Make a Swing with No Rope or Board or Nails" (see Poems) Finish Merrily We Roll Along Do Tightrope Tricks	Read *Hats Hats Hats* Do Tie Dye!	Do String Kabobs Do A Tisket A Tasket Tie It, Twist It for Snack
Thursdays	Read *The Big Ball of String* Do Tangled Do String of Pearls	Read *Kites Sail High* Fly Kites Spaghetti Ropes for Snack	Do Beautiful Bows Do Presents Pasta bows and butter for Snack	Read *Noisy Nora* Do Disappearing Ball Make Stompers
Fridays	Read "Eight Balloons" (see Poems) Do Flying High	Do Guessing Box Do Sneakers List things that tie	Read *Up, Up and Away* Do Crazy String Do You've Got the Beat	Do Three-Legged Walk Do Catch of the Day Spaghetti squash with butter and grated cheese for Snack

Theme Objectives

- To discover what can be tied
- To use things that can be tied in meaningful and creative ways
- To offer fine motor practice in threading, wrapping, lacing and tying

Learning Centers

Dramatic Play

- aprons
- ties—bowties, string ties, neckties
- hats with strings or bows
- shoes with ties or bows
- hair ornaments
- corsages
- dried bow-tie noodles
- clothesline
- beauty shop items: ribbons, bows and capes
- gift wrap store items: ribbons, bows, string, tape, paper, scissors and cards
- necklaces
- soap on a rope

Manipulatives

- lacing shoes or boards
- beads and lacing string
- lacing cards
- fishing poles and magnetic fish
- push pin stringing board
- assorted shoes to lace and unlace

Library

- marionette puppets
- flannel board with flannel pieces on string to create a flip board
- musical instruments—string variety

Blocks

- sports rackets from various sports
- rope ladder
- jump ropes, including Chinese jump ropes
- tetherball and punching ball
- kites and string
- tire swing
- yo-yo's
- fish net
- bow and arrows
- paddles with attached balls
- weights and pulleys
- Stompers (see activity in Music and Movement section)

Art

- bows—premade
- string—assorted sizes/colors
- ribbon in assorted thicknesses
- yarn
- colored dried bow tie macaroni
- bow-making kit
- garland pieces
- supplies for mobiles/stabiles

Writing

- string to tie homemade books together
- expanding file which ties shut
- pencil and pens attached to message center by string
- award ribbons

Science

- weights and pulleys
- string and rope of assorted lengths and thicknesses
- tree on which to hang items
- display of common knots
- bird's nest
- string beans or other climbing plants

Snacks

- long stringy licorice
- shoestring potatoes and dip
- spaghetti squash with butter and grated cheese
- cereal necklaces
- string cheese and crackers
- pasta bow ties with sauce
- spaghetti "ropes"
- fresh string beans
- Tie It, Twist It (see activity in Discovery section)

Discovery Activities

Tie It, Twist It

3+

Materials

- frozen bread dough, thawed
- melted butter
- cookie sheet

What to do

1. Give each child a portion of dough to roll out and tie in any shape.
2. Place them on a cookie sheet and brush them with butter.
3. Bake and eat.

All Tied Up

Take It Apart

Materials

- old bird's nest
- tweezers
- newspaper

What to do

1. Place the bird's nest on the newspaper and let the children carefully take the nest apart using tweezers.
2. Record the materials found, especially noting any string or yarn.

Race to the Top

3+

Materials

- pole bean or pea seeds, one per child
- potting soil
- dowel rods or sticks, one per child
- potting cups, one per child
- string lengths, one per child

What to do

1. Anchor strings to a hanging dowel rod or hang directly from the ceiling by a push pin.
2. Let each child plant her own bean/pea in a cup.
3. Tie the end of a string to a stick and insert the stick in a child's cup so the bean can climb up the stick and then on the string. Repeat with all the cups.
4. Water the beans periodically and watch them climb the string.

More to do

- Use climbing plant anchor in other ways your room/space allows.

Don't Forget the _____

Materials

- pieces of string or ribbon

What to do

1. Tie the string around the child's finger to remind him to do something. Some ideas: to bring an item to class for show and tell, to wear any kind of bow the next day, to tell his parents what he ate for snack.

Cut It Out

Materials

- scissors
- yarn, string, rope, garlands and thread

What to do

1. Let each child cut and explore various thicknesses and textures.

2. Ask, "Which is the hardest to cut? Which is the easiest? Which one is slippery?"

Hang It Up

Materials

- child's picture or name on a circular piece of construction paper
- hole puncher
- string

What to do

1. Have each child punch a hole above his picture, thread a string through the hole and tie the ends together.

2. Let him wear it as a necklace throughout the day.

More to do

- The child's name/picture can hang in an area where he is working to indicate his choice.

Grand Opening

Materials

- length of thick ribbon
- scissors

What to do

1. Rearrange a special area of your room and partition it off in anticipation of a grand opening.
2. Talk about what a grand opening is and then cut the ribbon!

Weave a Nest

Materials

- plastic berry baskets
- scraps of yarn or string
- scissors

What to do

1. Have the children loosely weave bits of yarn and string through a basket.
2. Turn the basket upside down and tie a string to the bottom, long enough to hang from a tree.
3. Hang the basket in a tree so birds can use the scraps of yarn to make their nests.

Line Them Up

Materials

- assorted lengths of string, rope and yarn
- sorting trays or cookie sheets

What to do

1. Ask the children to arrange the strands from the shortest to the longest.

More to do

- Add more lengths to the set. Ask the children to start with the longest and order to the shortest.

Over and Under and Under and Over

Materials

- loom
- yarn or ribbon

What to do

1. Have younger children weave pieces of yarn or ribbon over and under randomly on the loom.
2. Older children can weave a design with the yarn.

Darn It

Materials

- large-eyed needles
- two paper plates labeled "yes" and "no"
- thread, yarn, string and rope of varying types, cut into lengths

What to do

1. Have the children predict which thicknesses can go through the eyes of their needles.

2. Let each child try to thread his needle with one type of string.

3. Direct him to put the string on the correct plate according to how his experiment succeeded.

4. Repeat the activity.

Unstring It

Materials

- old tennis or badminton racket
- scissors
- magnifying glasses

What to do

1. Let the children try to unstring the racket by either cutting the strings or using their fingers to undo the weave.

2. Look at the weave under a magnifying glass.

More to do

- Cut open a golf ball or baseball to see all the string inside.

Measuring Up

Materials

- strings in one, three and six-foot lengths
- adding machine tape and pens

What to do

1. Give each child a length of string and ask her to find objects in the room that are as long as her string.

2. Record their responses on charts made from adding machine paper that are also one, three or six feet long to correspond with the children's measuring lengths.

String Kabobs

Materials

- string
- fat from meat
- fruit peels
- whole peanuts
- round dry cereal

What to do

1. Have the children tie the string around or through food scraps to form a string kabob about twelve to eighteen inches long.
2. Hang the kabob from a tree branch.
3. Enjoy watching the birds eat their meal.

Floaters

Materials

- handkerchiefs
- string
- washers or round-headed clothespins
- scissors

What to do

1. Tie a twelve-inch length of string to each corner of each handkerchief.
2. Gather the strings from each corner and tie them to a washer or around the round head of the clothespins.
3. Let the children toss them into the air and watch the parachutes float down.

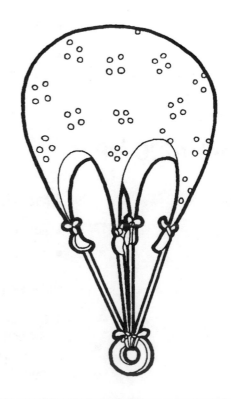

More to do

- Use different fabrics and graph their rates of descent. Create a parachutist out of the clothespin. Use heavier strings to see how it affects the parachute.

Art Activities

Tangled

Materials

- pieces of string, yarn, ribbon, garland, rope, bows and shoestrings
- paper
- glue or tape

What to do

1. Have the children make their own collage by using the above materials. Give them the option of using tape for the curlier and thicker materials.

Hanging by a Thread

Materials

- children's artwork
- string
- hooks, push pins or tape

What to do

1. Hang the children's artwork from the ceiling to decorate the room or to create a particular environment.

More to do

- Older children can do the planning, hanging, and designing.

Beautiful Bows

3+

Materials

- raffia bows
- glue
- confetti, jewels and glitter

What to do

1. Let each child drizzle glue on a bow.
2. Cover the glue with glitter, jewels and confetti.
3. Let dry.

Crazy String

3+

Materials

- string of various lengths
- paper
- tempera paint

What to do

1. Have each child fold his paper in half and then open again.
2. Have him dip his string into the paint and place it on half of the folded paper. Make sure the child maintains a firm grasp on one end of the string.
3. Fold the paper on top of the string.
4. Have him wiggle the string and pull through for a crazy design.
5. Repeat with different colors.

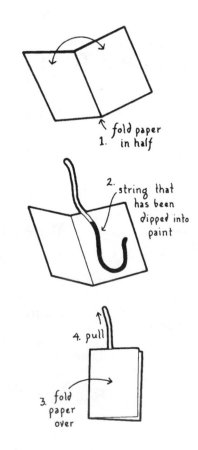

1. fold paper in half

2. string that has been dipped into paint

4. pull

3. fold paper over

Sticky String

Materials

- strings of assorted colors, lengths and thicknesses
- glue
- paper

What to do

1. Have each child select one string at a time and plan a design for her paper.
2. The string can either be immersed in glue or made to follow a glue design that the child makes on her paper.
3. Stick the string on the paper and let dry.

More to do

- Features can be added to this design with markers/crayons. The string can be covered with a watercolor wash once it is dry. You could dip the string in glue and arrange it to dry on wax paper. Peel off the paper, paint it and hang it as a decoration. The glue can be colored a couple days ahead of time by adding several drops of food coloring.

String of Pearls

Materials

- string, thread, yarn
- large-eyed needles
- buttons, beads, craft beads and styrofoam pieces

What to do

1. Let the children string their own necklaces with the available materials.

More to do

- Make this an extended project. Make your own beads with dry painted playdough.

What's the Catch?

Materials

- sandwich size plastic bags
- miscellaneous collage materials, especially bits of ribbon, yarn and string

What to do

1. Fill the bags from assorted collage materials using different textures and colors.
2. Tie the bags closed with a bit of yarn and fan out the tails.
3. Look at the fish and all the "worms" it swallowed!

Spin Me a Home

Materials

- an old tree branch with several forks in it
- string or yarn

What to do

1. Ask the children if they've ever seen a spider web nestled in a branch.
2. Invite them to make a web by weaving string or yarn through and around the tree branch.

Flying High

Materials

- plastic bags
- yarn
- scissors

What to do

1. Fold back the top edge of each bag about one inch to create a double thickness.
2. Punch a hole through each side and tie a piece of yarn through each hole.
3. Children can add any length of tail to the bottom of the bag.
4. Run as fast as you can holding on to the strings.

A Tisket, A Tasket

Materials

- plastic berry baskets
- lengths of ribbon in assorted colors

What to do

1. Invite the children to weave the ribbon in and out of the basket with assorted colors and widths.
2. Fill with a surprise for Mom or Dad.

Rippling Ribbons

Materials

- stiff paper or flexible cardboard
- lengths of ribbon in assorted colors

What to do

1. Cut the paper or cardboard into strips 6" wide and 18" long.
2. Bend the paper into a circular crown shape and staple together.
3. Have the children glue or staple ribbons all the way around the circular shape so that they hang free like a windsock.
4. Hang them in the wind and admire the blowing ribbons.

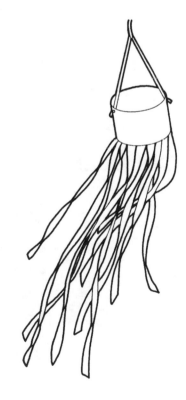

Merrily We Roll Along

4+

Materials

- empty toilet paper or paper towel tubes
- yarn
- scissors
- paper
- glue
- paint
- paintbrushes

What to do

1. On the first day, have each child glue yarn around the tube in any design he wants. Let it dry overnight.
2. On the next day, instruct the child to paint the string design, then roll the tube across a sheet of paper to print the design.

More to do

- For three-year-olds, have the design pre-glued. For older children, have them glue string on wooden blocks or larger tubes.

Gee! Oh! Board

Materials

- 1/2" plywood cut into 8" squares
- flat-headed nails
- hammers
- string

What to do

1. Let each child pound nails into her piece of plywood to make a pattern.
CAUTION: Supervise the children closely.
2. Have them use the string and wind around the nails to make a design.

Disappearing Ball

Materials

- balloons
- string
- diluted white glue, half glue and half water

What to do

1. Inflate and tie a balloon.
2. Take a length of string, dip it in the glue mixture and wrap it around the balloon.
3. Have the children follow your example as often as needed until the balloon is nearly covered by string and glue.
4. Let it dry overnight or as needed.
5. Once the creation is dry, pop the balloon with a pin. See what's left!

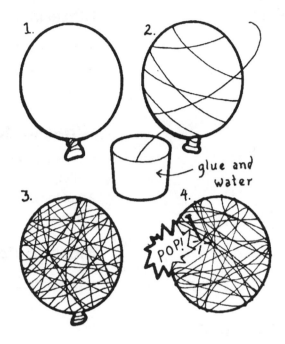

glue and water

POP!

Tie a Creature

Materials

- old pantyhose
- fiberfill
- yarn or ribbon
- miscellaneous items

What to do

1. Cut pantyhose so each child has about a leg length to use.
2. Let the children stuff the hose with fiberfill to make a snake-like creature.
3. Once done, let the children tie ribbons or yarn at intervals so the creature resembles a segmented caterpillar.
4. Decorate the creature with ribbons and bows.

Sew It Up

Materials

- paper plates or old greeting cards
- hole punchers
- yarn

What to do

1. Punch holes in the plates or greeting cards. Older children can probably punch their own holes.
2. Let the children use bright-colored yarn to sew in and out of the holes to make a design.

More to do

- Design your own set of lacing cards.

Tie Dye!

Materials

- 100% cotton white handkerchief, one per child
- cloth dye (any color)
- two-gallon bucket
- yarn or string
- tongs or slotted spoon

What to do

1. Prepare the dye according to the directions on the package.
2. Let each child wind a string around a segment of the handkerchief so that a tight band of string covers the white.
3. Cut the string and tuck the ends under.
4. Repeat in a new area as often as the child wants.
5. Dip the handkerchief in the dye according to package directions.

6. Lift the cloth out with the tongs or spoon and squeeze out the excess dye.

7. Unravel the strings and open the handkerchief.

8. Hang it out to dry.

9. Wear it as a scarf or bandanna!

Music and Movement Activities

Tightrope Tricks

Materials

- long rope

What to do

1. Extend a long rope on the floor.

2. Encourage the children to walk on or alongside the rope in various ways: balancing with an umbrella in your hand, walking slowly, walking quickly, walking on your toes, walking sideways, walking backwards or any other variation of direction, speed, level and props.

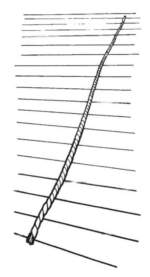

Stringing Along

Materials

- long rope

What to do

1. Have the children grasp a segment along the rope as they walk to the playground or around the block.

2. Discuss how it feels to hold on to the rope.

3. Ask if they notice any difference in movement using the rope.

All Tied Up

You've Got the Beat

Materials

- paper towel tubes
- crepe paper streamers or colored ribbons
- stapler

What to do

1. Measure and cut streamers or ribbon in lengths 12" or longer.
2. Staple the lengths around one end the of tubes, overlapping if necessary.
3. Turn on dance music and let each child move his body and shaker to the beat.
4. Store the shakers in the room for spontaneous movement.

More to do

- Use different tempos to create different ways to move. Children five and over can make their own shakers. Use scarves or 3" wide fabric lengths as streamers instead of shakers for movement.

Jump the River

2+

Materials

- a long rope

What to do

1. Have two adults hold a rope so that it stretches about one inch above floor.
2. Have all the children jump over the river. When it "rains" the river rises another inch. All jump.
3. Continue to raise and lower the rope to encourage balance and motor skills as well as visual perception.

More to do

- Let two children hold the rope for the others. Have children cross under the river, on their stomachs or on their back. Invent new ways to cross the river.

Getting in Touch

Materials

- piece of rope long enough to make a hoop-sized circle, one per child

What to do

1. Encourage following directions and body awareness by directing how to use the rope. For example, "make a circle with your rope. Step in the circle, step out of the circle; put one foot in, one foot out; put one elbow in the circle, put your whole body in the circle, place your hands outside the circle."

More to do

- Drape the rope around various body parts. Make different shapes. Give two-part commands.

Stompers

Materials

- two empty tuna cans per child for three and four year olds
- two empty coffee cans for five year olds and older
- tape
- heavy strings or ropes, 4' or 5' long, two per child
- scissors
- ice pick (for the teacher)

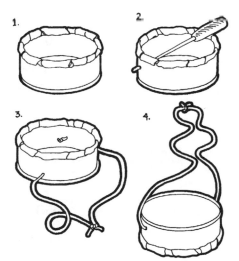

What to do

1. Remove or tape over any sharp edges on the cans.
2. Poke holes in opposite sides of the cans. (Teacher does this step.)
3. Thread the rope through both holes and tie ends together. (Teacher does this step.)
4. Turn the cans upside down so their bottoms face up.
5. Have the child stand on the cans and pull the ropes so that she is pulling the cans against her feet as an extension of her legs.
6. Stomp around the room.

Roll It Out

Materials

- big ball of yarn or string

What to do

1. Have the children stand or sit in a circle.
2. Toss the ball of yarn from one child to another, unraveling the yarn as it is tossed.
3. Observe the pattern the tangled yarn makes.

More to do

- Count how many throws it took to unravel the ball. Reverse the process and roll the ball back to its original shape.

All Tied Up

What to do

1. Have the children hold hands and make a long snake-like line.
2. Still holding hands, have the two ends weave in and out and over and under to make one giant knot of children.

Three-Legged Walk

Materials

- old pantyhose, leg portion only, or broad ribbon

What to do

1. Have two children stand side by side.
2. Tie their inside legs together at the knee and the ankle using pantyhose or ribbon.
3. Have the children try to walk around with their legs tied together.

All Tied Up

Math Activities

Calendar

Materials

* plain calendar or paper and markers

What to do

1. Make or purchase a plain calendar with only the days of the week marked on it.
2. Each month, make different paper patterns to fit your theme. For example: for the "All Tied Up" theme you may want to use three gift-wrapped packages—two squares and one rectangle made out of wrapping paper with a ribbon glued on. Children would identify the pattern as "square, square, rectangle,"; strung beads—a string with two beads on it, then a string with four beads strung on it. Mount these on a small piece of colored cardboard. The pattern would be: two beads, four beads, two beads, four beads.
3. The days of the week may be sung to the tune of "Frere Jacques." "Sunday, Monday, Tuesday, Wednesday, Thursday, Friday, Saturday. It's not Sunday, it's not Monday, it's not Tuesday, it is......" (Let the children fill in the blank for whatever day of the week it is.)
4. School Days Countdown — make an ongoing number line for the number of days the children have been at school. Follow the same pattern as your monthly calendar pattern.

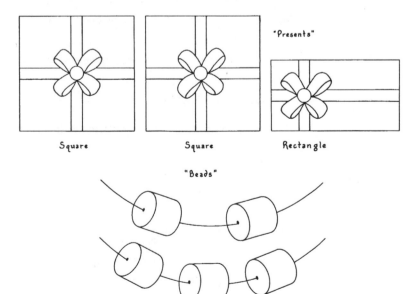

Calendar Patterns for All Tied Up

"Presents"

Square   Square   Rectangle

"Beads"

Suits Me

Materials

- legal-sized file folder
- assorted ties cut from wallpaper or wrapping paper

What to do

1. Make doubles of each tie pattern.
2. Glue one from each pair of ties on the inside of the folder.
3. Store the extra ties in an attached envelope.
4. Have the children match sizes, colors and patterns.

Make a Guess

4+

Materials

- a transparent recloseable plastic bag with around ten premade gift wrap bows
- chart with children's names on it

What to do

1. Show the children the bag. Let them look at it from all angles.
2. Have each child estimate how many bows he sees.
3. Record each child's guesses on the chart next to their name.
4. Remove bows and count as a group.
5. Congratulate those who guessed the closest.

More to do

- Estimate hair bows, necklaces, dried pasta bows.

Square One

Materials

- lengths of ribbon, string, rope, or yarn brought from home
- floor graph

What to do

1. Floor graph can be made out of an old twin sheet or solid-colored shower curtain. Mark off 12" squares across and down so the sheet resembles a grid.
2. Have each child display and describe her length of material.
3. Have the children decide some way of classifying these "ties." They could be sorted by length, color, use or thickness.
4. Starting at one end of graph, have the children place their ties in the appropriate boxes, as in one row for yarn, one row for string and one for ribbon. Note: only one item per box.
5. Count and decide which row has the most, the least or which have the same.

More to do

- Children can take off one shoe and decide how to graph them, for example ties vs. velcro vs. slip-ons. Have children bring in a wearable tie such as a necktie or hair bows to graph.

Presents

Materials

- small, medium and large-sized packages wrapped in gift wrap
- ribbon of assorted lengths to correspond with package sizes

What to do

1. In a small group, place the packages and ribbon on the table.
2. Decide which ribbon will fit best on each package.

More to do

- Add more packages and ribbons.

Guess My Rule

4+

What to do

1. Select a child on the basis of one attribute, such as one who is wearing a hair bow.
2. Have that child stand facing one direction.
3. Select a child without a bow to stand facing away from the first child.
4. Add another child to each side following the same criteria.
5. Have the children try to guess how they are being divided.
6. If they cannot decide, add more children to each side until the rule is discovered.

More to do

• The rule could be velcro vs. tie shoes, or strings on coats vs. non-strings. For older children, try two attributes such as tie shoes and ties anywhere else on child.

Finish the Bows

4+

Materials

• one legal-sized file folder
• bows cut out of either wrapping or wallpaper
• laminating film or clear contact paper
• envelope

What to do

1. Glue a row of bows inside the file to create a pattern. The pattern can be based on size, color or texture.
2. Repeat the pattern on the same line but leave off the final bow.
3. Have the extra bows in an attached envelope to finish the pattern or extend it.
4. Repeat several more patterns in the same file folder. Depending on the size of the bows, most files can accommodate four patterns on each side of the inner folder.
5. If possible, laminate or cover each piece with clear contact paper.
6. Ask the child to study the pattern and pick out the correct bow to extend the pattern.

Guessing Box

4+

Materials

- box or paper bag
- tennis shoe with colored laces
- hair bow
- gift-wrapped present with a bow
- fishing pole with line
- mittens with strings connecting them
- ball of yarn
- necktie
- jump rope
- yo-yo

What to do

1. Show a tying item such as a hair bow to the children and talk about its properties: shape, color, size and uses.
2. Bring out the guessing box with another tying item in it. Use the same box each time, no matter what size the item is. Storage boxes for clothing are the ideal size.
3. Say:

   "There is something in my guessing box.

   Would you like to guess?

   First you ask a question and

   I'll answer no or yes."
4. Children then ask questions. Encourage them to ask in the form of a question. "Is it.....?"
5. After a brief time, if you notice they aren't asking questions that pertain to the item in the box, give broad hints.

   "It's something that fits in your hand." Wait for guesses.

   "It's something round." Wait for guesses.

   "It's something with made from wool." Wait.

   "It's something you that can unravel." Wait for guesses.

   ("Yes, it's a ball of yarn!")

Language Activities

Catch of the Day

Materials

- large sheet of paper
- markers

What to do

1. On a large piece of paper record a list of things you could catch if you went fishing, as dictated by the children.

More to do

- List things that can be tied or are tied. Add to the list during the theme. Use imagination to decide what might be at the end of a string up in the clouds. Turn into an this into an art/language experience by having the children draw what is on the "sky hook" and record the details about the catch. This exercise could also be turned into a class book called "What's the Catch?"

Sneakers

Materials

- cardboard
- shoe box
- old shoestrings, one pair per child
- scissors
- markers
- hole punch

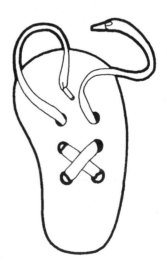

What to do

1. Trace around each child's shoes on cardboard.
2. Let the child cut out his shoes.
3. Punch holes for shoelace eyelets.

4. Let each child color his shoes and thread his laces through the holes.

5. Put all the shoes in the shoe box and make a class book—the shoe box being the binding.

More to do

● Have the children go through the book at later date and find their shoes. Have older children figure out "right" and "left" shoes.

Transition Activities

Keeping Us in Stitches

What to do

1. Hold up one hand and pretend to stitch your fingers together one by one, until all the fingers are stitched together. Have the children follow your actions.

More to do

● Stitch other body parts together, such as your hand to your head or your fingers to your leg.

Crank It Up

What to do

1. Have the children sit on the floor. Ask the children to attach an imaginary string to their foot and slowly pull their foot up.

2. Drop the "string" and the foot falls.

3. Repeat with the other foot, their arms or their head.

4. Pull up slowly, quickly, jiggly. Drop loudly, softly, or without any noise. Vary it in any way.

Muscle-Up

What to do

1. Pull an imaginary rope. Pretend to pull up a well bucket, a ship's anchor, a huge animal, a fish out of the water; pretend to pull a hot air balloon or kite back to earth, or pull back a bow to shoot an arrow.

All Tied Up

Songs and Chants

- "Do Your Ears Hang Low?"
    Do your ears hang low? Do they wobble to and fro?
    Can you tie them in a knot? Can you tie them in a bow?
    Can you throw them over your shoulder like a continental soldier?
    Do your ears hang low?

Theme Extensions and Variations

Field trips

- Have a fisherman come to class, show his tackle and demonstrate tying lures.
- Ask someone who spins wool into yarn to come demonstrate her technique. Check with area craft or nature centers for resources.
- Go window shopping. Walk around a several block area and notice how many things are tied and how many ways tying is used.
- Go fly a kite!

Variations

- Incorporate cowboys, using bandannas, spinning, weaving, quilting and lassoing.

Bibliography

- *Bear's Toothache, The*, David McPhail. Little, Brown and Company, 1988. Bear pulls his tooth by attaching a string and pulling.
- *Big Ball of String, A*, Marion Holland. Random House, 1993. Story of a boy and his adventures with his big ball of string.
- *Curious George Flies a Kite*, Margaret & H.A. Rey. Houghton Mifflin, 1958. George and his kite cause chaos.
- *Hats Hats Hats*, Ann Morris. Lothrop, Lee and Shepard Books, 1989. Introduces many kinds of hats, many that tie.
- *Kites Sail High*, Ruth Heller. Putnam Publishing Group, 1988. A book of verbs giving action words to kites and many more things.
- *Nathan's Fishing Trip*, Lulu Delacre. NY: Scholastic, Inc., 1987. Adventures of fishing with a pole and string and how to really catch fish!

All Tied Up

- *Noisy Nora*, Rosemary W. NY: Dial Press, 1973. Nora makes her presence known when her family seems to ignore her. One of her disasters involves wrapping a kite around furniture.

- *Up, up & Away*, Ruth Heller. Putnam Publishing Group, 1991. A book of adverbs describing movement of hot air balloons, sails and ballet shoes.

Poems

- "Eight Balloons," *A Light in the Attic*, Shel Silverstein. Evil Eye Music, Inc., Harper and Row Publishers, 1981, p. 58.

- "How to Make a Swing with No Rope or Board or Nails," *A Light in the Attic*, Shel Silverstein. Evil Eye Music, Inc., Harper and Row Publishers, 1981, p. 67.

- "Jumping Rope," *Where the Sidewalk Ends*, Shel Silverstein. Evil Eye Music, Inc., Harper and Row Publishers, 1974, p. 62.

Recordings

- *Counting Games and Rhythms for the Little Ones*. Ella Jenkins, Folkways Records and Service Corp., 1965. (Use with jump rope and streamers.)

- "Late Last Night," *Late Last Night*. Joe Scruggs, (Shadow Play Records & Video, c/o) Educational Graphics Press, Inc., 1984.

- "Petites Marionettes," *More Singable Songs for the Very Young*. Raffi, (Shoreline Records) Troubadour Records, 1977.

- "Bean Bag Shake," *Rhythms on Parade*. Hap Palmer, Hap-Pal Music, 1988. (Shake streamers to this song.)

- "I've Got No Strings," *Special Delivery*. Fred Penner, (Shoreline Records) Troubadour Records, 1983.

Through the Looking Glass

Mondays	Read _Look Again_ Do _Fun House Mirrors_ _Mirror Maniacs_	Do _Seascape in a Jar_ Window Walk: walk the blocks around school, looking at all the different windows Do _Window Watching_	Read _I Spy_ Do _I Spy_ Do _Copy Cat_	Start _Zip It Up_ Do _Color Race_ Do _Foiled Again_
Tuesdays	Do _A Cold Look_ Do _Solar Power_ _Flavored iced fizzy water_ for Snack	Read _It Didn't Frighten Me_ Do _Night Critters_ Make a Snack in a blender and watch it change	Do _Jack Frost_ Start _Greens Under Glass_ Frost a cake and eat for Snack	Read _The Hidden House_ Do _Cover-Ups_
Wednesdays	Field trip to a lumber yard to see window frames Do _Frame It_ Do _In and Out the Windows_	Read "Wavy Hair" (see Poems) Do _Mirror Images_ Do _All About Mirrors_	Do _Drink Up!_ Do _Who Nose?_ Have _Shake-Ups_ for Snack	Read _Goggles!_ Do _A Hole in One_
Thursdays	Read _Look! Look! Look!_ Do _Thoughtful Reflections_ Do _Catch the Sun #I_	Do _Guessing Box_ Start _Hatch a Rubber Egg_ _Peanut Butter Squeeze_ for Snack	Read _The Eye Book_ Do _I See Stars_ Do _Kaleidoscope_	Make _Bean Sprout Salad_ & eat for Snack Do _Suncatchers II_ Make a self-portrait looking in a mirror
Fridays	Read "Reflection" (see Poems) Do _Here's Looking at You_ Do _Guess What I See?_	Read _Simple Pictures Are Best_ Do _Blizzards_ Do _Frame It_	Start _Watch It Sprout_ Do _Sound of Music_	Do _Dot to Dot_ Do _Rose-Colored Glasses_ Do _Clearly a Guess_

Through the Looking Glass

Theme Objectives

- To observe, explore and manipulate the immediate environment
- To use glass, mirrors and instruments, not only with their original functions in mind, but also as a basis for creativity
- To experience basic scientific principles such as reflection, heat and magnetism

Learning Centers

Dramatic Play

- dressing mirror
- compact and hand mirrors
- swim goggles
- eyeglass frames
- eye doctor's office
- clear acrylic cutting board
- plastic wrap and foil
- old windowshades
- poster, framed to look like the view from a window
- sparkly crystal costume jewelry
- framed photos

Blocks

- wooden window frames
- telescope
- periscope
- binoculars
- safety glasses

Manipulatives

- assorted plastic boxes
- kaleidoscope
- marbles
- "waterful" toys
- collection of mirrors

Through the Looking Glass

- jar and lids to sort and match

Writing

- eyeglasses frames
- glass paperweights (supervise closely)
- transparent plastic pens
- envelopes with cellophane windows

Science

- butterfly farm
- ant farm
- prisms
- magnifying glasses, all sizes
- microscope
- telescope
- binoculars
- plastic wrap and foil
- Ocean Waves (see *Crash, Bang, Boom* theme)
- Tornado Tube (see *Crash, Bang, Boom* theme)
- terrarium
- foil in the bottom of water table before water is added
- lead filings in see-through plastic boxes and jars to use with magnets

Art

- acrylic easel
- clear contact paper
- transparent tape
- cellophane
- transparent glue sticks
- paper towel and toilet paper tubes
- wax paper

Environment

- If windows are high, have a step stool so children can look out.
- Mount mirrors at ceiling, feet, knee and face level.

Snacks

- ice water, flavored waters
- Shake-Ups (see activity in Discovery section)
- Peanut Butter Squeeze (see activity in Discovery section)
- Bean Sprout Salad (see activity in Discovery section)
- If you have access to an oven with a window or a microwave, cook any recipe and observe all the changes.

Discovery Activities

Peanut Butter Squeeze

Materials

- peanut butter
- bananas
- graham crackers
- pint-sized reclosable plastic bags
- scissors

What to do

1. Put two tablespoons of peanut butter in a plastic bag for each child.
2. Let each child add several slices of banana to his bag.
3. Seal the bag and squish the peanut butter and banana together.
4. Cut off a corner of the bag, squeeze the peanut butter-banana blend onto a cracker and eat!

Through the Looking Glass

Materials

- assorted collection of mirrors: compacts, hand held, purse-sized and make-up mirrors

What to do

1. Display the assortment of mirrors for the children to examine.

Through the Looking Glass

2. Ask a child to sort the mirrors in some way.
3. Talk about her classifications.
4. Repeat the activity with seriating and counting.

Shake-Ups

Materials

- 2-liter bottle of ginger ale
- one package frozen strawberries
- 1/2 gallon orange sherbet
- blender
- cups
- spoons

What to do

1. Pour a third of the two-liter bottle of ginger ale into the blender.
2. Add one pint (two cups) of the sherbet and one cup frozen strawberries.
3. Blend and watch the foods change properties.
4. Pour and serve.

Glass to Glass

What to do

1. Explain the concept of recycling to the children.
2. Encourage the children to save and wash out glass jars to be picked up or taken to a recycling center.

More to do

- Older children may want to use this as a class project, not only recycling but also sorting and tallying kinds, sizes, and colors.

Through the Looking Glass

Color Race

Materials

- several clear jars and lids
- food coloring
- water

What to do

1. Fill the jars with water.
2. Add several drops of food coloring to each jar. Make each jar a different color.
3. Without shaking the jars, observe how long it takes for the food coloring to diffuse and color the whole jar.

More to do

- Vary the amounts of water in each jar and observe which one is colored first. Vary the number of drops of food coloring per jar. Which one changes first? Put two different colors in one jar. Do they mix immediately? Is one color dominant?

Here's Looking at You

Materials

- mirror, foil, toaster, spoon, shiny pan or pot and any other reflecting objects

What to do

1. Have the children observe their reflections in the materials.
2. Ask them, "Which is clearest? Which one is hard to see into? Which one works best in the bathroom? Which one shows you upside down? Which one changes your shape or size?"

Through the Looking Glass

Solar Power

Materials

- windows with direct and indirect sunlight

What to do

1. Have the children sit in direct sunlight coming through a window and have them describe how it feels.
2. Have them sit in front of a window with indirect sunlight and have them describe how it feels.
3. Ask the children, "Which one was warmer? Why? Which one was cooler? Why? Which window felt more comfortable to you?"
4. Responses can be recorded as votes or tallies on a graph or chart.

More to do

- Repeat the process with car windows by having children sit in a car in full sunlight and one in the shade. Note: This may not be possible at school if your car is not near your building. You may want to send this idea home for parents to try.

Watch It Sprout

3+

Materials

- assorted dried beans: pea, navy, kidney, green
- quart-sized reclosable plastic bags
- paper towels
- water

What to do

1. Moisten paper towels and squeeze out excess water.
2. Fold the towels and place them in the bottom of the bags.
3. Add two or three of the same kind of bean to a bag and zip them closed.
4. Display all the bags and watch to see which kind of bean sprouts first.
5. Keep the bags long enough to see roots and shoots. See how long it takes each for bean to sprout.
6. Observations can be made into time graphs, sequence charts or pictorial murals.

Through the Looking Glass

Bean Sprout Salad

3+

Materials

- mung or alfalfa seeds (available at health food stores)
- an empty mayonnaise jar
- cheesecloth
- rubber band

What to do

1. Soak the seeds in water overnight in a mayonnaise jar.
2. Secure the cheesecloth over the mouth of the jar with a rubber band. Turn the jar over and drain the water off the beans.
3. Leave the jar turned upside-down on a paper towel to drain.
4. Every morning, fill the jar with water and drain immediately. Repeat this for several days until sprouts fill the jar.
5. Refrigerate and use as soon as possible on salad.

Guess Who?

3+

Materials

- mirror

What to do

1. Have the child look in the mirror and point out his facial features by touching his reflection.

More to do

- Show the child pictures of facial expressions and have him duplicate them in the mirror. Use magazines as a resource.

Through the Looking Glass

Hatch a Rubber Egg

Materials

- white vinegar
- glass jar about the size of a mustard jar
- raw egg

What to do

1. Put an egg carefully in clean jar.
2. Pour vinegar into the jar until the egg is covered.
3. Seal the jar.
4. Make observations of any immediate reaction between egg and vinegar.
5. Date the project.
6. Make a daily chart of any observations.
7. After about a week the eggshell will be completely dissolved. Remove the egg and carefully pass it around so the children can feel the rubber texture and peer into the insides of the egg.

NOTE: If the egg happens to break, there is a real mess but no odor.

Mirror on the Wall

3+

Materials

- face paints
- mirror

What to do

1. Let the children explore and pretend with face paints. Have them use the mirror to apply the paints and examine the results.

More to do

- Let the children use shaving cream and popsicle sticks to "shave" while watching themselves in the mirror.

State of Attraction

Materials

- magnetic wand
- baby oil or cooking oil
- paperclips, metal or plastic-covered
- transparent plastic bottle such as clear 1-liter bottle

What to do

1. Fill the plastic bottle with oil. Drop in the paperclips and seal the bottle well so the lid cannot be removed.
2. Let the children experiment with moving the paper clips throughout the bottle using the magnetic wand.
3. See how many paperclips the child can move to the top at one time.
4. Talk about how to keep the paperclips off the bottom for a time period.
5. Turn the bottle on its side to experiment more.

More to do

- Before adding the paper clips, link them in groups of twos, threes, or fours. Ask a child if she can move just the groups of four, or just the groups of two.

Sound of Music

Materials

- spoons or dowel rods
- four equal-sized glass jars
- water

Through the Looking Glass

What to do

1. Pour water into the glasses at four different levels.
2. Have a child tap each glass gently to experiment with sound.
3. Ask him to identify the glasses which make a high sound or a low sound.
4. Order the glasses from the least amount of water to the most. Play that tune.
5. Have the child order the glasses differently to create his own music.

More to do

- Add food coloring to different water levels and make up tunes using colors, for example, "tap two reds, one green, two yellow, stop." Fill all the glasses equally but use different tapping instruments such as tuning forks, pencils, spoons, pens or popsicle sticks. Chart which one is softest, highest, lowest. Use milk or juice or other liquid to see what difference the contents make. Tally votes for the most popular sound. Use different-sized glasses and see how sound is effected.

Picture It!

Materials

- camera and film

What to do

1. Show the children how to look through the camera viewer and frame a photograph.
2. Let the children take turns taking pictures.
3. Develop the film and mount the pictures for display.

More to do

- Let the children take photos according to a theme or to sequence an activity.

Drink Up!

4+

Materials

- assorted sizes of drinking glasses
- water pitchers
- measuring cups
- tub or tray to pour over

Through the Looking Glass

What to do

1. Have a child guess which glass will hold the most liquid.
2. Start with 1/4 cup measure and see how many are needed to fill the glass. Record with tally marks.
3. Continue with other glasses.

More to do

- Use other measurements to begin the experiment, such as a half-cup measure. Pour the water from the smallest glass to the largest to see how many small ones are needed to fill the large one. Or do the reverse and see how many smaller glasses can be filled by the larger's volume.

Tops and Bottoms

Materials

- jars and lids of extracts, shampoo, cupcake liners, spices, soaps and perfume, all washed well

What to do

1. Show the collection to the children for free exploration. They can sort or classify the jars, or describe their uses.
2. Have the children unscrew the lids from the jars and separate them into two groups, one for jars and one for lids.
3. Ask the children to find the correct lid for each jar and screw it back on.

More to do

- This works well with two children working together. Some make a game of it and good-naturedly "race" each other to see who can put the lids on the jars first.

Through the Looking Glass

Glass Magic

Materials

- large mirror laid flat on a table or firm surface
- glass cleaner
- rags, old newspaper, or paper towels

What to do

1. Let the children spray glass cleaner on the mirror to clean it.

More to do

- Experiment with different cleaning tools: rags, paper towels, newspapers, tissues, felt, paper. Experiment with different cleaning agents: bar soap, liquid soap, vinegar and water, water only. Decide which one cleans best.

Mirror Skating

Materials

- small hand-held mirror
- magnets, of any size
- magnetic wands

What to do

1. Hold the mirror horizontally in one hand.
2. Put a magnet on the top surface of the mirror.
3. Hold the wand in the other hand and run it along under the mirror to make the magnet on top "skate" around.

More to do

- Use different sizes and weights of magnets on the top and bottom. Put more than one magnet on top of the mirror and move them around.

Through the Looking Glass

A Cold Look

Materials

- ice cubes or icicles
- printed materials—magazines, newspapers
- wax paper or clear plastic wrap

What to do

1. Look through the ice at your surroundings. Talk about how things look.
2. Cover a page of a magazine or newspaper with clear plastic wrap or wax paper. Does it change the way the paper looks?
3. Set the ice on top of the plastic wrap or wax paper and see if the words appear larger, smaller or the same. Try different thicknesses and sizes of ice pieces.

More to do

- Let the ice melt and use a drop of water to look at a page.

Fun House Mirrors

Materials

- mirrors
- pictures either drawn by children or from magazines
- stiff paper
- glue

What to do

1. Mount the pictures on stiff paper.
2. Cut the pictures in half lengthwise.
3. Place the mirror's edge on the center of the picture so that when the child looks in the mirror she sees a whole picture!

More to do

- Use real objects such as small parquetry blocks and place the mirror on them as above. What does the new figure look like?

Greens Under Glass

Materials

- mayonnaise jars and lids
- pebbles
- sand
- peat moss
- potting soil
- plants

What to do

1. Layer pebbles and sand; then add a mixture of soil and peat moss.
2. Place the plants in the soil in the jars.
3. Moisten the soil.
4. Put the lids on the jars and place them in indirect sunlight.
5. Periodically moisten the soil if the plants show signs of drying out. (There will usually be visible moisture in the jar.)
6. Watch the plant grow in its own jar.

Zip It Up

Materials

- gallon-sized reclosable plastic bags
- steel wool
- string
- penny
- water

Through the Looking Glass

What to do

1. Put a piece of steel wool in each bag.
2. Add the string to one bag, the penny to the second and water to the last.
3. Zip the bags shut and leave them out so the children can see them.
4. Observe and record any changes over time: Does the steel wool change? How about the one with water? Do the string and its steel wool change? Do the penny and its steel wool change?

More to do

- Add water to each bag and observe. Add different objects to the bags such as pieces of foil or a paper clip.

Who Nose?

Materials

- small clear glass jars with lids
- cotton balls
- assorted extracts: vanilla, lemon, mint, almond, pickle juice

What to do

1. Put a cotton ball in each jar and saturate with a few drops of extract.
2. Have a child examine each jar and guess what might be on the cotton ball.
3. Have him open the jar, smell it and guess the fragrance.
4. Continue with all the jars.

More to do

- Have pictures of the scents, such as a picture of an orange for orange extract, candy cane for mint, and have the child match the pictures to the scents.

Through the Looking Glass

Art Activities

See-Through Painting

Materials

- large mirror laid flat on a table
- shaving cream

What to do

1. Squirt shaving cream on the mirror.
2. Encourage the child to move the shaving cream all over the mirror while watching her fingers move in the reflection.

More to do

- Use fingerpaint instead of shaving cream.

Window Painting

Materials

- sponges cut into specific shapes: hearts, ducks, flowers and so on
- paint
- classroom windows

What to do

1. Plan how you wish to decorate the windows with shapes and colors.
2. Dip the sponges in paint and print on the windows.
3. To extend this activity, print on paper so the children can take their own "windows" home.

More to do

- Older children can use brushes to paint scenes onto the windows.

Through the Looking Glass

Catch the Sun #1

3+

Materials

- clear contact paper cut into 6" circles, two circles per child
- bits of colored paper
- glitter
- small seeds
- buttons
- pieces or yarn, ribbon and string
- hole puncher

What to do

1. Have each child peel the protective coating off a circle of contact paper.
2. Have the child arrange the materials on the sticky side of the paper.
3. Have him peel off another contact circle and place it over the first.
4. Trim any overlapping edges.
5. Punch a hole in the circle near the edge.
6. Tie a string through the hole and hang in the window.

Catch the Sun #2

3+

Materials

- lids from margarine tubs, one per child
- white school glue
- collage materials

What to do

1. Fill each child's lid with glue.
2. Let her arrange the collage materials in the glue.
3. Let the glue dry for several days, and peel the suncatcher off the lid.
4. Punch a hole in the circle near edge.
5. Tie a string through the hole and hang it in the window.

Through the Looking Glass

Shady Deal

Materials

- old window shade
- paint

What to do

1. Unroll the window shade on the table.
2. Let the children paint pictures and designs and fill all the space on the shade.
3. Hang as a mural.

More to do

- Instead of painting, have the older children plan, design and cut out figures to make a 3-D mural on the window shade.

Reprints

Materials

- transparent acrylic easel
- tempera paint or fingerpaint
- paper
- brushes or sponges

What to do

1. Have a child paint with a brush, sponge or his fingers to create a design on the easel.
2. Press paper against the wet design and make a print from the original.
3. Wash off the easel and begin again.

Through the Looking Glass

Stained Glass Windows

3+

Materials

- wax paper, one piece per child
- colored tissue paper, cut into assorted pieces
- diluted white glue
- paintbrushes

What to do

1. Have the children brush diluted glue onto wax paper.
2. Have her place pieces of colored tissue onto the glue, and then brush more glue onto the tissue.
3. Continue to coat and overlay tissue to make desired design.
4. Let dry. The tissue paper will harden and lift off wax paper.
5. The child can hang the "stained glass" as is or cut it into a shape such as a heart, star or flower.

Rose-Colored Glasses

3+

Materials

- assortment of colored cellophane
- paper towel tubes
- rubber bands

What to do

1. Cut the cellophane into 6" squares.
2. Have each child select a color and cover one end of his tube with a piece of cellophane.
3. Secure the cellophane with the rubber band.
4. Look around the room!

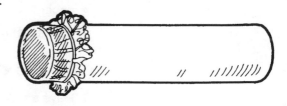

Through the Looking Glass

Frame It

Materials

- paint
- markers
- crayons
- pencils
- strips of cardboard or construction paper

What to do

1. Encourage the children to draw an outdoor scene. Have them look out different windows if they need some inspiration.
2. Help the children frame the scene by overlaying the cardboard or construction paper on the picture so the final product resembles a window.
3. Enjoy the view!

More to do

- Older children can look "into" a house or school room and draw what they see from the outside through the "window."

I See Stars

Materials

- toilet paper or paper towel tubes, one per child
- foil, cut into 6" squares, one per child
- rubber bands
- pushpin

What to do

1. Have each child cover one end of the tube with a piece of foil and secure it with a rubber band.
2. Poke tiny holes in the foil with the pushpin.
3. Hold the "telescope" up to the light and look at the stars!

Through the Looking Glass

Kaleidoscope

Materials

- large or small white paper plates, one per child
- markers or crayons
- pencils

What to do

1. Have the children use bright colors to make designs on their paper plates.
2. Poke a small hole in the center of the plate.
3. Poke the pointed end of a pencil through the hole in the plate and spin it around to make a kaleidoscope effect.

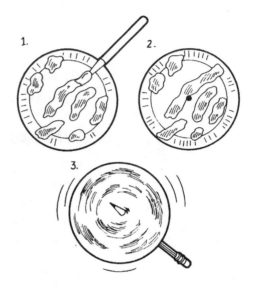

Seascape in a Jar

Materials

- colored sand in several colors
- toothpicks
- baby food jars and lids

What to do

1. Have the child layer colors of sand in his jar until it is about three-quarters full.
2. Have him carefully push a toothpick down the side of the jar to create designs in the sand.
3. Fill the jar to the top with more sand.
4. Seal the jar and handle carefully; don't shake!

Through the Looking Glass

See-Through Sea Creatures

Materials

- quart-sized plastic bags with twist ties, one per child
- collage materials such as styrofoam peanuts, yarn and string

What to do

1. Have the children fill the baggies about three-quarters full with any kind of collage stuffing.
2. Twist tie the bags shut.
3. Fan out the unstuffed portion of the baggie like a fish fin.
4. Display the fish and talk about all the "worms" and things it swallowed.

Blizzards

Materials

- baby food jars and lids
- hot glue gun and glue sticks
- small figures to put in jar
- confetti, glitter or styrofoam pellets
- water

What to do

1. Assemble all the materials and work one-on-one with the children.
2. Heat the glue gun. Always use caution when using a glue gun with children.
3. Have the child select the materials he needs.
4. Glue the figure to the inside of the jar lid. Do not allow the child to do this.
5. Fill the jar almost to top with the water.
6. Add the glitter or other snow-like filler.
7. Screw the lid on tightly.
8. Turn the jar over so the lid is on the bottom.
9. Shake the jar and watch the blizzard!

Through the Looking Glass

Mirror Images

Materials

- paper
- pencils
- mirrors

What to do

1. Have the children draw pictures of themselves.
2. Have the children look in a mirror, study their features and draw themselves again.
3. Compare the pictures. What differences do they notice between these two pictures?

Foiled Again

Materials

- hot tray on low setting
- crayons with the paper peeled off
- foil, cut in small sheets

What to do

1. Place the foil on the hot tray.
2. Have the children use the crayons on the foil, moving them around as they melt.
3. Continue changing colors until finished.
4. Remove the foil from the tray and take home.

More to do

- Sprinkle glitter on the wet crayon melt. Try wax paper instead of foil. Frame and hang when done.

Through the Looking Glass

Jack Frost

Materials

- can of spray snow or shaving cream
- mirrors or accessible window

What to do

1. Use the spray can as directed or spread shaving cream on mirror.
2. Let the shaving cream dry.
3. Etch the dry snow or shaving cream to make snowflakes, snowmen or other designs.

Music and Movement Activities

Copycat

What to do

1. Make simple movements and have the children mirror them.

More to do

- For older children have more complicated movements. Let a child be the lead copycat and the rest follow her.

Mirror Maniacs

Materials

- room with several full length mirrors
- music

What to do

1. Turn on the music and have the children watch themselves in the mirrors as they develop moves to the music.

Through the Looking Glass

Dot to Dot

3+

Materials

- hand-held mirror
- sunlight

What to do

1. Position the mirror to reflect the sunlight onto the walls and ceiling. Have the children chase the dot around the room.

Math Activities

Calendar

3+

Materials

- plain calendar or paper and markers

What to do

1. Make or purchase a plain calendar with only the days of the week marked on it.
2. Each month, make different paper patterns to fit your theme. For example: for the "looking-glass" theme you may want to make one set of mirrors by drawing and cutting out circles of paper, then smaller circles of foil. Glue foil circles on the large ones to be "mirrors." Make another set of squares and draw simple lines to represent "windows." A simple pattern could be "mirror, mirror, window." On day one of the month, place "mirror" on the calendar and continue, repeating the pattern as the days pass. These pattern pieces can also be used in your number line for numbering how many days you've been at school.
3. The days of the week may be sung to the tune of "Frere Jacques." "Sunday, Monday, Tuesday, Wednesday, Thursday, Friday, Saturday. It's not Sunday, it's not Monday, it's not Tuesday, it is. . . " (Let the children fill in the blank for whatever day of the week it is.)
4. School Days Countdown—make an ongoing number line for the number of days the children have been at school. Follow the same pattern as your monthly calendar pattern.

Through the Looking Glass

More to do

- Children can put actions to the pattern. For example, "mirror, mirror" could be looking at their right and left palms as if they were mirrors. "Window" could be peering out with hands framing eyes.

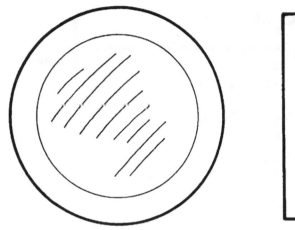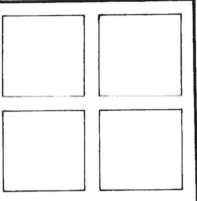

Cover-Ups

Materials

- graph showing five columns: blinds, curtains, shades, other and none
- markers

What to do

1. Ask the children to describe what covers the windows in their living rooms. Discuss their responses and the variety of window treatments.
2. Have the children mark their responses in the appropriate columns.
3. Tally the responses. Report on which window cover is used the most, and which is used the least. Seriate the responses.

Through the Looking Glass

In and Out the Windows

Materials

- simple map of the school building, or of just one floor
- pencil

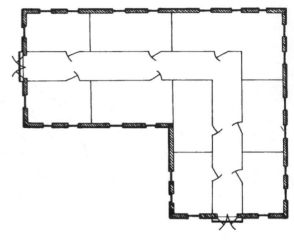

What to do

1. Talk about windows and where they are usually located.
2. Talk about the usual shape of windows and how they can be represented in drawings as a square.
3. Take a tour of the school and let the children draw in windows in their approximate locations on the map.
4. Return to the room and count all the windows on the map. Record.
5. Notice if there is one room that has more windows or fewer windows than other rooms. Do any rooms have the same number?

More to do

- Let older children go in teams and do their own map. Have children tally the number of windows in their homes with parent's help. Repeat the process with mirrors.

Guessing Box

Materials

- box or paper bag
- eye glasses
- mirror
- picture frame with glass
- telescope
- binoculars
- magnifying glass

Through the Looking Glass

What to do

1. Show a "looking-glass" item such as a telescope to the children and talk about its properties, such as its shape, color, container, size and uses.

2. Bring out the guessing box with another "looking-glass" item in it. Use the same box each time, no matter what size the item is. Storage boxes for clothing are the ideal size.

3. Say:

> "There is something in my guessing box.
>
> Would you like to guess?
>
> First you ask a question and
>
> I'll answer no or yes."

4. Children then ask questions. Encourage them to ask in the form of a question. "Is it. . . ?"

5. After a brief time, if you notice they aren't asking questions that pertain to the item in the box, give broad hints.

> "It's something small." Wait for guesses.
>
> "It's something round with a handle." Wait for guesses.
>
> "It's something that makes things look bigger." Wait for guesses.
>
> ("Yes, it's a magnifying glass!")

Thoughtful Reflections

What to do

1. Place a child facing a window, but do not tell the children your criteria.

2. Place another child back-to-back to the first child.

3. Ask the class, "Can you guess my rule? Why is one facing this way and the other child another way?"

4. Add children to each line.

5. If the children have difficulty guessing, say, "What do these children see as they look straight ahead?"

6. Continue giving hints if children are unable to see the pattern.

More to do

- Repeat above activity with those wearing glasses vs. those who don't. Face some children towards a mirror and some away. Repeat questioning.

Guess What I See?

Materials

- recloseable plastic bags
- any collection of similar items, such as buttons, straws or marbles
- chart

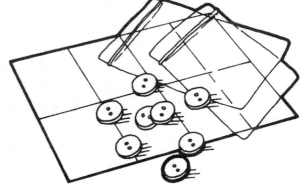

What to do

1. Fill the bag with a few of the objects.
2. Ask the children to estimate how many items are in the bag.
3. Record the guesses on a chart.
4. Remove and count the items, and circle the closest estimate.

More to do

- Using the same collection, add or subtract more each day and continue to record the estimates. Hang several reclosable plastic bags with the same objects and have the children order them from least to most using only estimating skills. For older children, use mixed collections such as straws to buttons.

Clearly a Guess

Materials

- clear glass jar filled with beads, beans or small stones

What to do

1. Let the children look at the jar, turn it around and shake it.
2. Have them estimate how many items are in the jar.
3. Record the guesses.
4. Take the lid off the jar and count the items.
5. Who was closest?

Through the Looking Glass

Language Activities

I Spy

2+

Materials

- old magazines and school supply catalogs
- large poster showing children at play
- scissors
- glue

What to do

1. Cut out small pictures from the magazines and catalogs such as animals, lamps, food and jewelry. Simple, easy-to-identify pictures work best.
2. Glue onto the poster in different areas, for example a glass in a boy's hand, earrings in a girl's ear, and other items in unique places.
3. Have the children examine the poster. Make the statement, "I spy a. . ." and have the children find it on the poster.

More to do

- Children five years old and up are able to cut and glue to make the class poster.

Window Watching

3+

Materials

- posterboard marked off to resemble a window
- markers

What to do

1. Go for a walk around several blocks, looking especially at windows.
2. When you return to school, record some of the things the children saw either in or through windows. Have the children describe some of the shapes and styles of windows they saw.

Through the Looking Glass

All About Mirrors

Materials

- paper shaped like a hand-held mirror

What to do

1. Ask the children what they know about mirrors. Ask them, "How do we use mirrors. . . at home? In stores? In cars? In beauty parlors? In a dentist's office?" Record their responses on paper shaped like a hand-held mirror.

A Hole in One

4+

Materials

- magazines
- scissors
- glue
- construction paper, one sheet per child

What to do

1. Have the children cut out pictures of objects, especially larger ones.
2. Have them glue the pictures on a piece of construction paper.
3. With your help, have them cut a square or circle in another piece of paper so that when it is laid over the photo, only a small part shows through the hole.
4. Repeat with several pictures and "holey" pages.
5. Put all the pages together in a book.
6. Show the book to children. Have them guess what each picture is behind its hole.

More to do

- A simpler version for younger kids is to cut one square in the middle of a large manilla envelope, mount magazine pictures on sheets of paper and slide the pictures into the envelope. Older children can make their own books. They can make the cutouts as tiny or as abstract as they would like.

Through the Looking Glass

Magnificent Magnifier

Materials

- photocopies of a giant magnifying glass
- pens and pencils

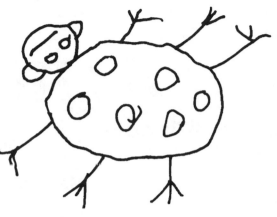

What to do

1. Ask the children to imagine what a tiny bug looks like under a magnifying glass. Then ask them to draw that bug in great detail.

More to do

- Use any other topic and have children draw the close-up. These can be made into a class book.

Night Critters

4+

Materials

- *It Didn't Frighten Me* by Janet Goss and Jerome Harste
- paper
- markers

What to do

1. Read the story *It Didn't Frighten Me* aloud to the class.
2. Have the children draw their own imaginary creatures.

More to do

- Make them into a book for the class to read.

Through the Looking Glass

Transition Activities

Looking at Plans

What to do

1. As the children are deciding which activity to choose, give a child a mirror to look into and ask, "Mirror, mirror in your hands, please tell me *(child's name or day of the week)* plans."

Magic Window

3+

Materials

- An 8 1/2" by 11" window made with a cardboard frame and a heavy clear plastic insert (decorate the window frame in an attention-getting way)
- tape

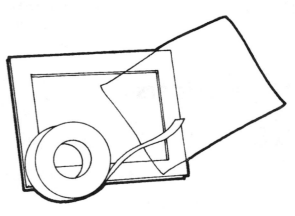

What to do

1. Use this window to highlight certain areas of your room. For example: place the magic window over a sign in your block area. At circle time, discuss where the window was found and what it highlighted.
2. Place the window over certain children's names. Perhaps they will be the leaders that day or the one who will tell what they did during work time.
3. Use the window as a focal point for any feature you may introduce to the class. You may put it on a planning sheet or over some special artwork.
4. The children could hold the window up to their eyes and look around the room to decide where they would like to play first.

Through the Looking Glass

Looking Around

Materials

- real or homemade telescope

What to do

1. To bridge waiting time between activities, hold telescope to eye and say, "I see something *(name a color or shape)*."
2. Let the children guess what you spy.

Songs and Chants

> Mirror, mirror on the wall
> Who's the _____ of them all?

- Insert tallest, oldest, shortest, and so on to include an attribute your children have.

Theme Extensions and Variations

Field Trips

- **Lumber Yard**—Lumber yards frequently have assorted window frames that are used in homes. All shapes and sizes make for interesting looking.
- **Neighborhood Walk**—Walk for several blocks near the school and notice the many different shapes and sizes of windows. If you are lucky enough to have a church nearby, stained glass windows are particularly interesting to observe from both inside and outside the church.
- **Window Shopping**—Visit a small shopping area that appears to be safe for a group of children. Walk past several stores and look in their windows. Talk about what services each store provides and look for surprises in each window. This is especially effective during seasonal displays.
- **Eye Doctor**—Arrange a visit to an eye doctor's office and peer through eye machines as well as look at frames and other eye aides.

Bibliography

- *Arthur's Eyes*, Marc Brown. Boston: Little, Brown & Co., 1986. His friends tease Arthur when he gets glasses, but he soon learns to wear them with pride.

Through the Looking Glass

- *Eye Book, The*, Theo Le Sieg. NY: Random House, 1968. Eyes see a lot of things in various shapes and colors.

- *Goggles!* Ezra Jack Keats. NY: Macmillan, 1987. Peter and Archie find a pair of motorcycle goggles, but some bigger boys chase after them! Willie, the dog, saves the day.

- *Hidden House, The*, Martin Waddell and Angela Barrett. NY: Putnam Publishing Group, 1990. With the owner gone, three dolls watch from a window as their house becomes hidden by growing plants and trees until a family discovers the residence and moves in.

- *I Spy*, Jean Marzollo and Carol Carson. NY: Scholastic, Inc., 1992. A picture riddle book.

- *It Didn't Frighten Me*, Janet L. Goss and Jerome C. Harste. Worthington, Ohio: Willowisp Press, Inc., 1985. A predictable book in which a little boy imagines seeing all sorts of weird creatures out his bedroom window, but doesn't get scared until he sees the only "real" creature. . . an owl!

- *Look Again*, Tana Hoban. NY: Macmillian Publishing Co., 1971. Look through a square window to discover what is hiding beyond the frame.

- *Look! Look! Look!* Tana Hoban. NY: Greenwillow Books, 1988. Photographs of familiar objects are viewed first through a cut out hole and then in their entirety.

- *Simple Pictures Are Best*, Nancy Willard. NY: Harcourt Brace Jovanovich, 1978. A shoemaker and his wife being photographed for their wedding anniversary keep adding items to the picture, despite the photographer's admonition that "simple pictures are best."

Poems

- "Reflection," *A Light in the Attic*. Shel Silverstein, NY: Evil Eye Music Co., Harper and Row Publishers, 1981, p. 29.

- "Wavy Hair," *A Light in the Attic*. Shel Silverstein, NY: Evil Eye Music Co., Harper and Row Publishers, 1981, p. 38.

- "Jimmy Jet and His TV Set," *Where the Sidewalk Ends*. Shel Silverstein, Evil Eye Music Co., Harper and Row Publishers, 1974, p. 29.

- "Stone Telling," *Where the Sidewalk Ends*. Shel Silverstein, Evil Eye Music Co., Harper and Row Publishers, 1974, p. 147.

Through the Looking Glass

Recordings

- "Shadow Dancing," *Kids in Motion*. Greg and Steve, Youngheart Records, 1987.
- "Brown Bear, Brown Bear, What Do You See?" *Playing Favorites*. Greg and Steve, Youngheart, 1991.
- "Watch Me," *Sally the Swinging Snake*. Hap Palmer, Activity Records, Inc., 1987.
- "Just Like Me," *We All Live Together*. Greg and Steve, Youngheart Records, 1987.

Picture This!

Mondays	Read *The Legend of the Indian Paintbrush* Do Mixing a Rainbow Do Brushless Painting	Start Maché Masterpieces Do Fold 'n' Cut	*Simon's Book Continued* Read *Simon's Book* Do Simple Simon Do More Copy Cat Drawings	Do Action Painting Do Blended Paper
Tuesdays	Do Bumpy Pictures Have Masterpiece Sandwiches for Snack	Read *Why Worms?* Do Scribble Pictures Do Wall to Wall	Do Finish the Masterpiece Do Clay Play	*EXIT* Read *The Sign-Maker's Assistant* Do Signs, Signs Everywhere Signs
Wednesdays	Read *No Good in Art* Do What Does An Artist Do? Do Copy Cat Drawings	Read "The Painter" (see Poems) Finish Maché Masterpieces	Visit a local artist's studio Do Whip It Up	Read *The Mitten* Do Brett's Borders Paint on Blended Paper
Thursdays	Start Soft Sculpting Clay Field trip to art gallery	Do Freeform Cutting Visit a high school art class	Purple Day Read *Harold and the Purple Crayon* Do Purple Painting Jelly and grape juice for Snack	Prepare and hold an open house to exhibit artworks Do More Copy Cat Drawings
Fridays	Picasso Read *Matthew's Dream* Do Soft Sculpting Clay Do True Blue Drawings	Read *Purple, Green and Yellow* Do a Fistful of Markers	Read *Mouse Paint* Do Mixed-Up Paint yellow blue red	Do Shiny Art Read *Draw Me A Star* Do Things Are Looking Up

Theme Objectives

- To explore many different kinds of art mediums, emphasizing "process" rather than "product"
- To provide an "art-rich" environment to expose young children to many different types and works of art
- To enable children to express themselves in a creative and appropriate way
- To foster within children a sense of pride and accomplishment in their own work

Learning Centers

Dramatic Play

- class art museum (display framed artwork reproductions)
- art studio
- easels
- smocks and berets

Manipulatives

- mosaic tiles

Library

- books containing works of art by various artists

Blocks

- pictures of famous buildings such as the St. Louis Arch, the Pyramids and the Eiffel Tower

Science

- water
- food coloring
- eyedroppers for mixing colors

Writing

- blank books for illustrating stories

Art

- easels
- sculptor's clay
- pottery wheel
- weaving loom
- papermaking supplies

Snacks

- Masterpiece Sandwiches (see activity in Discovery section)

Discovery Activities

Masterpiece Sandwiches

Materials

- various lunchmeats
- cheeses
- different types of bread
- lettuce
- tomatoes
- onions
- ketchup
- mustard
- mayonnaise
- pickles

What to do

1. Set up a "sandwich bar."

2. Have the children come through and prepare their own masterpiece sandwich.

Mixing a Rainbow

Materials

- eyedroppers
- small clear plastic containers or cups
- red, yellow and blue food coloring
- water

What to do

1. Mix up three different cups of food coloring and water.
2. Have the children use eyedroppers and mix the colored water to make new colors.
3. Ask them, "Which colors make purple? Which make green? or orange?" Let the children discover how secondary colors are made.

More to do

- Let the older children drip food coloring directly from the bottles to explore dark and light hues.

Blended Paper

Materials

- paper scraps of different colors, kinds and grades
- newspaper strips
- paper towels
- piles of newspaper
- blender
- food coloring or powdered tempera paint
- styrofoam meat trays
- piece of window screen
- duct tape
- cotton towels
- sponge
- dishpan
- water

What to do

1. Make a screen mold by cutting out the inside of a meat tray, leaving a "frame." Cut the window screen to fit the inside of the frame and use duct tape to attach it to the tray.
2. Fill the dishpan half full of water.
3. Let the children tear up paper scraps, newspapers or paper towels into one or two inch pieces. Fill the blender with two parts water to one part paper pieces.
4. Blend the mixture for about two minutes, stopping frequently to avoid overheating.
5. Pour the pulpy mixture from the blender into the dishpan.
6. Have a child use the screen mold to "pick up" the floating pulp by dipping the screen down into the water and lifting it up. A layer of pulp will catch on the screen.
7. Carefully flip the screen onto a wet towel. Pat the screen with a sponge to release the pulpy layer.
8. Fold the other end of the wet towel on top of the paper (or use several layers of newspaper) and press out as much moisture as you can.
9. Place the pressed-out paper onto a dry piece of newspaper or wax paper and let dry for a day or two.
10. Children may paint on it when dry.

More to do

- Add a few drops of food coloring or a couple tablespoons of powdered tempera paint to blender before mixing. Add glitter to the pulpy mixture in the dishpan before dipping screen. Press leaves or flower petals into paper before letting it sit to dry. Be creative. Experimenting, whether it works or not, is the name of the game!

Art Activities

Puff Paint

Materials

- empty plastic dish detergent, ketchup or other squeeze bottles
- flour
- water
- bowl
- spoon
- dry tempera paint

What to do

1. Mix equal parts of flour and water, making sure the consistency is runny enough to squeeze out of the bottles. (It should be the consistency of pancake batter.)
2. Add tempera to color your puff paint, and fill a number of empty squeeze bottles.
3. Have the children make designs or write their name with the puff paint.
4. Add glitter for an attractive touch.

Scribble Pictures

Materials

- paper
- markers
- crayons

What to do

1. For younger children, draw scribbles on the paper ahead of time.
2. Have the children color in each section or loop a different color to resemble a "modern art painting."

More to do

- Older children may draw their own scribbles before coloring them in.

Whip It Up

Materials

- soap flakes
- water
- electric mixer
- tempera paint
- combs
- popsicle sticks
- cardboard
- large mixing bowl

What to do

1. Place one cup of flakes in a large mixing bowl.
2. Add water and mix until thick. Add more water or soap flakes if needed.
3. Add a tablespoon of tempera to the mixture.
4. Whip the mixture until it is the consistency of mashed potatoes.
5. Have the children use popsicle sticks to "paint" and sculpt the whipped paint on the cardboard.
6. Children may use old combs to give the paint a textured design. This is a good recipe to use as Van Gogh's thick paint.

Clay Play

3+

Materials

- plastic knives
- popsicle sticks
- different types of clay: artists' sculpting clay, commercial playdough, homemade playdough, beeswax, modeling clay

What to do

1. Encourage the children to explore the clay by sitting down and sculpting with them. Experiment with sculpting tools such as plastic knives and popsicle sticks.
2. Talk about how the clay feels, looks and smells.
3. Display the masterpieces by placing them on styrofoam trays and labeling them with the children's names and the titles of their sculptures.

Watercolor Impressions

3+

Materials

- watercolors
- water
- paintbrushes
- heavy paper or lightweight cardboard
- bubble packing plastic
- crumpled plastic wrap
- crumpled aluminum foil
- netting
- heavy books for weight

What to do

1. Have the children paint with watercolors as they normally do.
2. When they are done, place one item (foil, plastic wrap, netting or bubble packing) on top of the watercolor before it dries. Use one item per painting for best results.
3. Place under heavy books and let dry overnight.
4. When dry, carefully remove the pressed item from each painting. This process gives the paintings added texture. For instance, the foil makes the painting look like a frosted windowpane. You will get wonderful results!

More to do

- Instead of using items to make impressions, sprinkle salt over the watercolor painting. This will give it a glistening effect!

Shiny Art

Materials

- shiny Christmas tree garland
- aluminum pie pans or trays
- foil gift wrap
- glitter
- metallic ribbons and bows

- glue

What to do

1. Have the children glue shiny scraps and pieces in different shapes and sizes on pie pans or trays.
2. Sprinkle with glitter.

Bumpy Pictures

Materials

- cardboard
- textured items, such as netting, popsicle sticks, corrugated cardboard, textured wallpaper samples, toothpicks or bubble packing material
- glue
- tempera paint
- paintbrushes

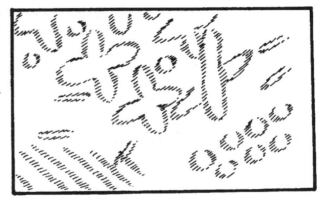

What to do

1. On the first day, have the children glue items of different textures, such as those listed above, onto a piece of cardboard to make a collage.
2. Let dry overnight.
3. On the second day, encourage children to paint over the entire collage with one or two colors, giving it a "textured effect."

More to do

- Display "bumpy pictures" on a homemade kiosk by covering tall boxes with colored paper or wallpaper.

Upside Down Drawings

3+

Materials

- low table
- paper
- masking tape
- markers
- optional—pictures of the Sistine Chapel as painted by Michelangelo

What to do

1. Show pictures of the Sistine Chapel and discuss how Michelangelo spent years lying on his back to do this artwork.
2. Let the children discover how it feels to draw while lying on their backs. Tape drawing paper to the underside of the low table.
3. Have the children lie down on their backs and reach up to draw on the paper.
4. Ask the children how it feels to draw this way. "Does it hurt your arms?" "Would you like to draw for eight hours every day for years like this?"

Brushless Painting

3+

Materials

- tempera paint
- paper
- various objects to use instead of a brush, such as sticks, a potato masher, popsicle sticks, a sponge, a toothbrush, a feather, a plastic spoon, a knife or a fork, a comb, a corn cob, a plastic dish-scrubber, a pine tree branch, or a crumpled ball of aluminum foil, plastic wrap, wax paper or newspaper

What to do

1. Encourage the children to paint using some of the objects listed above.
2. Ask which new way of painting they liked best.

More to do

- Older children can bring in or find unusual items around the classroom with which to paint.

Action Painting

Materials

- paint smocks
- mural-sized paper
- tempera paint
- newspapers
- paintbrushes
- pictures of Jackson Pollack's abstract wall murals

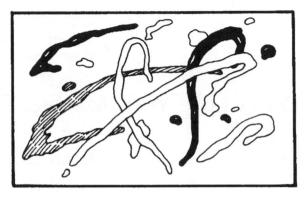

What to do

1. Cover a large area of the floor with newspaper.
2. Show pictures of Jackson Pollock's abstract wall murals.
3. Discuss how he "flung" the paint or dripped it from his brush.
4. Let each child try.
5. Limit this activity to two children at a time to minimize the mess.

Geometric Pictures

- electric warming tray
- aluminum foil
- paper
- black permanent marker
- old crayons
- ruler
- reproductions by Mondrian

What to do

1. For younger children, you may need to draw geometric designs with a marker and ruler.
2. Cover the warming tray with aluminum foil for easy cleanup.

3. Show examples of Mondrian's works.

4. Let the children color in each section a different color by using crayons on the warming tray. Watch the crayons melt.

5. Mount the artwork on black construction paper.

More to do

- Older children may use rulers and markers to design their own pictures. Some children may want to watercolor each section. Some children may want to use crayon without a warming tray.

Don't Lose Your Marbles

Materials

- shoeboxes
- construction paper
- marbles
- tempera paint
- plastic spoons

What to do

1. Precut the paper to fit inside the shoebox.

2. Place the paper in the shoebox.

3. Dip a marble into the paint using a spoon.

4. Place the coated marble inside the box.

5. Gently tip the box from side to side and from front to back, rolling the marble around.

More to do

- Roll several different marbles at a time. Put lid on box and shake the marble around. Place a stencil on top of the paper and remove after rolling to leave a blank design on the paper.

Get to the Point

Materials

- pencils
- tempera paint
- paper
- reproductions of pictures by a Pointillist artist such as Georges Seurat

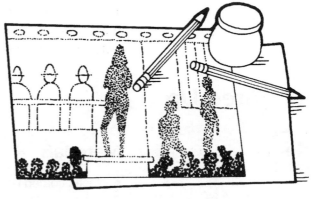

What to do

1. For young children, you may wish to pre-draw simple shapes (butterfly, heart, circle) or designs for children to fill in.
2. Show the children examples of Pointillism paintings.
3. Have them dip the eraser ends of their pencils into the paint and dot inside their designs to fill them completely with dots of color.

Recycled Sculptures

Materials

- styrofoam packing sections (not peanuts)
- toothpicks
- scraps of yarn or string
- nails
- screws
- straws
- pantyhose eggs
- corrugated cardboard
- bubble packing
- styrofoam meat trays
- used aluminum foil
- Easter grass
- plastic lids from detergent bottles or shampoo
- glue

- paint

What to do

1. Display the recyclable junk on a large table.
2. Have the children choose several items and let them create creatures, machines, tools, robots or anything else they can devise.

All Wired Up

Materials

- plastic-coated flexible colored craft wire
- old playdough
- styrofoam trays

What to do

1. Have the children create wire sculptures using craft wire.
2. Stick the wire sculpture into balls of old playdough so the sculpture will be free-standing.
3. Place the sculptures on styrofoam trays for display.

Fold 'n Cut

Materials

- white or colored thin paper (such as typing paper)
- scissors
- glue
- construction paper

What to do

1. Demonstrate how to fold the paper and cut around the fold so the shape or design will be symmetrical.
2. Let the children experiment with folding and cutting.

3. Glue design onto construction paper for display.

Freeform Cutting

Materials

- white or colored thin paper (such as typing paper)
- scissors
- glue
- construction paper

What to do

1. Encourage the children to cut out designs and shapes with scissors.
2. Glue the shapes and designs onto construction paper for display.

Finish the Masterpiece

Materials

- easel paper
- tempera paint or watercolors
- paintbrushes

What to do

1. Prepare each piece of paper ahead of time by cutting a hole of any size in the paper, or gluing on a construction paper flower pot or vase. Try gluing a yellow construction paper sun with rays on the paper, or perhaps glue on white construction paper clouds. And, of course, one could simply paint a line across the paper. These are all "starters."
2. Have the children choose a piece of paper with one of the "starters" and complete the picture with paints.

Copy Cat Drawings

Materials

- drawing paper
- pencils, markers, crayons
- various drawing tableaus such as a clock, a bowl of fruit and a vase with flowers; a book, a candle and eyeglasses; or a coffee mug and a sandwich

What to do

1. Every few days while exploring this theme, set up objects to draw in a designated area.
2. For the first couple of tries, sit with the children and draw just as you would expect them to. Talk while you draw, discussing the colors, the placement on the paper, the lines and the shading. Encourage the children's efforts.

More to do

- Mounting the still life drawings give the children's drawings special attention. Display still life reproductions and talk about what the children "see." Display the children's drawings along with the real objects they drew from.

Soft Sculpting Clay

Materials

- plaster of Paris
- empty yogurt cups
- vermiculite
- spoons
- mixing bowl
- water

What to do

1. Prepare plaster of Paris according to package directions.
2. Add an equal amount of vermiculite and mix.
3. Fill yogurt cups about 3/4 full with this mixture and let them stand overnight.
4. Peel away the yogurt cup when the plaster has hardened.
5. Give the children spoons with which to sculpt the mixture.

Mache Masterpieces

Materials

- clean, empty dish detergent or plastic bottles
- newspaper
- flour
- water
- tempera paint
- paintbrushes
- junk pieces such as lids, Easter grass, buttons, pipe cleaners
- glue

What to do

1. Make a flour and water mixture in a large bowl by using several cups of flour and slowly adding water to get the thick paste used for papier mache.
2. Tear the newspapers into 1" wide strips.
3. Have the children dip the newspaper strips into the paste and squeeze out the excess paste by running the strip between their fingers.
4. Completely cover the plastic bottle with a single layer of newspaper strips.
5. Let it dry for a day or two.
6. Have the children paint it, letting dry overnight.
7. The children can glue on junk materials to turn papier-mache bottles into robots, people, vehicles or rockets.

True Blue Drawings

4+

Materials

- a reproduction of one of Pablo Picasso's works during his "Blue Period"
- blue construction paper
- blue drawing utensils such as markers, chalks, pastels, crayons, pen and ink, and colored pencils

What to do

1. Show a blue Picasso reproduction such as "Le Gourmet."
2. Tell the children that for a couple of years this particular artist painted all in blues.
3. Let the children draw a portrait or scenery all in blue hues.

More to do

● Let older children give their pictures a title.

Math Activities

Calendar

Materials

● plain calendar or paper and markers

What to do

1. Make or purchase a plain calendar with only the days of the week marked on it.
2. Each month, make different paper patterns to fit your theme. For example: for the "Picture This" theme you may want to use three paint palettes each with a spot of paint of a different color. For example, one paint palette with a red spot, one with a blue spot and one with a yellow spot. Repeat the red, yellow blue pattern throughout the calendar.
3. The days of the week may be sung to the tune of "Frere Jacques." "Sunday, Monday, Tuesday, Wednesday, Thursday, Friday, Saturday. It's not Sunday, it's not Monday, it's not Tuesday, it is. . . " (Let the children fill in the blank for whatever day of the week it is.)

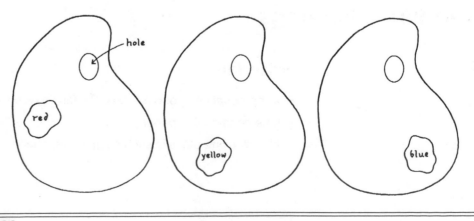

Calendar Patterns for Picture This...

4. School Days Countdown—make an ongoing number line for the number of days the children have been at school. Follow the same pattern as your monthly calendar pattern.

More to do

- For older children, a blue star or some other designation may be used for numbers ending in five.

Guessing Box

Materials

- box or paper bag
- picture frames
- artists' canvas
- smock and beret
- paint palette
- paintbrush

What to do

1. Show a "Picture This" item such as a picture frame to the children and talk about its properties: shape, color, container, size, uses and so on.
2. Bring out the guessing box with another "Picture this" item in it. Use the same box each time, no matter what size the item is. Storage boxes for clothing are the ideal size.
3. Say:

   "There is something in my guessing box.

   Would you like to guess?

   First you ask a question and

   I'll answer no or yes."
4. Children then ask questions. Encourage them to ask in the form of a question. "Is it. . . ?"
5. After a brief time, if you notice they aren't asking questions that pertain to the item in the box, give broad hints.

   "It's something long." Wait for guesses.

   "It's something ticklish." Wait for guesses.

   "It's something red." Wait.

   "It's something you paint with." Wait for guesses.

   ("Yes, it's a paintbrush!")

Tallyho!

Materials

- art reproductions, attractively mounted
- posterboard
- marker
- scissors
- blue ribbon or blue construction paper

What to do

1. Write each child's name on a 1" x 2" card cut from posterboard.
2. Make a blue ribbon out of ribbon or construction paper.
3. Display various masterpieces around the room.
4. Have each child vote for her favorite masterpiece by placing her name card under the reproduction of her choice.
5. Count the votes.
6. Place the blue ribbon by the masterpiece with the most votes.

Language Activities

Simple Simon

Materials

- *Simon's Book* by Henrik Drescher
- various colored ink pens
- paper

What to do

1. Read *Simon's Book* aloud to the children.
2. After reading the book, the children can draw monsters or other pictures using ink pens only.
3. Laminate the pictures or cover them with contact paper, and bind them into a class book entitled *Simon's Book Continued*, or use your school's name.

A Fistful of Markers

Materials

- thin and fat markers in all colors
- paper
- *Purple, Green and Yellow* by Robert Munsch

What to do

1. Read *Purple, Green and Yellow* aloud to the class.
2. Tell the children to grab as many markers in one hand as they can and try to draw, scribble or write their name.
3. How many fat markers could they hold?
4. How many thin markers could they hold?

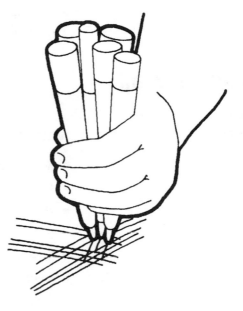

More to do

- This is a good time to reinforce that markers or crayons are used only on paper!

Purple Painting

Materials

- *Harold and the Purple Crayon*, by Crockett Johnson
- purple paint
- purple markers
- purple crayons
- purple pencils
- paper

What to do

1. Read *Harold and the Purple Crayon* aloud to the children.

2. Give the children the opportunity to use any of the purple tools available to draw or paint a purple picture.

More to do

• Declare this day Purple Day and wear purple, eat a purple snack like jelly and grape juice, or bring in an item or picture of something purple to display.

Wall to Wall

4+

Materials

• watercolors
• *Why Worms?* by Gillian Davies
• sheet of mural-sized paper
• paint
• scissors
• paintbrushes
• glue
• collage materials

What to do

1. Read *Why Worms?* aloud to the children.
2. Tell the children they will be making a wall mural of things that live under the ground, like worms, and things that live on top of the ground, like butterflies.
3. Draw a horizontal line across the mural to designate the ground level.
4. Have the children paint above the ground with watercolors.
5. Have the children draw or paint worms, snakes, or ants under the ground.
6. Show the children how to create bugs by making a thumbprint and drawing in legs and eyes.
7. Show a picture of an ant tunnel and have a child draw one.
8. Have the children paint or cut out and glue flowers, leaves and butterflies above the ground.
9. The children can glue cotton balls on cloud shapes and place in the sky.
10. Have a child paint a sun in the sky.
11. Display on the wall for everyone to see!

What Does an Artist Do?

Materials

- half a piece of posterboard
- marker

What to do

1. A few days into the theme, ask, "What does an artist do?"
2. The children will give examples of kinds of art work such as painting, drawing or sculpting. Record all responses given by the children.
3. Add to the list throughout the theme.

Things Are Looking Up

Materials

- *Draw Me a Star* by Eric Carle
- blue mural paper
- glitter
- glue
- collage materials
- pictures of the planets
- star stencils
- scissors
- colored construction paper

What to do

1. Read *Draw Me a Star* aloud to the children.
2. Tell the children they are going to make a ceiling mural of things in the sky.
3. Have some children trace a star, cut it out, and glue on glitter.
4. Ask a child to paint a yellow sun or a white moon or both.

5. Using pictures of planets, have the children decorate colored construction paper circles to make their own planets.

6. Have the children make shooting stars by making a brushstroke with glue and sprinkling glitter on it.

7. Children can add rocket ships or satellites to their mural.

8. Tack your heavenly mural onto the ceiling to display!

Mixed-Up Paint

Materials

- red, yellow and blue tempera paint
- paintbrushes
- paper
- *Mouse Paint* by Ellen Stoll Walsh
- small cups

What to do

1. Read *Mouse Paint* aloud to the children.

2. Let the children randomly mix paint to make new colors.

3. After exploring, tell them two colors to mix. You might say, "Mix red and yellow. What new color did you make?"

Signs, Signs, Everywhere Signs

Materials

- *The Signmaker's Assistant* by Tedd Arnold
- commercial or homemade sign flashcards of real signs: street signs, road signs and signs of restaurants, fast food chains or stores in your local area
- posterboard
- markers

Picture This!

What to do

1. Read *The Signmaker's Assistant* aloud to the children.
2. Show them the flashcards and let the children "read" them. They will readily recognize most of them.
3. Let the children use books, pictures, or dictation to design their own signs to post at school, in the classroom or at home.

Brett's Borders

Materials

- some of Jan Brett's books, but especially *The Mitten*
- paper
- markers
- book binding material

What to do

1. Read one or several books by Jan Brett, including *The Mitten*. Be sure to point out her technique of using borders around her pictures.
2. Have each child draw an animal that went into the mitten.
3. Ask him to draw a border around his picture.
4. Laminate or cover the pictures with contact paper and bind into a class book for your library.

More to do

- For younger children, a rolling stamp wheel is a quick way to "border" a picture.

Transition Activities

Mime It

What to do

1. Mime an artist such as a painter or sculptor at work.
2. Have the children guess what she's doing step by step.

Theme Extensions and Variations

Field trips

- Art gallery
- Art museum
- Crafts store
- Local artist's studio
- High school art class
- Invite a local artist or graphic artist to your classroom.
- Culminate this theme by holding an open house art gallery for parents to view their children's masterpieces. Mounting, laminating and framing the art work can really make a beautiful difference. Display pieces on homemade kiosks, walls, from the ceiling, and on dividing screens. Send home an invitation to families and offer simple refreshments. We suggest that you do not judge the children's art work or award ribbons because we feel they are all winners!

Bibliography

- *Draw Me a Star*, Eric Carle. NY: Putnam Publishing Group, 1992. An artist's drawing of a star begins the creation of an entire universe around him as each successive pictured object requests that he draw more.
- *Harold & the Purple Crayon*, Crockett Johnson. NY: HarperCollins, 1958. Harold can draw himself in and out of trouble with his purple crayon.
- *Legend of the Indian Paintbrush, The*, Tomie dePaola. NY: Putnam Publishing Group, 1988. Little Gopher follows his destiny as revealed in a Dream-Vision of becoming an artist for his people, and eventually he is able to bring the colors of the sunset down to earth.
- *Matthew's Dream*, Leo Lionni. NY: Alfred A. Knopf, 1991. A visit to an art museum inspires a young mouse to become a painter.
- *Mitten, The*, Jan Brett. NY: Putnam Publishing Group, 1990. Several animals sleep snugly in Nicki's lost mitten until the bear sneezes.
- *Mouse Paint*, Ellen Stoll Walsh. San Diego: Harcourt Brace Jovanovich, Publisher, 1989. Three white mice discover jars of red, blue and yellow paint and explore the world of color.
- *No Good in Art*, Miriam Cohen. NY: Dell Publishing, 1980. Everyone is supposed to paint a picture of what they want to be when they grow up. But Jim isn't feeling confident about his ability to do art.
- *Purple, Green and Yellow*, Robert Munsch. Toronto, Canada: Firefly Books, Ltd., 1992. Brigid's mother buys her 500 super-indelible-never-come-off-till-you're-

dead-and-maybe-even-later coloring markers with strict instructions not to draw on the floor, walls, or herself.

- *Signmaker's Assistant, The*, Tedd Arnold. NY: Dial Books, 1992. A young sign-maker's apprentice dreams of having his own shop but creates havoc when he is left in charge by himself.
- *Simon's Book*, Henrik Drescher. NY: Lothrop, Lee & Shepard Books, 1983. Simon's story and illustrations come to life one night when he is asleep.
- *Why Worms?* Gillian Davies. Lake Forest, IL: Forest House Publishing, 1990. Andrew loves to draw worms in all sorts of places—that is, until Mom finds out!

Poems

- "The Painter," *A Light in the Attic*. Shel Siverstein, NY: Harper and Row Publishers, 1981, p. 123.

Teacher Resources

Books

- *Art for Children*, series by Ernest Raboff. Each of the 16 books in the series offers a biography, painting interpretations, and 15 color reproductions of the world's most recognized artists.
- *Artworks*, Harriet Hodgson. Palo Alto, CA: Monday Morning Books, Inc., 1986. Fifty activities stressing process not product.
- *Come Look With Me: Exploring Landscape Art With Children*. Gladys S. Blizzard. Charlottesville, VA: Thomasson-Grant, Inc., 1992. Present twelve color reproductions of landscape paintings by such artists as Vincent vanGogh, M.C. Escher and Georgia O"Keefe. With questions to stimulate discussion and background information on each artist and painting. One book in a series.
- *How to Teach Art to Children*, Joy Evans and Jo Ellen Moore. Monterey, CA: Evan-Moor Corp., 1992. Activities designed to encourage children to explore materials and techniques in a large-group, a small-group or independently.
- *Let's Meet Famous Artists*, Harriet Kinghorn, Jacqueline Badman and Lisa Lewis-Spicer. Minneapolis, MN: T.S. Denison and Co., 1991. Includes background information on 19 artists from Alexander Calder to Frank Lloyd Wright.
- *Masterpiece of the Month*, Jennifer Thomas. Huntington Beach, CA: Teacher Created Materials, Inc., 1990. Lessons focus on the elements of design: line, color, texture, shape, space and form, and are based on an art history approach which incorporated learning about art as well as doing art.

Picture This!

- *Paint! Make Prints! Make Sculptures!* and *Draw!* These four books are by Kim Solga. Cincinnati, Ohio: North Light Books, 1991. Filled with wonderful activities for young children.

- *Paint Without Brushes*, Liz and Dick Wilmes. Elgin, IL: Building Blocks, 1993. Children experiment with a wide variety of paints, props and textures.

- *Preschool Art.* MaryAnn Kohl. Mt. Rainier, MD: Gryphon House, 1994. Seasonally organized, with over 200 open-ended art activities including drawing, painting, collage, sculpture and construction.

- *1-2-3 Art*, Jean Warren. Everett, WA: Warren Publishing House, Inc., 1985. Over 200 open-ended art activities for young children.

Catalogs

National Gallery of Art
Mail Order Dept.
2000 B South Club Drive
Landover, MD 20785

- They offer a very reasonably priced selection of post cards and posters to use as fine art examples.

Mini-Units

Mondays	Read Goldilocks and the Three Bears Do Bear Drama Three Bears Porridge for Snack	Read The Three Silly Goats Gruff Soup - Goat Style for Snack	Read The Three Little Pigs Do Act It Out!	Read Three Little Kittens Do Qust Visiting Tuna and Crackers for Snack
Tuesdays	Do Bear Hunt Do Size Sort Small, Medium, Large Mmm! for Snack	Do Picture This Do Tally the Goats and Cows	Do Qust Like the Pigs Do Which is Stranger? Pigs-in-a-blanket for Snack	Do Mitten Lace- Do Mouse, Mouse, Cat!
Wednesdays	Read The Three Wishes Do Make a Wish Toast and Honey for Snack	Do And Then What Happened? Do Picture Me Ugly! Goat cheese and crackers for Snack	Field trip to a pig farm Do Let's Make Plans	Read Mystery of The Missing Red Mitten Do Hide the Mitten
Thursdays	Do Corny Recipes Corn on the Cob for Snack	Do The Grass is Greener Do Guessing Box	Read Pigs in Hiding Do Pigs in Hiding	Do Mitten Match Do Mitten Safari Milk and cookies for Snack
Fridays	Read Three Little Ducks Do Corn Mosaic Cornbread for Snack	Read Gregory the Terrible Eater Do Goat Stew Recipes	Read Magic Fish Do Yarn Mosaic	Do Let's Compare! Read Lost Do Bubbling Berries for Snack

Theme Objectives

- To illustrate the quantity "3"
- To understand the concepts of seriation and sequence
- To explore and experience the techniques and concepts of story development
- To provide materials and opportunities to develop original stories

Learning Centers

Dramatic Play

- cake pans
- seriated sizes of mixing bowls
- empty cake mix boxes
- empty oatmeal boxes
- bowls
- cups
- eating utensils
- seriated sizes of chairs
- several sizes of blankets
- several pairs of mittens
- clothesline and clothespins
- big cooking pot with lid
- measuring cups
- plastic birthday cake
- cake decorating utensils

Blocks

- planks
- hollow blocks
- box of Easter grass
- cardboard brick blocks
- two large boxes for house construction
- mother and baby farm animals
- fishing poles
- Lincoln logs

Art

- Easter grass
- straw
- toothpicks
- craft sticks
- corrugated cardboard
- pre-cut mitten shapes
- dried corn (including Indian corn)
- wood scraps of assorted shapes and sizes

Manipulatives

- collections of plastic farm animals in several sizes

Writing

- blank paper books in three sizes
- pig, cat and bear hole punches
- animal stamps and stamp pads

Discovery

- materials for growing several varieties of grass
- straw
- sticks
- bricks
- several pieces of log

Library

- flannel board
- flannel board figures for the Three Billy Goats Gruff, the Three Bears, the Three Little Pigs and the Three Little Kittens
- tape recorder
- a teddy bear
- pig, cat and goat puppets

Snacks

- goats' milk
- goat cheese and crackers
- "grass" (select a variety of greens from the produce section of your grocery store)
- porridge (oatmeal) with brown sugar
- toast and honey
- jam with biscuits
- pigs-in-a-blanket (hot dogs cooked in biscuit dough)
- cornbread
- corn chowder
- corn meal mush
- tuna and crackers
- berries and whipped cream
- Soup—Goat Style (see activity in Discovery section)
- Bubbling Berries (see activity in Discovery section)
- Three Bears Porridge (see activity in Discovery section)

Discovery Activities

Just Like the Pigs

Materials

- dirt
- water
- a large tub
- measuring and mixing tools
- smocks to cover clothing

What to do

1. Discuss what children think pigs like to do. Most of them will say, "play in the mud."
2. Have the above materials available in the discovery center and allow a limited number of children at one time to "play in the mud." Helpful hint: Limit the amount of water available.

Soup—Goat Style

3+

Materials

- *Gregory the Terrible Eater* by Mitchell Sharmat
- note to parents about bringing a vegetable
- large cooking pot
- stove or hot plate
- table knives
- vegetable peelers
- cutting boards
- bouillon cubes for broth
- paper
- marker

What to do

1. Send the note home to parents several days in advance, asking each child to bring a vegetable to school.
2. Read *Gregory, the Terrible Eater* to the children.
3. Discuss the project with the children.
4. Start the pot with a small amount of water warming and two or three bouillon cubes. Supervise closely.
5. Help the children add their ingredients as they arrive.
6. As each child puts his vegetable in, write that vegetable down as part of the recipe for "Soup—Goat Style."
7. Let the soup simmer during choice time and serve for snack.
8. Talk about all the good things to eat in the soup.

Just Visiting

Materials

- live kittens

What to do

1. Find someone whose cat has recently had kittens and ask her to bring them to school.
2. Allow the children to gently pet the kittens to feel how soft they are.
3. Have the children observe the size and actions of the kittens.

More to do

- You may want to jot down some of the observations the children make while the kittens are at school.

Three Bears Porridge

Materials

- oatmeal
- electric pot
- water
- salt
- measuring cups
- spoons
- bowls
- honey or brown sugar
- timer
- paper
- marker
- laminating film or clear contact paper

What to do

1. Draw the recipe using pictures, following the directions on the oatmeal box. Laminate or cover with contact paper if possible.
2. Make this activity available during choice time for those children who are interested in cooking.
3. Follow the directions and allow each child a chance to stir. Caution: The cooking pot will need close supervision.
4. Serve for snack with honey or brown sugar.

More to do

• For variation add raisins, diced apples or nuts.

Which Is Stronger?

Materials

• straw
• craft sticks or small sticks collected outside
• a brick
• *The Three Little Pigs* told by Jean Claverie

What to do

1. Read *The Three Little Pigs* aloud to the children.
2. Put the materials on the table. Ask the children to take turns trying to blow them across the table. If they don't have enough air power to move the sticks, assist them.
3. Ask them, "Which one is the strongest? Which one would you rather build a house out of? Why?"

The Grass Is Greener

Materials

• potting soil
• several varieties of grass seed
• planting containers
• *The Three Billy Goats Gruff* retold by Paul Galdone
• water

What to do

1. Read *The Three Billy Goats Gruff* to the children.
2. Talk with the children about why the three Billy Goats Gruff wanted to cross the bridge.
3. Have the children fill the planting containers with potting soil, water them, and sprinkle grass seed on top.
4. Use a different container for each seed variety.
5. Place them in a windowsill and watch your grass grow. Is one variety greener than the others? Are they all about the same?

Bubbling Berries

Materials

- berries
- sugar
- fruit pectin
- electric pot
- colander for washing berries
- timer
- water
- paper
- marker
- measuring cups
- biscuits or toast

What to do

1. Draw the recipe for making jam on a large sheet of paper, following the directions on the pectin package.
2. Determine the quantity of berries you will need.
3. Supervise the children as they wash the berries.
4. Follow the recipe with them step by step while they measure ingredients.
5. Follow the cooking instructions on the recipe and let cool when finished. CAUTION: The cooking pot will need close supervision.
6. Serve the jam on biscuits or toast for snack.

Art Activities

Yarn Mosaic

Materials

- assortment of colored yarn pieces
- paper cut into the shape of a mitten
- glue or tape

What to do

1. Allow each child to choose the colors of yarn pieces she likes best.
2. The child can glue or tape her yarn pieces onto her mitten-shaped paper in any pattern or design she chooses.

Make a Wish

Materials

- paper
- pencils
- markers
- crayons

What to do

1. Ask the children to draw a picture of something they might wish for if they had three wishes.
2. They may draw one thing or all three things they would wish for if they had three wishes.

More to do

- Make the drawings into a Wish Book by adding a cover and binding. Make it available in the classroom library.

Picture Me Ugly!

4+

Materials

- *The Three Billy Goats Gruff* retold by Paul Galdone
- large paper plates with two large eyeholes cut out, one per child
- glue or tape
- stapler
- collage material, such as yarn, feathers, Easter grass, tin foil, styrofoam pieces, short cardboard tubes, corrugated card board, colored tissue paper, construction paper scraps, wallpaper scraps, pieces of wrapping paper.

What to do

1. Read *The Three Billy Goats Gruff* to the children and talk about the physical characteristics of the troll.
2. Allow each child to choose the collage materials he wants for his troll mask.
3. Let each child glue or tape the materials to his mask.

More to do

- Act out the story of the Three Billy Goats Gruff and let each child take a turn being the troll and using his troll mask.

Corn Mosaic

Materials

- ears of dried field corn, Indian corn, popcorn
- glue
- heavy paper
- large bowl or tub

What to do

1. Allow the children to remove the corn from the cob over the bowl or tub.
2. Let them pick out kernels of corn to glue in a pattern, shape or design on her paper. Supervise closely.

Mitten Lace

Materials

- cardboard, one piece per child
- hole punch
- yarn
- tape

What to do

1. Cut cardboard into large mitten shapes.
2. Punch holes around the edge of the mitten shape about an inch from the edge.
3. Cut the yarn into 18" lengths, taping one end of each length to facilitate "sewing."
4. Tie the untapped yarn ends through one of the holes on each piece of cardboard.
5. Each child can sew in and out of the holes with his length of yarn.

Let's Make Plans

Materials

- blueprints of a home
- paper
- crayons
- markers
- pencils
- rulers

What to do

1. Show the children the set of blueprints and explain that they are the plan a builder uses when she is building a house.
2. Ask the children to draw a "blueprint" of their homes or their rooms.
3. Leave the blueprints out so they can see how rooms are drawn.

Music and Movement Activities

Pigs in Hiding

Materials

- little plastic pigs
- *Pigs in Hiding* by Arlene Dubanevich

What to do

1. Hide the small plastic pigs throughout the classroom.
2. Read *Pigs in Hiding* to the class.
3. Have the children hunt for the hidden pigs.

Mouse, Mouse, Cat!

3+

What to do:

1. Have the children sit in a circle.
2. One child walks around the outside of the circle touching each head as she says, "Mouse, mouse, mouse, mouse," until she comes to the person she wants to be "it" and she says, "Cat!"
3. The person whose head she touches when she says "Cat!" gets up and races around the circle after her.
4. The child who was "it" races around to the space vacated by the child she tagged. (This is a variation of the game, "Duck, Duck, Goose.")

Hide the Mitten

3+

Materials

- one bright-colored pair of mittens
- *The Three Little Kittens* retold by Paul Galdone

What to do

1. Let the children know the previous day that when they come in the next day, one of the mittens will be hidden somewhere in the classroom.
2. Have your assistant hide one mitten from the pair each morning while the children are listening to you reading *The Three Little Kittens*.
3. Lay the unhidden mitten out in plain sight as a reminder to hunt for the other one.

Bear Hunt

3+

Materials

- bear footprints cut from construction paper
- tape

What to do

1. Mark the path of the hunt by taping sets of bear footprints to the floor.
2. Decide what will be at the end of your destination. It could be a snack, a special treat, the story for the day, or a bear hunter's badge held by a teddy bear.
3. As a group, follow the footprints. Talk about the direction they go.
4. Have the children predict where they'll end, and what size and kind of bear they'll find.

Math Activities

Mitten Safari

3+

Materials

- real mittens or mitten pairs cut from wallpaper sample books, one pair per child

What to do

1. Hide one mitten of each pair in the classroom.
2. Distribute the leftover mittens to the children and instruct them to find the lost mitten.
3. Remind the children not to pick up a mitten that does not match theirs.

Calendar

Materials

- plain calendar paper and markers

What to do

1. Make or purchase a plain calendar with only the days of the week marked on it.
2. Each month, make different paper patterns to fit your theme. For example: for the "3's Weeks" theme you may want to use three mittens in different sizes, or three different colors of mittens.
3. The days of the week may be sung to the tune of "Frere Jacques." "Sunday, Monday, Tuesday, Wednesday, Thursday, Friday, Saturday. It's not Sunday, it's not Monday, it's not Tuesday, it is. . ." (Let the children fill in the blank of whatever day of the week it is.)
4. School Days Countdown—make an ongoing number line for the number of days the children have been at school. Follow the same pattern as your monthly calendar pattern.

Mitten Match

Materials

- a basket
- one pair of mittens or gloves from each child

What to do

1. Put all the mittens and gloves together in a basket and mix them up.
2. Have each child find her own pair of mittens or gloves.

More to do

- Make ten pairs of mittens out of wrapping paper or wallpaper scraps. Laminate or cover with contact paper one of each pair onto the inside of a file folder. Laminate or cover with contact paper the other mitten of each pair and place them in an envelope attached to the front of the file folder. The object of the game is to match the mittens in the envelope to the corresponding mitten inside the folder.

Tally the Goats and Cows

Materials

- goat's milk
- cow's milk
- small cups
- stickers
- tally chart

What to do

1. Prepare a tally chart with two columns. Put a picture of a goat over one column and a picture of a cow over the other.
2. At snack time, serve a small portion of goat's milk and cow's milk to each child.
3. Ask the children to taste each one and vote for the one they prefer by putting a sticker under the picture of the animal whose milk they liked the best.
4. Count after everyone has voted.

Size Sort

Materials

- three baskets (small, medium and large)
- three sizes of ten to twelve different items such as pencils, balls, blocks and crayons

What to do

1. Put the baskets on the table. Sort one set of objects with the children to give them an idea of how to sort.
2. Ask the children to sort the remaining items.

Small, Medium, Large, Mmmmm!

Materials

- several rolls of prepared cookie dough
- an oven
- rolling pin
- flour
- cookie sheets
- three sizes of the same shape of cookie cutter

What to do

1. Have the children roll out a portion of the dough. Allow each child to cut one small, one medium, and one large cookie.
2. Bake them and serve them for snack. Discuss the size differences while you eat.
3. Count how many bites it takes to eat each size.

Guessing Box

4+

Materials

- box or paper bag
- mittens
- box of oatmeal
- small, medium and large bowl
- straw
- sticks
- a brick

What to do

1. Show a "3's Weeks" item such as a brick to the children and talk about its properties, such as its shape, color, size, uses.
2. Bring out the guessing box with another "3's Weeks" item in it. Use the same box each time, no matter what size the item is. Storage boxes for clothing are the ideal size.
3. Say:

   "There is something in my guessing box.

   Would you like to guess?

   First you ask a question and

   I'll answer no or yes."

4. Children then ask questions. Encourage them to phrase their responses in the form of a question. "Is it . . ."
5. After a brief time, if you notice they aren't asking questions that pertain to the item in the box, give broad hints.

   "It's something small." Wait for guesses.

   "It's something warm." Wait for guesses.

   "It's something red." Wait.

   "It's something you wear on your hands." Wait for guesses.

   ("Yes! It's a mitten!")

More to do

- If you choose bowls. . .

   estimate their number,

   sort and classify them by color,

   count the number of each size, and then

   turn them upside down and use them as drums!

Language Activities

Act It Out!

Materials

- straw
- sticks
- two large cardboard boxes
- cardboard brick blocks
- headbands with pink ears attached
- plastic pig noses
- step stool
- *The Three Little Pigs* retold by Jean Claverie

What to do

1. Read *The Three Little Pigs* to the children.
2. Talk to the children about acting out the story of the three little pigs.
3. Choose three volunteers to be the pigs and one to be the wolf.
4. Place the headbands and noses on three children who volunteer to be the pigs.
5. The first pig begins to place some straw on top of his cardboard box like he is building his house.
6. The second pig begins to place some sticks on top of his cardboard box like he is building his house.
7. The third pig uses the cardboard brick blocks to begin building his house.
8. Along comes the big bad wolf volunteer. He huffs and puffs and pretends to blow down the first pig's house. The first pig runs to the second pig's house.
9. Mr. Wolf does the same thing to the second pig's stick house. Both pigs run to the third pig's brick house.
10. The wolf huffs and puffs but he cannot blow the brick house down.
11. The wolf uses the step stool to pretend he is climbing up the roof of the brick house and jumps down off of it into the boiling pot. The wolf then jumps up and runs away.
12. Act this out several times because most of the children will want a chance to be in the play.

Troll-n-Tell

Materials

- paper
- markers
- crayons
- watercolors
- colored chalk
- *The Three Billy Goats Gruff* retold by Paul Galdone

What to do

1. Read *The Three Billy Goats Gruff* to the children several times.
2. Have the children draw or paint the scariest or ugliest troll they can imagine.

Corny Recipes

Materials

- note to parents
- copier
- pencils
- crayons
- markers
- stapler

What to do

1. Send a note home to parents asking them to send in the recipe for their favorite way to fix corn.
2. Have the children illustrate the recipes they bring in. Make copies and staple them into a book for each child to take home.

Bear Drama

Materials

- three sizes of chairs, bowls, and blankets
- a table
- bear costumes (optional—instead of costumes you may use a baby hat, a women's hat, and a men's hat to represent baby, mama, and papa bear)
- *Goldilocks and the Three Bears* retold by Jan Brett

What to do

1. Read *Goldilocks and the Three Bears* to the children.
2. Ask for volunteers to play Goldilocks and the three bears, and dress them accordingly.
3. Place the three bowls on the table, the three chairs next to the table, and the blankets, representing the beds, a short distance away from the chairs.
4. Direct and narrate the story as the children act it out.
5. Act the story out several times because most of the children will want to be a bear or Goldilocks.
6. Leave the props and costumes out in pretend play center the next day for the children to use on their own.

And Then What Happened?

Materials

- paper
- markers
- *The Three Billy Goats Gruff* retold by Paul Galdone

What to do

1. Read *The Three Billy Goats Gruff* to the children.
2. Ask the children what they think happened to the troll after the Great Big Billy Goat Gruff knocked him off the bridge.
3. Have the children draw a picture or dictate a story about their idea of what happened to the troll.

More to do

- This could be bound and made into a class book.

Goat Stew Recipes

Materials

- *Gregory the Terrible Eater* by Mitchell Sharmat
- paper
- crayons
- markers
- pencils

What to do

1. Read *Gregory the Terrible Eater* to the children.
2. Have the children name some of the things Gregory ate in the story.
3. Let them dictate things to put in a stew or soup for Gregory to eat.
4. Have the children draw the item they want to add to the recipe.

More to do

- If each child draws an item for the stew, you could make this into a class book.

Let's Compare!

Materials

- chart
- stickers
- *Goldilocks and the Three Bears* retold by Jan Brett; *The Three Little Pigs*, retold by Jean Claverie; *The Three Little Kittens* by Paul Galdone and *The Three Billy Goats Gruff* retold by Paul Galdone
- pictures of a bear, pig, kitten, and goat

What to do

1. Prepare a chart with four columns, one for each story. Place a picture of a bear over one column, a pig over the next column, a kitten over the third, and a goat over the last; or photocopy the covers of the books and place them at the top of each column.
2. Ask the children to recall what happened in each story.
3. Have each child choose the story she liked best and place a sticker in the column representing that story.

Transition Ideas

- Walk like a bear.
- Walk like the baby Billy Goat Gruff.
- Walk like a great big Billy Goat Gruff.
- Walk like a cat.
- Be a pig and roll around in the mud.
- Count, "one, two , three, hop!" hop as you walk.
- If you have a mitten like this one, you may. . .
  (Pass out one of each pair first or have several mittens alike to speed things along.)
- If these are your mittens, you may get your coat.
- If you had hot cereal (porridge) for breakfast, you may. . .
- If you had cold cereal for breakfast, you may. . .
- If you have a cat at home, you may. . .
- If you have a teddy bear at home, you may. . .

Theme Extensions and Variations

Field Trips

- Visit a farm that has goats.
- Take a walk in the woods like Goldilocks did.
- Go berry picking or go to the grocery store to pick out berries.
- Visit a cave.
- Visit a pig farm.
- Visit a home construction site.

Extensions for older children

- Construct a bridge out of wood scraps.
- Construct a cave out of a large box and mud.
- Make bear costumes, wolf costume, troll costume.

Bibliography

- *Goldilocks and the Three Bears*, retold by Jan Brett. NY: Putnam Publishing Group, 1987. Lost in the woods, a tired and hungry girl finds the house of the three bears where she helps herself to food and falls asleep.
- *Gregory the Terrible Eater*, Mitchell Sharmat. NY: Macmillan Publishing Company, 1980. A very picky eater, Gregory the goat refuses to eat the usual goat diet of shoes and tin cans in favor of fruits, vegetables, eggs and orange juice.
- *Lost*, David McPhail. NY: Little, Brown & Co., 1990. A story of how a little boy helps a big bear find his way back home and how the bear reciprocates.
- *Magic Fish*, retold by Freya Littledale. NY: Scholastic, Inc., 1986. Traditional tale of a magic fish who grants a fisherman wishes until his wife gets too greedy.
- *Mystery of the Missing Red Mitten*, Steven Kellogg. NY: Dial Books, 1974. A young girl out for a day's adventure in the snow loses her red mitten, but finds it as her snowman's heart when the snow begins to melt.
- *Pigs in Hiding*, Arlene Dubanevich. NY: Macmillan, 1983. A pig hide and seek game. The "it" pig cleverly puts out a tray of food when he is unsuccessful in finding the hiding pigs.
- *Three Billy Goats Gruff, The*, retold by Paul Galdone. NY: Houghton Mifflin Co., 1979. The traditional version of the fairy tale in which three goats outwit a mean troll.
- *Three Little Ducks*, June Melser and Joy Cowley. San Diego: The Wright Group, 1980 (NIP). A mother duck teaches her three little ducks how to paddle, waddle, snuggle, hide and fly.
- *Three Little Kittens*, Paul Galdone. NY: Clarion Books, Houghton Mifflin Co., 1988. Three little kittens lose, find, soil and wash their mittens.
- *Three Little Pigs, The*, Jean Claverie. NY: North-South Books, 1989. The adventures of three little pigs who leave home to seek their fortunes and their encounters with the big bad wolf.
- *Three Wishes, The*, Charles Perrault. Mahwah, NJ: Troll Associates, 1979. A woodsman encounters a tree fairy who grants him 3 wishes which get foolishly used in an argument with his nagging wife.

Recordings

- "Eight Piggies in a Row," *Everything Grows*. Raffi, Troubador Records, 1987.
- "The Three Little Pig's Blues," *Playing Favorites*. Greg and Steve, Youngheart Records, 1991.
- "Across the Bridge," *We All Live Together*. Greg and Steve, Youngheart Records, 1980.

Mondays	_Read Peter's Pockets_ Do Count Your Pockets Pita Bread for Snack	_Read Benny Bakes a Cake_ Do Liquid Gold Butter and crackers for Snack		
Tuesdays	Read A Pocket for Corduroy Do Painted Dust Tacos for Snack	_Read Marcel the Pastry Chef_ Do Guess Who I Am # 1		
Wednesdays	Read There's a Wocket in my Pocket! Do Something in My Pocket	_Read Thunder Cake_ Do It Says Me		
Thursdays	_Read Pancakes for Breakfast_ Do Flip It for Snack	Do Me, a Builder! Read Block City Do Be Our Guest with a builder Do Shave It off		
Fridays	Read Tony's Bread Field trip to a Bakery	Read Big Red Barn Do Guess Who I Am # 2		

Theme Objectives

- To explore how pockets are used by children and the larger society

Learning Centers

Dramatic Play

- a mailbox
- muffin tin
- egg beater
- mixing bowls
- cake pans
- bread pans
- spatula
- empty cake mix boxes
- empty muffin mix boxes
- empty pancake mix boxes
- measuring cups
- measuring spoons
- cake decorating utensils
- a pretend birthday cake
- hot pads
- skillet
- recipe book
- food magazines

Blocks

- tractors
- plows
- discs
- harvesters
- planters
- mail delivery truck
- pickup trucks
- sawhorses

Mini-Units

- planks
- hollow blocks
- cardboard brick blocks
- materials for making signs

Discovery

- planting containers and planting materials
- a variety of seeds
- field corn on the cob
- stalks of wheat
- incubator
- pictures of hatching chick
- pictures of germinating seed
- yeast growing in a cup

Work Bench

(limit number of children and supervise closely)

- wood
- hammer
- nails
- screws
- screwdriver
- Phillips screwdriver
- saw
- hacksaw
- clamps
- plane
- pliers
- ruler and measuring tape
- T-square
- level
- tool box or peg board for storing tools
- safety glasses
- child-sized work gloves
- sandpaper

Library

- flannel board with barn and farm animals
- farm animal puppets
- seed catalogs
- cookbooks

Writing

- envelopes
- postal stamps and stamp pad
- canceled stamps
- junk mail stamps
- pocket-shaped paper
- egg-shaped paper
- blueprints
- graph paper
- rulers
- protractors
- triangle and circle stencils
- slotted box for sorting
- bread-shaped paper
- barn-shaped paper
- recipe cards

Art

- feathers
- felt
- seeds
- grain
- fabric scraps to make pockets
- cooking utensils for printing
- wood scraps for gluing and painting

Mini-Units

Snacks

- pocket pita bread with filling
- tacos
- Liquid Gold (see activity in Discovery section)
- It Says Me (see activity in Discovery section)
- Flip It (see activity in Discovery section)

Discovery Activities

Liquid Gold

3+

Materials

- cream
- salt
- four small jars with tight lids (baby food jars are good)

What to do

1. Since this theme involves pockets like in a cook's apron, try to do a lot of cooking during this theme.
2. Place about 1/4 cup of cream into four jars.
3. Make sure lids are tightly secured.
4. Let four children start shaking the jars. Explain to them that if you shake the cream long enough it will turn to butter.
5. After a few minutes, let four other children take a turn shaking the jars.
6. When a child feels a lump bumping around in his jar, he knows his butter is ready.
7. Open the lid and pour off the excess liquid. Salt lightly.
8. Use for snack on crackers, biscuits or homemade bread.

Guess Who I Am #1

3+

Materials

- chef's hat
- chef's apron
- four to six utensils used in baking such as a pastry cutter, wire whisk, wooden spoon, spatula and vegetable peeler

What to do

1. Put on the hat and apron with utensils.
2. At group time, have the children guess who you are dressed up to be. Show them the utensils in the cook's pockets and have them guess what they are used for in cooking.
3. Give clues if necessary.

Guess Who I Am #2

3+

Materials

- blue work shirt
- coveralls
- seed company hat
- boots
- bandanna handkerchief
- four to six item for farmer's pockets such as keys, rope, pliers and seed packets

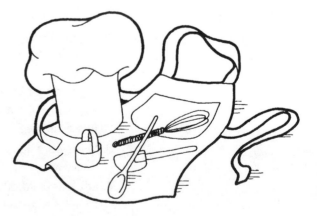

What to do

1. Put on farmer's clothes.
2. At group time, have the children try to guess who you are dressed up to be. Show them each tool in the farmer's pockets and let them decide what he uses each tool for.
3. Give clues if necessary.

Mini-Units

Guess Who I Am #3

Materials

- blue jeans
- blue work shirt
- boots
- carpenter's apron
- four to six items in the carpenter's pockets such as a hammer, nails, plane, screwdriver and level
- hard hat

What to do

1. Dress as a carpenter.
2. Have the children try to guess who you are dressed to be. Show them each tool in the carpenter's pockets and explain what each one does, or let them guess.
3. Give hints if necessary.

Something in My Pocket

Materials

- a note to parents
- anything that will fit in a pocket

What to do

1. Send a note home two or three days ahead of time asking parents to have their child choose something to bring to school for show and tell in his pocket. It can be anything, as long as it fits in her pocket.
2. At group time have each child show and tell about what she brought in her pocket.

Be Our Guest

| 3+ |

Materials

- community contacts

What to do

1. If possible, make arrangements for a farmer, a mail carrier, cook or baker and a carpenter to visit your classroom on different days. Ask them to come dressed as if they were going to work, and to bring with them some "tools of their trade."
2. At group time, have your guest speaker talk to the children about what he or she does at his or her job. Let the children guess at some of the things the guest might have in his or her pockets.

Shave It Off

| 4+ |

Materials

- wood plane
- wood
- work bench
- safety goggles

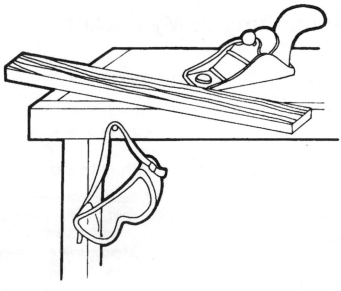

What to do

1. Let the children experience using a wood plane on wood at the work bench. Show them the wood shavings that fall off when they plane the wood.

CAUTION: Supervise this activity closely.

Me, a Builder!

Materials

- wood scraps
- work bench
- hammers
- nails
- safety goggles

What to do

1. Let the children experiment by nailing wood scraps together at the work bench.
2. Save and display some of their creations. CAUTION: Supervise closely.

It Says Me

Materials

- frozen bread dough, thawed
- prepared cookie sheets
- foil
- oven

What to do

1. Give each child a small amount of bread dough on a piece of foil.
2. Let each child roll the dough between her hands to form a long snake-like piece.
3. Help each child form her initial with her piece of bread dough.
4. Let the dough rise and then bake, let cool, and eat at snack time with some home-made butter.

Flip It

Materials

- pancake recipe
- recipe ingredients

- measuring spoons
- water
- small paper cups
- electric skillet
- spatula
- syrup
- margarine
- paper plates
- knives
- forks

What to do

1. Draw the recipe on a card, and display it on the worktable with the pancake materials.
2. Let each child follow the recipe for mixing pancakes in his cup.
3. By looking at the pictures, he should know how many spoonfuls of pancake mix to use and how many spoonfuls of water.
4. When he has stirred his mix up, assist him in pouring it on the electric skillet.
5. Let each child flip his pancake over when it is ready.
6. Most children enjoy this cooking a great deal and can do it with some supervision.

Art Activities

Print It

3+

Materials

- kitchen utensils with unique shapes: whisks, apple slicer, forks, spatulas, slotted spoon, potato masher
- paint
- paper
- styrofoam trays

What to do

1. Let the child choose a utensil to dip in a small amount of paint on a styrofoam tray.
2. Let the child print with the utensil on her piece of paper.
3. Let each child use several different utensils with several different colors of paint.

Painted Dust

Materials

- tempera paint
- paintbrushes
- small containers
- sawdust
- paper

What to do

1. Pour several different colors of tempera paint into the small containers. Add sawdust to each container of paint to give it texture.
2. Let each child paint with the textured paint.
3. Ask the children to guess what is in the paint. Give clues if necessary.
4. Let the paintings dry.

Stamps Galore

Materials

- canceled stamps
- junk mail stamps
- paper
- glue

What to do

1. Ask parents to send in canceled stamps.
2. Let each child make a stamp collage using the canceled stamps and the junk mail stamps. Encourage creativity.

Math Activities

Calendar

Materials

- plain calendar or paper and markers

What to do

1. Make or purchase a plain calendar with only the days of the week marked on it.
2. Each month, make different paper patterns to fit your theme. For example: for the "pockets" theme you may want to use red, blue and yellow pockets, or three different-sized pockets. (See the illustration for calendar patterns.)
3. The days of the week may be sung to the tune of "Frere Jacques." "Sunday, Monday, Tuesday, Wednesday, Thursday, Friday, Saturday. It's not Sunday, it's not Monday, it's not Tuesday, it is. . . " (Let the children fill in the blank for whatever day of the week it is.)
4. School Days Countdown—make an ongoing number line for the number of days the children have been at school. Follow the same pattern as your monthly calendar pattern.

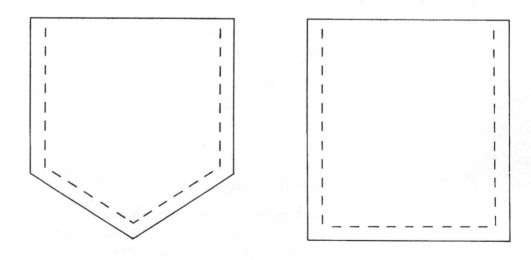

Count Your Pockets

Materials

- posterboard
- stickers

What to do

1. Draw a graph on the poster-board. Have a column for each child with his name at the top.
2. Let each child come up and count how many pockets he has in his clothing that day.
3. For each pocket he has, let him put a sticker in a square under his name. If he has three pockets, he puts three stickers in the three squares going down from his name.

Annie	David	Mark	Gina	Amy
☆	☺		♡	
☆	☺		♡	
	☺		♡	
			♡	

4. Who had the most pockets? Who had the least? Did anyone have the same amount?

Guessing Box

Materials

- box or paper bag
- aprons
- shirt with a pocket
- stuffed kangaroo doll
- pita pocket bread

What to do

1. Show a "Pockets" item such as an apron or a shirt to the children and talk about its properties such as its shape, color, size and uses.
2. Bring out the guessing box with another pocket item in it. Use the same box each time, no matter what size the item is. Storage boxes for clothing are the ideal size.

3. Say:

> "There is something in my guessing box.
>
> Would you like to guess?
>
> First you ask a question and
>
> I'll answer no or yes."

4. Children then ask questions. Encourage them to ask in the form of a question. "Is it. . . ?"

5. After a brief time, if you notice they aren't asking questions that pertain to the item in the box, give broad hints.

> "It's something big." Wait for guesses.
>
> "It's something soft." Wait for guesses.
>
> "It's something a cook uses." Wait.
>
> "It's something you wear." Wait for guesses.
>
> ("Yes, it's an apron!")

Language Activities

Exactly Right

Materials

- *Benny Bakes a Cake by Eve Rice*
- paper
- markers
- crayons

What to do

1. Read *Benny Bakes a Cake* to the children.
2. Ask the children to draw a picture of their birthday cake. How would they like their birthday cakes to look?
3. Take dictation if needed.

More to do

- These drawings could be bound into a class book.

What's a Wocket?

Materials

- *There's a Wocket in My Pocket!* by Dr. Seuss
- paper
- markers
- crayons

What to do

1. Tape a small piece of paper over the picture of the wocket on the cover of the book.
2. Read *There's a Wocket in My Pocket!* to the children.
3. Ask the children to draw what they think a wocket looks like.
4. When they are finished drawing, remove the paper from the front of the book so that they can see what Dr. Seuss thought a wocket looked like.

Transition Ideas

- If you have one pocket, you may. . .
    (continue with two pockets, three pockets or four pockets)
- If you have a mailbox on your house. . .
- If you have mailbox by your driveway. . .
- Walk like a duck to. . .
- Gallop like a horse to. . .
- Flap like a chicken to. . .
- Walk like a tired cow to. . .

Theme Extensions and Variations

- Visit a bakery.
- Visit a home construction site and have the builder give the children a tour.
- Visit the post office.
- Visit a farm. Ask the farmer to give the children a tour of the farm animals, barn and some farm machinery.

Bibliography

- *Benny Bakes a Cake*, Eve Rice. NY: William Morrow & Co.

- *Big Red Barn*, Margaret Wise Brown. NY: HarperCollins Books, 1989. Rhymed text and illustration introduces the many different animals that live in the big red barn.

- *Block City* Robert Louis Stevenson. NY: E.P. Dutton, 1988. A child creates a world of his own which has mountains and a sea, a city and ships, all from toy blocks.

- *Marcel the Pastry Chef*, Marianna Mayer. NY: Little Rooster, Bantam Books, 1991. A dishwasher practices pastry making in the palace kitchen each night as the rest of the world sleeps. Then one night the king discovers one of his delicious cream puffs. Confusion and justice follow.

- *Pancakes for Breakfast*, Tomie dePaola. NY: Harcourt Brace Janovich, Inc., 1978. A little old lady's attempts to have pancakes for breakfast are hindered by a scarcity of supplies and the participation of her pets.

- *Peter's Pockets*, Eve Rice. NY: Greenwillow Books, 1989. Peter's new pants don't have any pockets, so Uncle Nick lets Peter use his until Peter's mother solves the problem in a clever and colorful way.

- *Pocket for Corduroy, A*, Don Freeman. NY: Viking Children's Books, 1978. Corduroy, the bear, gets separated from Lisa and finds that a pocket would be a useful thing to have.

- *There's a Wocket in My Pocket!*, Dr. Seuss. NY: Random House, 1974. A young boy gives the reader a tour of his house which has strange creatures inhabiting every corner. Written in Dr. Seuss's classic rhythmic text.

- *Tony's Bread*, Tomie dePaola. NY: Putnam Publishing Group, 1989. A baker loses his daughter but gains a bakery in the grand city of Milano after meeting a determined nobleman and baking a unique loaf of bread.

- *Thunder Cake*, Patricia Polacco. NY: Putnam Publishing Group, 1990. Grandma finds a way to dispel her grandchild's fear of thunderstorms.

Recordings

- "Biscuits in the Oven," and "Oats and Beans and Barley," *Baby Beluga*. Raffi, (Shoreline Records) Troubadour Records, 1977.

- "Barnyard Talk," and "Happiness Cake," *Happiness Cake*. Linda Arnold, Ariel Records, 1988.

- "In My Garden," and "Down on Grandpa's Farm," *One Light One Sun*. Raffi, (Shoreline Records) Troubadour Records, 1985.

Mini-Units

Mondays	Read *Truck* Field trip to a tire store Carrot wheels for Snack	Read *Bigmama's* Do Guessing Box		
Tuesdays	Read *Truck Song* Do Tire Rubbing	Read *School Bus* Do Making Circles Round cereal and milk for Snack		
Wednesdays	Read *Trucks* Do Truckload Pancakes and syrup for Snack	Read *Wheels* Do Find the Wheel "Edible Wheel" or pizza for Snack		
Thursdays	Read *Wheels on the Bus* Do Wheel Tally Sing Wheels on the Bus	Field trip to a car dealership Orange slices and round crackers for Snack		
Fridays	Read *Carousel* Visit a carousel or Ferris wheel car | van | truck | bike Wheel pasta and butter and cheese - Snack	Read *Wheel Away!* Do Wheels on a String Do Rounds of Paint		

Theme Objectives

- To discover the functions of wheels and how wheels are used in our environment

Learning Centers

Dramatic Play

- pizza pans
- pizza cutter
- small clock
- wheel pasta

Writing

- round and car-shaped paper
- car-shaped hole punch
- tire advertisements

Blocks

- pickup trucks
- fire truck
- ambulance
- school bus
- police car
- construction vehicles: crane, bulldozer, road grader
- train and tracks
- barn and farm vehicles

Manipulatives

- small cars
- interlocking plastic miniblocks with lots of wheel pieces
- garage
- fire station

Library

- car magazines

Discovery

- pieces of tires with different treads
- tire casts
- collection of wheel tools and utensils
- clock with gears
- a system of small pulleys

Snacks

- wheel pasta
- pinwheel cookies
- round crackers
- pizza
- round cereal
- carrot coins
- orange slices (cut across the orange)
- pancakes
- An Edible Wheel (see activity in Discovery section)

Discovery Activities

Find the Wheel

Materials

- an assortment of tools and kitchen utensils which use wheels in some way, such as wrenches, pizza cutters, and small pulleys

What to do

1. Put the tools and utensils on a tray and allow the children to explore and experiment with them.
2. Ask the children to pick one tool and point out its wheel.

An Edible Wheel

4+

Materials

- canned biscuits, one biscuit per child
- pizza sauce
- shredded cheese
- cookie sheet
- spoons
- oven

What to do

1. Have each child flatten a biscuit and spoon on pizza sauce.
2. Have the child spread the sauce around on his biscuit and sprinkle a little cheese on top.
3. Place them on a cookie sheet, bake them and serve for snack.

Tire Rubbings

4+

Materials

- paper
- chalk or crayons

What to do

1. Peel the paper off of the crayons.
2. Take the children out to the school parking lot.
3. Show them how to place a paper on a tire and rub the crayon or chalk over the paper to get a print of the tire tread.

CAUTION: Supervise children closely.

More to do

- Visit a tire store or garage that sells tires and get some prints from different types of tires.

Art Activities

Wheels on a String

Materials

- buttons
- spools
- plastic or metal washers
- yarn
- scissors
- tape

What to do

1. Cut an 18" piece of yarn for each child and wrap tape around one end.
2. Have each child string wheels on his piece of yarn.
3. After it is completed, the "Wheels on a String" can be a necklace!

Rounds of Paint

Materials

- round items, such as spools, lids, round beads and cups
- paper
- paint
- styrofoam trays

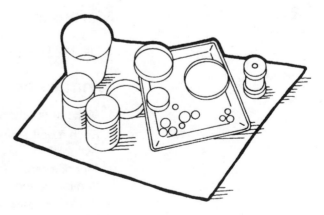

What to do

1. Pour a small amount of each color of paint onto several trays.
2. Let each child dip the round objects into the paint and print with them on her paper.
3. Overlap the circles to make it look like a page full of wheels.

Making Circles

Materials

- paper plate
- scissors
- markers
- record player

What to do

1. Cut the paper to fit on the record player.
2. Each child can place his paper on the record player. (You may have to help push it down in the center to make a hole.)
3. Have the child hold a marker in one spot and turn on the record player. He will draw a perfect circle!
4. Give the child a different-colored marker and have him hold it in a different spot. He will get a smaller or larger circle than the first one, depending on where he holds the marker.

Math Activities

Calendar

3+

Materials

- plain calendar or paper and markers

What to do

1. Make or purchase a plain calendar with only the days of the week marked on it.
2. Each month, make different paper patterns to fit your theme. For example: for the "wheels" theme you may want to use a car wheel and a bicycle wheel; three or four different colors of wheel or small, medium, or large wheels. (See the illustration for calendar patterns.)
3. The days of the week may be sung to the tune of "Frere Jacques." "Sunday, Monday, Tuesday, Wednesday, Thursday, Friday, Saturday. It's not Sunday, it's not Monday, it's not Tuesday, it is. . . " (Let the children fill in the blank for whatever day of the week it is.)

4. School Days Countdown—make an ongoing number line for the number of days the children have been at school. Follow the same pattern as your monthly calendar pattern.

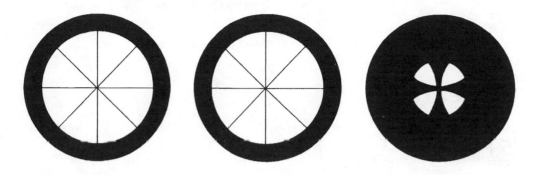

Guessing Box

Materials

- box or paper bag
- steering wheel
- flywheel
- tricycle wheel

What to do

1. Show a "wheel" item such as a steering wheel to the children and talk about its properties such as its shape, color, size and uses.
2. Bring out the guessing box with another "wheel" item in it. Use the same box each time, no matter what size the item is. Storage boxes for clothing are the ideal size.
3. Say:

   "There is something in my guessing box.

   Would you like to guess?

   First you ask a question and

   I'll answer no or yes."
4. Children then ask questions. Encourage them to ask in the form of a question. "Is it. . . ?"

5. After a brief time, if you notice they aren't asking questions that pertain to the item in the box, give broad hints.

> "It's something small." Wait for guesses.
>
> "It's something round." Wait for guesses.
>
> "It's something rubber." Wait.
>
> "It's something that rolls." Wait for guesses.
>
> ("Yes, it's a wheel!")

Wheel Tally

Materials

- paper
- pencils

What to do

1. Make a large tally sheet with four columns, labeled car, van, truck and bicycle. (Include motorcycles with bicycles since they have the same number of wheels.)
2. Go outside and sit as a group on a corner, well back from the street.
3. Tell the children to count how many cars, vans, trucks, and bicycles they see going down the street.
4. Tally each one as they call them out.
5. Limit your time outside to ten to fifteen minutes, then go back inside and count how many of each type of vehicle you saw.
6. Talk about how many wheels each vehicle has.

car	van	truck	cycle

Language Activities

Truckload

Materials

- paper
- markers or crayons

What to do

1. Cut the paper in the shape of a semi-truck. Make sure there is one sheet for each child.
2. Ask each child to draw what he thinks the truck is hauling or delivering.
3. Make into a class book and place in the classroom library.

Transition Ideas

- Pretend you're balancing on a unicycle to. . .
- Pretend you're driving a truck to. . .
- If your bike has three wheels, you may. . .
- If your bike has two wheels, you may. . .
- If you have a scooter, you may. . .
- If you have a wagon, you may. . .
- If you have a skate board, you may. . .
- If you have buttons on, you may. . .
- If you have snaps on, you may. . .

Theme Extensions and Variations

Field Trips

- Visit a car dealership.
- Visit a hardware store.
- Ride a carousel and/or a ferris wheel.
- Visit a fire station. Count the wheels.
- Take a bus ride.
- Visit a tire store.

Bibliography

- *Bigmama's*, Donald Crews. NY: Greenwillow Books, 1991. Visiting Big Mama's house in the country, young Donald Crews finds his relatives full of news and the old place and its surroundings just the same as the year before.

- *Carousel, Donald Crews. NY: Greenwillow Books, 1982. Brief text and illustrations recreate a ride on a merry-go-round.*

- *School Bus*, Donald Crews. NY: Greenwillow Books, 1984. Follows the progress of school buses as they take children to school and bring them home again.

- *Truck*, Donald Crews. NY: Greenwillow Books, 1980. A wordless picture book that follows the journey of a truck full of tricycles through a tunnel, through the night, through the rain, through a maze of highway interchanges and across a bridge to its destination.

- *Trucks*, Gail Gibbons. NY: HarperCollins, 1981. Pictures a variety of trucks that work around us every day.

- *Truck Song*, Diane Siebert. NY: HarperCollins, 1984. Rhymed text and illustrations describe the journey of a transcontinental truck.

- *Wheels*, Jane Resh Thomas. NY: Houghton Mifflin, 1986. Five-year-old Elliot learns that winning isn't everything when he begins to race with the big wheel he got for his birthday.

- *Wheel Away!* Dayle Ann Dodds. NY: HarperCollins, 1989. A bicycle wheel gets loose and rolls away. Many position words and phrases are used.

- *Wheels on the Bus, The*, Maryann Kovalski. Boston, MA: Little, Brown and Co., 1987. While a grandmother and grandchildren wait for the bus, they sing the title song with such gusto that they miss their bus.

Recordings

- "Morningtown Ride," *Baby Beluga*. Raffi, (Shoreline Records) Troubadour Records, Ltd., 1977.

- "Skateboard," *Deep in the Jungle*. Joe Scruggs, (Shadow Play Records & Video) Educational Graphics Press, Inc., 1987.

- "Wheels on the Bus," *Rise and Shine*. Raffi, (Shoreline Records) Troubadour Records, 1982.

Index

Materials Index

adhesive paper
Catch the Sun #1   262
Sticky Side Up   29
Stickers by Me   33

aluminum foil
Foiled Again   268
I See Stars   265
Teeny Tiny Town   88
Watercolor Impressions   290

balloons
Balloon Race   65
Disappearing Ball   229
100th Day   195
Sit On It   61
Static in Your Attic   28
The Enormous Turnip   94
Unbirthday Day   196

baking soda
Blow Your Top   56
Bubbling Raisins   124
Bubble Mountains   132

bandaids
Bandaid Match   39
It Hurts!   43
Sticky Guesses   42

beans
Bean Mix-Up   106
Bean Sort   177
Can You Believe Your Eyes?   107
Giant Bean Count   106
Growing a Beanstalk   159
Jack's Beans   156
Race to the Top   217
Watch It Grow   161
Watch It Sprout   251

biscuits
An Edible Wheel   354
Marshmallow Surprise   191

blocks
Cooperation   91
Cooperative Castle Building   164
Step Aerobic—Dinosaur Style   102

bread
Giant Jam Sandwich   85
Tie It, Twist It   216

bubbles
Blowing Bubbles   124
Catch the Bubbles   124
Good Clean Fun   23

buttons
String of Pearls   225
Wheels on a String   355

cans
Song Can   62
Stompers   233

cardboard
King (or Queen) for a Day   172
Mitten Lace   321
Teeny Tiny Town   88

cardboard tubes
Parading Around   75

catalogs
Match the Gifts   205

cellophane
Rose-Colored Glasses   264

chalk
Chalk Maze   95
Giant Canvas   97
Where Did It Go?   145

cheese
Hungry Thing Foodles   158

clothespins
Floaters   222
Little People   99
Squish Painting   135
This is the Way We Wash   126

coffee filters
Filter Fantasy   191
Racing Colors   190

cookies
Plant Pudding   128
Sandy Cups   129

construction paper
Bear Hunt   323
Coat of Arms   172
Corn Mosaic   320
Dragon Wigglers   170
Finish the Masterpiece   297

Free Form Cutting   297
Flower Power   199
Getting Ahead   170
Gift Wrap Collage   200
Hat Day   194
It Didn't Frighten Us   183
It's a Dragon!   169
Magic Drawings   138
Make-Believe   182
Pack a Bubble   137
Print It   344
Stamps Galore   345
Where Did the Color Go?   199
Yarn Mosaic   319

cornstarch
Goop II   22
Slime!   162

cotton swabs
Monster Toast   157
Secret Surprise Messages   203
Where Did the Color Go?   199

crayons
Corny Recipes   329
Geometric Pictures   293
Goat Stew Recipes   331
It's Raining Pizza!   146
Lace Rubbings   198
Let's Make Plans   321
Magic Crayon Mixture   160
Make a Wish   319
Monster Crayon Mess   161
Troll-n-Tell   329
Surprise Pictures   198
Tire Rubbings   354

cups
Big-Little Surprise   88
Hauling Big and Small   87
One Drop at a Time   92
Race to the Top   217

cupcake liners
Flower Power   199
Magic Crayon Mixture   160
Surprise Muffins   192

dirt
A Can of Worms   126
Cake, Slime or Pie, Please   131

Index

Dirt, Dirt and More Dirt   130
Just Like the Pigs   314
Robin Red Breast's Nest   131
The Grass is Greener   317

dowel rod
Hocus Pocus   173
Race to the Top   217

dryer vent hose
It's a Dragon!   169

eggs
Dragon Eggs   158
Effervescent Eggs   125
Hatch a Rubber Egg   253

face paints
Mirror on the Wall   253

fiberfill
The Big Stuff   109
Tie a Creature   229

file folders
Finish the Bows   238
Match the Bows   206
Suits Me   236
Match the Gifts   205

flour
Monster Mache   168
Muddy Playdough   135
Puff Paint   287
The Enormous Turnip   94

food coloring
Beastly Bubble Bath   171
Catch the Bubbles   137
Color Race   250
Decorate the Cake   202
Dragon Eggs   158
Making Meanie Bathwater   163
Mixing a Rainbow   286
Monster Toast   157
Racing Colors   190
Rainbow Glue   30
Slime!   162
Surprise Pudding   190
Tilt-a-Swirl   200

fruit
Bubbling Berries   318

garbage bags
Hauling Big and Small   87

garden catalogs
Pick a Seed   148

glitter
Beautiful Bows   224
Catch the Sun #1   262
Coat of Arms   172
Decorate the Cake   202
King (or Queen) for a Day   172
Nasty Faces   167
Party on a Plate   201
Princess' Nightmare Collage   165
Touch of Gold   166

glue
Clean Collage   138
Coat of Arms   172
Dragon Wigglers   170
Eat It Up   31
Finish the Masterpiece   297
Getting Ahead   170
Goop I   22
King (or Queen) for a Day   172
Nasty Faces   167
Pick a Seed   148
Princess' Nightmare Collage   165
Rainbow   30
Slime Two!   162
Touch of Gold   166

grass seed
The Grass is Greener   317

gum
Guessing Box   40
Sticky Tally   42

hair gel
Gel-O   21

handkerchiefs
Floaters   222
Tie Dye   230

hole punchers
Catch the Sun #1   262
Colorful Confetti   101
Hang It Up   218
Sew It Up   230
Sneakers   240

honey
Sticky Icky   24
Tacky Dough   26

instant pudding
Surprise Pudding   190

instruments
Name That Tune   62
Place 'n Trace   57
Stormy Weather   65
Wild Rumpus   72

jars
Bean Sprout Salad   252
Blizzards   267
Can You Believe Your Eyes?   107
Clearly a Guess   274
Color Race   250
Giant Bean Count   106
Greens Under Glass   259
Hatch a Rubber Egg   253
Seascape in a Jar   266
Sound of Music   254
Tops and Bottoms   256
Who Nose?   260

jelly or jam
Surprise Muffins   192

lamp
Me And My Shadow   159

lemon juice
Secret Surprise Messages   203

magazines
A Hole in One   276
I Spy   275
Oh Say Can You See?   93

magnets
Magnetic Mounts   34
Mirror Skating   257
Opposites Attract   23
State of Attraction   254

magnifying glass
Monster Tracking Tool   165
Oh Say Can You See?   93
Unstring It   224

marbles
Don't Lose Your Marbles   294
Have You Lost Your Marbles   58

markers
A Dragon's Fare   181
And Then What Happened   330
Copy Cat Drawings   298

Index

Corny Recipes   329
Eating Big   208
Fifth Dragon Story   179
Fistful of Markers   303
Flower Power   199
Goat Stew Recipes   331
How to Catch a Dragon   181
If I Were a King/Queen   180
It Didn't Frighten Us   183
It's Raining Pizza!   146
Let's Celebrate   208
Let's Make Plans   321
Make a Wish   209
Make a Wish   316
Making Circles   356
Mean Nasty, Downright Disgusting
   Germs   179
Make-Believe   182
Monster Tracking Tool   165
Once Upon a Time   180
Pajama Day   194
Picnic Day   195
Picture This   329
Racing Colors   190
Sail Away   147
Soup—Goat Style   315
Stormy Weather   147
Three Bears Porridge   316
Wacky! Wacky! Wacky!   207
What's a Monster Look Like?   178
100th Day   195

marshmallows
Marshmallow Surprise   191

measuring tape
Where Did It Go?   145

milk
Tally the Goats and Cows   325

mirror
Dot to Dot   270
Fun House Mirrors   258
Glass Magic   257
Guess Who?   252
Here's Looking at You   250
Mirror Images   268
Mirror Maniacs   269
Mirror Skating   257

Mirror on the Wall   253
See-Through Painting   261
Through the Looking Glass   248

muffin tray
Bean Sort   177
Surprise Muffins   203

mural paper
Action Painting   293
Giant Collage   93
Giant Paper Dolls   98
It's Small   97
Larger Than Life   96
Stuffed Animals   99
Things Are Looking Up   305
Wall to Wall   304

nature items
Birds of a Feather   27
Catch a Ray   33
Nature's Nasties   24

newspaper
Crumpled Paper Painting   59
Monster Mache   168
Secret Surprise Messages   203
Stuffed Animal   99

oatmeal
Three Bears Porridge   316

oil
State of Attraction   254

paint
Mixed-Up Paint   306
Monster Mache   168
Muddy Footprints   122
Muddy Tire Tracks   134
Pack a Bubble   137
Painted Dust   345
Print It   344
Rain Painting   134
Rounds of Paint   355
Slippery Soap Paint   136
Squish Painting   135
Touch of Gold   166

pantyhose
Three-legged Walk   234
Tie a Creature   229
The Big Stuff   109

paper
Blended Paper   286
Castle Caricature   167
Copy Cat Drawings   298
It's Raining Pizza!   146
Muddy Footprints   122
Once Upon a Time   180
Sail Away   147

paper bag
It's a Dragon   169
The Giant Paper Sandwich   95

paper clips
Surprise! Two Drawings   203

papier mache
Mache Masterpieces   299

paper plates
Flip It   343
Kaleidoscope   266
Nasty Faces   167
Party on a Plate   201
Picture Me Ugly!   320
Sew It Up   230
Tilt-a-Swirl   200

paper towel
One Drop at a Time   92
Watch It Grow!   161
Water on Glass   121

paper towel tubes
I See Stars   265
Merrily We Roll Along   228
Monster Mache   168
Rose-Colored Glasses   264
You've Got the Beat   232

pasta
Hungry Thing Foodles   158
Sticky Icky   24

peanut butter
Tacky Dough   26

pencils
Copy Cat Drawings   298
How To Catch a Dragon   181
Mean, Nasty, Downright Disgusting
   Germs   179
Penned Up Monster   178
Sail Away   147

Index

pennies
Count and Clink   41
pens
How to Catch a Dragon   181
Penned Up Monster   178
pie tins
Giant Crayons   100
Robin Red Breast's Nest   131
pizza sauce
An Edible Wheel   354
plants
Greens Under Glass   259
plaster of Paris
Catch That Muddy Track   139
Soft Sculpting Clay   298
plastic bags
Flying High   226
Guess What I See   274
Peanut Butter Squeeze   248
See-Through Sea Creature   267
Watch It Sprout   251
What's the Catch?   226
Zip It Up   259
playdough
Blow Your Top   56
Clay Play   289
Green Sculpture   171
Muddy Playdough   135
Sticky Fingers   25
plywood
Gee! Oh! Board   228
pipe
PVC Pipe Phone   53
popcorn
Corn Mosaic   320
Corny Counting   69
Pop Up   70
Weird Week   193
popsicle sticks
Tilt-a-Swirl   200
Which Is Stronger?   317
posterboard
Bubble Gum Tally   144
Catch That Drop!   143
Evaporation Investigation   145
Rain or Shine   143

Think Big, Think Small   111
Window Watching   275
potatoes
Veggie Scrub   133
potting soil
Big-Little Surprise!   88
Bury It!   120
Greens Under Glass   259
Growing a Beanstalk   159
Race to the Top   217
pudding
Plant Pudding   128
Sandy Cups   129
raisins
Bubbling Raisins   124
record player
Making Circles   356
ribbon
A Tisket, A Tasket   227
Grand Opening   219
Hat Day   194
Over and Under and Under and
Over   220
Presents   237
Rippling Ribbons   227
Square One   236
Tie A Creature   229
You've Got the Beat   232
Tangled   223
Party on a Plate   201
rickrack
Hat Day   194
rope
Darn It   220
Getting In Touch   233
Jump the River   232
Line Them Up   220
Square One   236
Stompers   233
Stringing Along   231
Tangled   223
Tightrope Trick   231
ruler
Evaporation Investigation   145
Let's Make Plans   321

safety goggles
Me, A Builder   343
Shave It Off   342
salt
Liquid Gold   339
Muddy Playdough   135
Salty Surprises   201
sand
Greens Under Glass   259
Seascape in a Jar   266
sawdust
Painted Dust   345
scissors
Fold 'n Cut   296
Free Form Cutting   297
How High Will They Go?   175
Pick a Seed   148
seeds
Bean Sprout Salad   252
Big-Little Surprise!   88
Bury It!   120
Catch the Sun #1   262
Flower Power   89
sequins
King/Queen For a Day   172
Princess' Nightmare Collage   165
shaving cream
Jack Frost   269
See Through Painting   261
soap
Beastly Bubble Bath   171
Car Wash   123
Dig That Soap   140
Magic Drawings   138
Mix It Up   59
More to Wash   127
Rub-a-Dub Classroom   123
Slippery Soap Paint   136
Soapy Mud   130
Soap Sort   144
Splish, Splash   125
This Is the Way We Wash   126
Whip It Up   288
soap wrappers/containers
Clean Collage   138
Soap Sort   144

Index

socks
Sticky Socks   21

sponges
Car Wash   123
Reprints   263
Squish Painting   135
Window Painting   261

spools
Rounds of Paint   355
Wheels on a String   355

starch
Goop I   22
Slime Two   162

stencils
Surprise Pictures   198

stickers
Count Your Pockets   347
How Old Are You?   205
Let's Compare!   331
Lick 'Em and Stick 'Em   32
Tally the Goats and Cows   325

string
Catch the Sun #1   262
Crazy String   224
Cut It Out   218
Darn It   220
Disappearing Ball   229
Don't Forget the _____   218
Floaters   222
Flower Power   89
Hanging By a Thread   223
Line Them Up   220
Measuring Up   221
One Giant Step   108
Race to the Top   217
Roll It Out   234
Spin Me a Home   226
Square   236
Sticky String   225
String Kabobs   222
String of Pearls   225
Stuffed Animals   99
Tangled   223
Tie Dye   230
Weave a Nest   219

sugar
Bubbling Berries   318
Marshmallow Surprise   191

syrup
Ooey Gooey   28
Sticky Icky   24

tape
Bear Hunt   323
Jump the River   35
Mitten Lace   321
Monster Tracking Tool   165
Poor Old Peg   25
Sticky Hunt   22
Sticky Surprise   32
Tape Tangle   30
The Dragon's Lair   167

tea
Muddy Brew II   127

tissue paper
It's A Dragon!   169

toilet paper
Soapy Mud   130

toothpicks
Green Sculpture   171
Toothpick Stick   34

tweezers
Take It Apart   217

vinegar
Bubble Mountains   132
Bubbling Raisins   124
Dragon Eggs   158
Effervescent Eggs   125
Hatch a Rubber Egg   253

wallpaper
How High Will They Go?   175
Match the Bows   206
Mitten Safari   323

warming tray
Foiled Again   268
Magic Crayon Mixture   160
Monster Crayon Mess   161

water
Bubbling Berries   318
Car Wash   123
Evaporation Investigation   145
Filter Fantasy   191

Flip It   343
Just Like the Pigs   314
More to Wash   127
Racing Colors   190
Rub-a-Dub Classroom   123
Salty Surprise   201
Splish, Splash   125
The Grass Is Greener   317
This is the Way We Wash   126
Three Bears Porridge   316
Washing Water   128
Water on Glass   121
Where Did the Color Go?   199

watercolors
Magic Drawings   138
Salty Surprise   201
Surprise Pictures   198
Troll-n-Tell   329
Watercolor Impressions   290

wax paper
A Cold Look   258
Stained Glass Windows   264

windowshade
Shady Deal   263

wire
All Wired Up   296

wood
Me, A Builder!   343
Shave It Off   342

yarn
Catch the Sun #1   262
Darn It   220
Human Web   36
Line Them Up   220
Merrily We Roll Along   228
Mitten Lace   321
Over and Under and Under and Over   220
Picture Me Ugly!   320
Roll It Out   234
Sew It Up   230
Square One   236
Weave a Nest   219
Weave-a-Web   37
Wheels on a String   355
Yarn Mosaic   319

Index

Book Index

Angry Arthur   73, 77
Art for Children   309
Arthur's Eyes   279
Artworks   309
Baby's Boat   147, 150
Bartholomew and the Oobleck   46
Bear's Toothache, The   242
Benny Bakes a Cake   348, 350
Ben's Trumpet   78
Big Ball of String, A   242
Big Fat Enormous Lie, A   114
Bigmama's   360
Big Red Barn   350
Big Toe, The   109, 114
Birthday for Frances, A   210
Bread and Jam for Frances   46
Bringing the Rain to Kapiti Plain   150
Carousel   360
Clifford the Big Red Dog   114
Cloudy with a Chance of Meatballs   146, 150
Come Look With Me: Exploring Landscape Art with Children   309
Crash! Bang! Boom!   78
Curious George Flies a Kite   242
Dark, Dark Tale, A   114
Draw Me a Star   305, 308
Enormous Turnip, The   94, 114
Eye Book, The   280
Eyes of the Dragon   185
Fin M'Coul   114
Fire Station, The   71, 78
Flash Crash Rumble & Roll   78
Giant Jam Sandwich, The   46, 85, 114
Gift, The   210
Gobble Growl Grunt   78
Goggles!   280
Goldilocks and the Three Bears   330, 331, 333
Gregory the Terrible Eater   315, 331, 333
Growing Colors   150
Hand Rhymes   151

Harold and the Purple Crayon   303, 308
Hats Hats Hats   242
Hidden House, The   280
How to Teach Art to Children   309
Hungry Thing, The   158, 185
Hurricane   147, 150
I Hear a Noise   78
Imogene's Antlers   210
I Spy   210, 280
It Didn't Frighten Me!   183, 185, 277, 280
Jack and the Beanstalk   115, 156, 159, 165, 185
Kids Pick the Funniest Poems   78, 186
Kites Sail High   242
Knight and the Dragon, The   164, 181, 185
Legend of the Indian Paintbrush, The   308
Let's Meet Famous Artists   309
Light in the Attic, A   79, 115, 151, 186, 211, 280, 309
Lion for Lewis, A   185
Listening Walk, The   78
Listen to the Rain   150
Little Mouse, The Red Ripe Strawberry, and the Big Hungry Bear   115
Look Again   280
Look! Look! Look!   280
Lost   333
Magic Fish   333
Marcel the Pastry Chef   350
Masterpiece of the Month   310
Matthew's Dream   308
Miss Rumphius   148, 150
Mitten, The   307, 308
Mouse Paint   306, 308
Mud Pony, The   150
My Mama says There Aren't Any Zombies, Ghosts, Vampires, Creatures, Demons, Monster, Fiends, Goblins or Things   185
Mystery of the Missing Red Mitten   333
Nathan's Fishing Trip   242
Night Noises   78, 210

No Bath Tonight   150
No Good in Art   308
Noisy Nora   73, 78, 243
Mouse Paint   46
Oh, Were They Ever Happy!   46
Paint! Make Prints! Make Sculptures! & Draw!   310
Paint Without Brushes   310
Pajamas   194, 210
Pancakes for Breakfast   46, 350
Parade   75, 78
Peanut Butter and Jelly   46
Peter's Pockets   350
Peter Spier's Rain   150
Pigs in Hiding   322, 333
Pocket for Corduroy, A   350
Poems to Read to the Very Young   210
Polar Bear, Polar Bear, What Do You Hear?   74, 78
Preschool Art   310
Prince Has a Boo-Boo, The   46
Princess and the Pea, The   157, 165, 171, 175, 185
Purple, Green and Yellow   303, 308
Ruby Mae Has Something to Say   194, 210
Secret Birthday Message, The   210
School Bus   360
Signmaker's Assistant, The   306, 309
Simon's Book   178, 185, 302, 309
Simple Pictures Are Best   280
Sing a Song of Popcorn   151
Something Big Has Been Here   78, 115, 186, 211
Storm in the Night   147, 150
Strega Nona   46
Surprise Party, The   210
There's a Nightmare in My closet   185
There's a Wocket in My Pocket!   349, 350
Three Billy Goats Gruff, The   317, 320, 329, 330, 331,333
Three Little Ducks   333
Three Little Kittens, The   322, 331, 333
Three Little Pigs, The   317, 328, 331, 333

Three Wishes, The 333
Time of Wonder 147,150
Those Mean Nasty Dirty Downright Disgusting But...Invisible Germs 109, 115, 179, 186
Thumbelina 115
Thunder Cake 350
Tony's Bread 350
Truck 360
Trucks 360
Truck Song 360
Up, Up & Away 243
Very Busy Spider, The 46
Wacky Wednesday 193, 207, 210
Walk in the Rain, A 150
Wednesday Surprise, The 210
Wheels 360
Wheel Away 360
Wheels on the Bus, The 360
Where the Sidewalk Ends 78, 115, 151, 186, 243, 280
Where The Wild Things Are 72, 78, 174, 182, 186
Why Worms? 304, 309
Wolf's Chicken Stew, The 195, 210
1-2-3 Art 310

Song Index

Across the Bridge 333
Ain't Gonna Rain No More 157
Barnyard Talk 350
Bathtime 151
Bean Bag Shake 243
Biscuits in the Oven 350
Brown Bear, Brown Bear, What Do You See? 281
Bubble Gum 47
Clap, Clap, Clap 76
Counting Games and Rhythms for the Little Ones 243
Dinosaurs 116

Do Your Ears Hang Low 242
Down By the Bay 151
Ducks Like Rain 151
Don't Drink the Water 151
Don't Step on the Rain 151
Down on Grandpa's Farm 350
Eeensy Weensy Spider 45, 113
Eight Little Piggies in a Row 333
Five Little Ducks 151
Five Little Frogs 151
Flight of the Bumblebee 47
Friendly Giant 116
Giant, Teeny, Tiny 113
Grape Jelly Cure 47
Hammer Song, The 79
Happiness Cake 211, 350
Happy Unbirthday 209
Hear the Wind Blow 76
Incey Wincey Spider 116
I'm a Little Teapot 116
If I Had a Dinosaur 115
In My Garden 151, 350
I've Got No Strings 243
Just Like Me 281
King in the Castle, The 184
Late Last Night 243
Little Ants 116
Little Elf 116
Little Raindrop 76
Little White Duck 151
Mice Go Marching 115, 186
Monsters Never Comb Their Hair 186
Morningtown Ride 360
Mr. Wind Is a Mischief 76
Muddy Water Puddle 151
Oats and Beans and Barley 350
Peanut Butter 47
Pass the Elf Round and Round 113
Petite Marionettes 243
Play Your Instrument 79
Please Don't Bring a Tyrannosaurus Rex to Show & Tell 115
Popcorn 211
Puff the Magic Dragon 186
Rain, Rain Go Away 151

Robin in the Rain 151
School Glue 47
Shadow Dancing 281
Skin and Bones 211
Shout and Whisper 79
Skateboard 360
So Much to Hear 79
Tap Your Sticks 79
Teddy Bear's Picnic, The 211
This Little Light of Mine 116
Three Little Pigs' Blues, The 333
Two Little Blackbirds 76, 113
Watch Me 281
Wheels on the Bus, The 360